Conference Papers Series
No. 11

The Basque Fiscal System Contrasted to Nevada and Catalonia:

In the Time of Major Crises

Edited by Joseba Agirreazkuenaga and Xabier Irujo

Center for Basque Studies Press
University of Nevada, Reno

This book was published with generous financial assistance from the Basque Government, the Documentation Centre for the Economic Agreement and the Foral Treasuries of the University of the Basque Country, and Agirre Lehendakaria Center

Conference Papers Series, No. 11
Series Editor: Xabier Irujo
Center for Basque Studies
University of Nevada, Reno
Reno, Nevada 89557
http://basque.unr.edu

Cover design: Zaloa Ipina

Library of Congress Cataloging-in-Publication Data
Names: Agirreazkuenaga, J. (Joseba), editor. | Irujo Ametzaga, Xabier, editor.
Title: The Basque fiscal system contrasted to Nevada and Catalonia : in the time of major crises / edited by Joseba Agirreazkuenaga and Xabier Irujo.
Description: University of Nevada, Reno : Center for Basque Studies Press, [2017] | Series: Conference papers series ; No. 11 | Includes bibliographical references and index.
Identifiers: LCCN 2017006425 | ISBN 9781935709749 (pbk. : alk. paper)
Subjects: LCSH: Finance, Public--Spain--País Vasco. | Finance, Public--Spain--Catalonia. | Finance, Public--Spain--Navarre.
Classification: LCC HJ1249.P35 B37 2017 | DDC 336.946/6--dc23
LC record available at https://
na01.safelinks.protection.outlook.com/?url=https%3A%2F%
2Flccn.loc.gov%2F2017006425&data=01%7C01%7Cdmontero%
40unr.edu%7C7ef97cd2035e48aee8de08d4bb057c85%
7C523b4bfc0ebd4c03b2b96f6a17fd31d8%
7C1&sdata=mtIYoz1gp2XSBSAx3W5Gn29vRFkomvyuxmPZ4GUf
LQ0%3D&reserved=0

Contents

Preface

In 2012 the Center for Basque Studies issued a new call for the William A. Douglass Distinguished Visiting Scholar for the 2013–2014 academic year, in order to promote a new line of research on taxation and management of public finances in the Basque Country. The Basque language together with self-government in taxation and public finances are the most significant elements of Basque identity in the twenty-first century. Taxation was linked to the representative assemblies and it articulated the Kingdom of Navarre and the territories of Araba, Bizkaia, and Gipuzkoa for 500 years as a component of the composite Spanish monarchy; the territories of Lapurdi, Navarre and Zuberoa were articulated in similar terms within the French composite monarchy until 1789. "No taxation without representation" (1769) was the cry of the inhabitants of Boston and the British American Colonies, promoting the process of US independence. After the abolition of the Basque representative assemblies in 1877, a specific tax culture persisted in the Basque provinces by means of the Economic Agreement between the Basque territories and the central Spanish government.

In 2014 the CBS published the book *The Basque Fiscal System*, with which it inaugurated the diffusion of the research on Basque taxation and the program of the William A. Douglass Distinguished Visiting Scholar 2013–2014, which was intended to implement and develop the fieldwork. On March 26, 27, and 28, 2014, the Thirteenth Annual International Conference of the CBS was organized at the University of Nevada, Reno. The Conference proposed to analyze the Basque Fiscal Systems in the context of the 2008 financial crisis. It also aimed to develop a comparative vision with the state of Nevada and Catalonia. The subjects of the conference were: the politics of finance in multi-level public institutions during the current economic crisis; long-term fiscal policies for dealing with economic downturns during the past twenty years; the development of treasuries in federal states, in non-federal states, and in complex unions (Europe); taxation and citizenship in a globalized world; long-term trends for dealing with the current crisis and strategies for the future in European and North American contexts (the Basque Country, Catalonia, Spain, Ireland, and Nevada). The Conference had been organized with the support of the Basque Government, the Documentation Center of the Economic Agreement and the Foral Treasuries in the University of the Basque Country with the support of the regional government of Bizkaia, Ad Concordiam (Association for the Promotion and Diffusion of the Economic Agreement), and the Emilio Soldevilla Foundation of the College of Economics and Business at the University of the Basque Country.

This book is a compilation of the contributions submitted to the Conference. Additionally, the thirteenth conference and this book also serve as a meeting point for university academics and officials from the public treasuries and finances of the institutions of the Basque Country. To create new knowledge we have to take into account the contexts of practical application. The comparative dimension was more limited than we had anticipated, however the contribution of Professor E. Parker of the University of Nevada offers a general comparative framework. The contribution of Professor A. Segura of the University of Barcelona once again establishes the close link between fiscal awareness and the process of independence in Catalonia in favor of self-government. To emphasize the practical dimension, officials from the Foral Treasury of Bizkaia, Gemma Martinez and Jose Rubi, members of the association Ad Concordiam, as well as Mikel Aranburu from the Foral Treasury of the Government of Navarre, present their experiences. M. Aranburu, following his participation in Reno, was appointed Minister of the Foral Treasury of the Government of Navarre in 2015. A member of the Arbitration Board of the Economic Agreement, the lawyer J. Muguruza, analyzes the trajectory of the body that settles the conflicts between the Basque and Spanish parties. In his contribution J. J. Ibarretxe, Vice-President of the Basque Government and later President (1999–2009), and Councilor of Finance and Public Administration (1995–1998), addresses a significant issue that he dealt with in his capacity as vice president when relevant aspects of the current Economic Concert were negotiated in 1997 between the Basque and Spanish governments. Currently, as head of the Agirre Lehendakaria Center he has collaborated in the edition of this book. Another of the participants, the academic Andrés Araujo also held the post of Deputy Minister for the Economy of the Basque Government (2009–2012). His contribution is situated in the field of public economics. Another contribution by J. Landeta analyzes the effects of taxation on other specific phenomena, such as industrial cooperatives.

Most of the contributions relate to the Basque Country, providing an analysis of fiscal policies or the evolution of public finances. A contribution on taxation and gambling is also offered.

In short, this book aims to be a new contribution to studies on fiscal federalism in Europe and America. At present the regional governments of Araba, Bizkaia and Gipuzkoa and their representative assemblies exercise fiscal powers and the Basque parliament plays a role of harmonization. These institutions jointly negotiate the Economic Agreement with the Spanish government to establish the quota: the Basque Autonomous Community's contribution to the Spanish Treasury as its input to the activities not managed by the Basque institutions. For its part, the government and parliament of Navarre have a similar agreement and negotiate a quota with the Spanish government. But as demonstrated by a judicial decision of the European Court, the Basque treasuries are independent of Spanish public finances and assume a unilateral risk. The Court of Justice of the European Union is the last instance of appeal (a higher instance than even "national" Supreme or Constitutional Courts). In general and European terms, the Basque fiscal system is not peculiar. But one kind of particularity consists in the implementation of the Basque fiscal state without political sovereignty. In this sense, it is a state within the Spanish sovereign state and the European Union. It is not part of the fiscal decentralization of the Spanish state, but a fiscal state within another political sovereignty, which is part of the European Union of sovereign states.

We hope that these reflections serve as a turning point to promote debate and for the formulation of future research. Fiscal analysis is now an important research line in the CBS, promoted by the

Regional government or Deputation of Bizkaia, with an agreement since 2014 for organizing workshops and research in a comparative view.

— Joseba Agirreazkuenaga and Xabier Irujo

1

Small States in a Time of Big Crises: Nevada, Ireland, and the Basque Autonomous Community during the Great Recession

Elliott Parker

The Basque Country has many cultural ties to Nevada, and shares some other historical similarities with Ireland. In this chapter, I suggest that there are economic lessons as well; that both Nevada and Ireland—like the Basque Country—are small parts of larger economies sharing a common currency, and there are lessons from the housing bubbles and financial crises that preceded their recessions and the deflationary pressures and public austerity which followed.

I first consider how recessions caused by financial crises are fundamentally different from normal recessions, especially when they occur in low-inflation or deflationary environments, and I also note issues related to fiscal intervention and common currency areas. I then review the unique characteristics of Nevada's economic development, and explain why it became the U.S. state with the most severe experience during the Great Recession. I next consider Ireland's economic development, and ponder what lessons it holds for Nevada. I end with a brief review of the economy of the Basque Country, along with its similarities and contrasts with both Nevada and Ireland, and conclude by considering any lessons that small states responding to big crises may hold for each other.

Factors in Short-Run Economic Performance

Small market economies need to integrate with larger economies in order to grow, in order to gain access to foreign trade and investment, but these benefits come with a price. The small economy needs some advantage in what it offers, whether tourist services or exports, and the demand for these is affected by relative prices and exchange rates. The small economy is cushioned from its own recessions by external demand, but is unable to prevent external events from affecting domestic demand. Small economies can get access to foreign investment, but when financial markets are unregulated these inflows can lead to asset bubbles and currency instability. Small states are more likely to use a currency managed by larger economies, and this implies that monetary and exchange policies are unlikely to be in the small economy's interest.

In addition to the many factors that contribute to economic growth and the ability to find export markets, such as public investment in education and infrastructure, some factors play a major part in how a small market economy responds to an economic crisis. One key is the economy's tax structure, not only to finance investment in education and infrastructure that supports market-driven growth, but also to provide a stable stream of government revenue during downturns. Small states with unstable revenues need access to capital markets to prevent untimely austerity. With common currency areas that do not easily allow for secular readjustment through higher inflation rates or currency depreciation, participation in a federal system helps to spread the cost of adjustment.

Economic activity can slow for many reasons. However, most shocks to aggregate demand or supply tend to be relatively short-lived, and in the postwar period, most developed-economy recessions have lasted a year or less. Growth during the following recovery is typically faster than usual, as potential GDP is not much affected, and economic growth soon catches up, back to its prior path. In normal recessions, what matters more is the long-term structure of the economy.

Balance Sheet Recessions

Financial markets are fundamental to economic development in a market economy, but they are particularly prone to market failure. Financial markets are inherently risky, of course, because they are pricing future uncertainties, but information is often asymmetric, and investors are often unaware of actual risks and returns. The externalities of contagion can be severe in countries with an inadequate regulatory structure. However, with regulation come implicit guarantees, and insurance—whether explicit and private or implicit and public—often creates moral hazard incentives that lead to excessive risk-taking. When investments pay off, the returns remain private, but when risky investments go bad many of the costs are borne by the rest of the economy.

When financial crises occur, they can lead to a much deeper and longer recession, which Minsky (1986) defined as a depression. Koo (2009) calls this a "balance-sheet" recession, since a financial crisis which significantly reduces asset values for firms and consumers can lead to a long period of deleveraging. Earnings and savings that might have been available for spending are instead used to reduce liabilities, and net wealth declines for a significant portion of the population. One person's spending is another person's income, and the effect is a long-lived recession. The longer people remain unemployed as a result, the less likely they will ever reenter the work force and regain their prior productivity. The recovery tends to be slower, and because potential GDP is adversely affected by long periods of high unemployment and low investment, the economy never regains its former growth path.

Since the Panic of 1792 following Hamilton's establishment of the Bank of the United States, depressions set off by financial panics were common in United States until the Great Depression of 1929–33, and they have been common in other more developed economies as well. On average, this type of recession tends to last twice as long as other recessions, and the decline in GDP is twice as large. Following these recessions, GDP remained roughly 10% below its prior path even seven years after the event (Reinhardt and Rogoff 2009). In the postwar period, the two best examples of this type of recession are the lost decade following the collapse of Japan's *Baburu* economy, and the Great Recession of 2007–09.

The normal mechanisms of monetary policy, such as reducing short-term interest rates, do not work in such an economy, especially if price inflation is already low. Financial institutions seek safer assets such as government bonds to reduce the overall risk of a portfolio of non-performing loans, and both consumers and firms move their financial assets into cash. This move out of traditional lending puts downward pressure on money supply even as money demand rises, and this can push an economy with already weak demand for goods and services into price deflation (Cargill and Parker 2003). Real interest rates rise with expected price deflation even with a low nominal rate of interest on interbank loans, and spending is delayed. On average, price deflation slows subsequent growth (Guerrero and Parker 2006). As both Japan and the United States have shown, it is difficult to reverse the problem even with a policy of quantitative easing.

Of course, the economic damage done by a financial crisis depends on the severity of the crisis, which is determined in part by the government regulatory structure, and the size of the financial sector relative to the overall economy. Real estate bubbles tend to affect consumer wealth for a large share of the population, many of whom have credit constraints, while stock market bubbles tend to affect a smaller share of the population, most of whom are more likely to reduce their savings than cut their spending.

Fiscal Intervention and Austerity

In a typical recession, government fiscal intervention beyond automatic stabilizers such as taxes (which decline during recessions) and social spending (which rises during recessions) is often ineffective and poorly timed, and the crowding-out effects on private spending or the increase in public debt can be counterproductive. Monetary intervention by the central bank is usually more effective in restoring spending, though it may be destabilizing and inflationary if used excessively.

In a balance-sheet recession, public spending and private spending are more likely to be complements rather than substitutes, and large, developed nation-states with access to capital markets have the option of fiscal intervention. Tax cuts for those with credit constraints not affecting consumption are not likely to be effective, since the resulting savings go primarily toward paying down debt. Public spending can raise private incomes for those who will spend it, and if spending focuses on the development of productive infrastructure, the result can be increases in the nation's potential output. While the central bank may act as the lender of last resort, the government in effect becomes a borrower of last resort in an economy wary of other financial assets.

For a small state, however, significant public borrowing is often not an option. During a typical recession, these states usually have financial reserves sufficient to weather the likely declines in revenue. In a balance-sheet recession, however, these financial reserves can be quickly used up. In such a situation, the fiscal policy of a small state becomes an automatic destabilizer. States are forced to engage in austerity by raising taxes, cutting public spending, or both, and this further reduces private incomes and makes the recession deeper or the recovery slower.

During the Great Recession, state and local governments were forced by effective credit limits and reduced tax revenues to cut spending significantly, particularly on education and infrastructure investments that have positive long-term effects. Because state and local governments cumulatively provide the lion's share of public purchases, Krugman (2008) predicted this would serve as "fifty Herbert Hoovers" in depressing overall demand, unless the federal government could overcompensate with fiscal policy. This occurred in 2009–10 because of the American Reinvestment and Recovery Act, but by 2011, public austerity was the net effect.

A Common Currency

As one of the United States, Nevada shares a common currency that allows it to trade with other states without exchange risk, and without the transactions cost of currency conversion. Like the Basque Country, Ireland has become part of the euro area, and this eases trade and investment with its neighbors. Unlike Nevada, Ireland is a sovereign state, and this makes it more difficult to receive interstate fiscal transfers during a crisis.

A common currency reduces both transaction costs and risk for trade and investment. Monetary policy is turned over to a central authority such as the Federal Reserve System or the European Central Bank, effectively preventing a small economy from access to this as a tool. To be "optimal" in an economic sense, countries need to have integrated product and capital markets, labor mobility between countries, similar fiscal characteristics, and similar types of economic shocks. The establishment of the euro led many economists to conclude that the euro area was not an optimal currency area, at least not in an economic sense. Unlike in the United States, Europe does not share a fiscal system that allows fluid and, often, indirect transfers between states.

With a common currency, countries with markets that overheat during booms are unable to easily adjust their real prices downward through currency depreciation. Only if core countries (like Germany in the euro system) are willing to tolerate high inflation is it possible to deflate relative prices in countries on the periphery (like Spain, Ireland, and Greece) without forcing them into nominal price deflation, a result that can lead to a downward spiral in economic activity. Economies with their own currencies may choose to have them depreciate, so their international competitiveness is restored, but small states within a larger currency union do not have this option. Giving up monetary policy in such a circumstance has a very high cost.

Nevada's Economy

Once Nevada's mining economy collapsed in the wake of the Mint Act of 1873, which demonetized silver, its population declined, and it struggled for decades to maintain a viable economy. Liberal divorce laws, prizefighting, and similar activities drew in some tourists from out of state, but it was only during the Great Depression that the legalization of casino gambling and federally financed public investment in the construction of Hoover Dam on the Colorado River created conditions for economic growth in the state.

With tax revenues from the casinos, the state followed an approach that became known as the "One Sound State" policy. With no personal income tax or corporate tax, the state offered itself as a haven for wealthy individuals fleeing other states. Though revenues were in time augmented by sales taxes and a "pick up" estate tax, the state maintained a relatively small government and put only minimal investment into public infrastructure, social services, and public education (Parker 2011).

Out-of-state investment in casino resorts began to grow after World War II. Federal interstate highway construction in the 1960s improved access from California to the southern part of the state, and in the 1970s, the construction of I-80 better-connected northern Nevada with its western neighbor. The population of Clark County, the home of Las Vegas, grew from about 8,500 people in 1930, or 9.2% of the state's population, to over 2 million people by 2012, or 73% of the state. This annualized rate of almost 7% made Nevada the fastest-growing state for several decades. Nonetheless, even with this rapid growth, Nevada still contains less than 1% of the U.S. population.

Beginning in the 1990s, however, Nevada began to lose its virtual monopoly on legal casino gambling in the United States. As the growth of casino construction and employment began to slow, however, a new engine of growth emerged. Financial deregulation and low interest rates in the late 1990s enabled rapid growth in housing finance, and home prices began to grow much faster than inflation in desirable relocation destinations such as Florida, Arizona, and California. Rapid rises in home prices then began to spill over to neighboring regions, where construction boomed. By 2005, Nevada's construction sector was the largest in the nation, as a share of total state employment. Both Nevada's cost of living and personal income per capita exceeded the national average, and Nevada remained the fastest-growing state in the nation.

Most jobs in casino gaming and construction open to workers in their twenties and thirties do not require much education, and state spending on public education as a share of GDP was the lowest in the nation, about half of what was spent by its neighbor Utah, a state with a similarly-sized population and at least one major private university. With no income taxes, Nevada did attract retirees and others seeking to shield their incomes, but the state also had the fewest government employees in the nation as a share of population, and provided relatively minimal social services. Nevada was among states with the lowest high school graduation rates and share of adults with a college education, but Nevada's economic growth was driven by population in-migration.

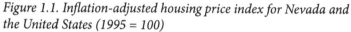

Figure 1.1. Inflation-adjusted housing price index for Nevada and the United States (1995 = 100)

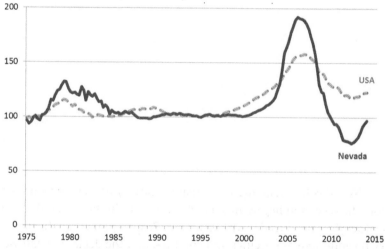

The housing bubble peaked in 2006, and then prices began to collapse. As figure 1.1 shows, between April 2006 and January 2012, inflation-adjusted housing prices fell by 60% in Nevada, compared to 26% nationwide and more than any other state, while foreclosure rates and share of mortgages underwater rose to the highest levels in the nation. Construction effectively halted, and because of the decline in construction employment, Nevada's unemployment rate rose to 14%, the highest in the nation. Adjusting for inflation and population, Nevada's fell by 15.5%, twice the national decline.

As we would expect with a balance-sheet recession, the state economy has been slow to recover, but Nevada also has long-term structural problems because of the decline in its major industries.

Exactly six years after the March 2008 peak, employment finally recovered, even though the state's population has continued to
grow (albeit much more slowly). Housing prices declined for twen-
ty-three straight quarters, and though prices have been recovering
ever since, they have yet to catch up to the inflation-adjusted 1975–
2000 average. As figure 1.2 shows, average real GDP per capita in
Nevada has remained flat since it hit bottom in 2010, while it has
been growing for the rest of the country since the recession ended
in 2009.

Figure 1.2. Real per capita GDP for United States and Nevada

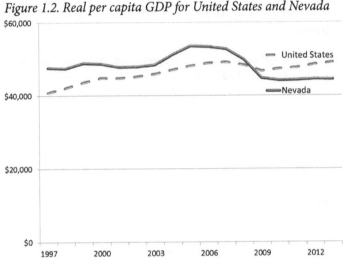

Nevada's tax structure has remained largely unchanged since before the recession began, in spite of the growth in the demand for social services produced by the recession. Property taxes are the primary revenue source for cities and counties, and the decline in assessed
property value from $144 billion in Fiscal Year 2009 to $82 billion in
FY 2013 has significantly reduced these. Unfortunately, the state caps
how fast assessed values can rise, so the loss of revenue is unable to
quickly rebound.

The largest source of state revenue is the sales and use tax, with
a state rate of 6.85% plus up to 1.25% for local governments. This
tax is expected to provide 31% of total state general fund revenue at
present, though many services are exempted and U.S. states are still
struggling to tax Internet commerce. For casinos, the state charges a
low gaming tax of 6.75% on the gross win; this used to be the largest
source of state revenue, though it is now down to 23% of the total.
The third largest revenue source for the state is a decade-old modified

business tax, currently 1.2% of payroll for large firms, which provides 12% of state revenue.

The state tax on insurance premiums accounts for 9% of revenue. The state constitution limits taxes on mining to 5% of net proceeds, even though Nevada is one of the largest producers of gold in the world, so this only contributes 3% of state revenue. Other miscellaneous taxes include those on entertainment, cigarettes, recordings, and real estate transfers. The state has no income tax, no corporate profits tax, and no value-added tax, and the "pick up" tax was phased out a decade ago. Voters rejected a margins tax in 2014, as well as a change to the constitutional limitation on mining taxes. But in 2015, the state nonetheless passed a plan that increased business license fees and added a sector-specific commerce tax on gross receipts for large firms. Figure 1.3 shows the state government's tax revenue for its general fund, both unadjusted and smoothed, so that the ratio does not jump up in a recession when the denominator declines. By 2000, state tax revenue had fallen to the lowest share of Gross State Product of any state in the union, a status not substantially changed by the implementation of the modified business tax. As casino gaming has become increasingly competitive, this ratio has shown a general downward trend.

Figure 1.3. Nevada state general fund revenue (share of gross state product.

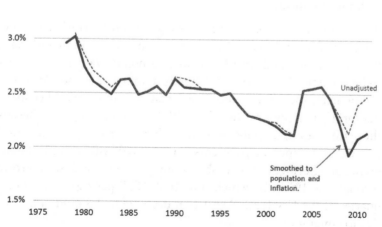

Like many states, Nevada is required to balance its general fund budget, allowing a 5% cushion and a small contribution to a "rainy day" stabilization fund. Borrowing for the capital budget is limited by the state's assessed value, and this has been a real constraint. Thus, falling tax revenues during the recession forced the state and its local governments to impose austerity. Even though the state already had the smallest government workforce in the country and one of the smallest state budgets, Nevada cut public spending at a time when private spending had already plummeted, exacerbating an already-slow recovery.

Nevada accounted for a much larger share of the U.S. financial crisis than its share of population would explain. Had Nevada been an autonomous nation with its own currency, it is likely that significant currency depreciation would have made recovery a little easier, but Nevada is part of the U.S. dollar area.

However, being part of a federal system has helped Nevada significantly. The federal government took responsibility for ensuring that the financial system did not collapse. Taxes paid by Nevadans to the federal government fell significantly during the recession, but federal spending in the state was not tightened in the state as a result. To the contrary, the federal fiscal stimulus of 2009 (the American Reinvestment and Recovery Act) increased public spending in the states, most significantly with support for higher education; this reduced cuts the state government would have otherwise implemented. As the U.S. economy began to recover after 2009, the economy of Nevada gradually stabilized, though its fiscal system continued to face structural problems.

Ireland's Economy

After centuries of conflict in a struggle against British rule, most counties of Ireland joined in a Free State in 1922, and then declared themselves a Republic in 1937. Under Éamon de Valera's Fianna Fáil, Ireland followed conservative Church-dominated economic and social policies, and became relatively isolated from the world economy due largely to a poor relationship with the United Kingdom. Because the Irish pound, or punt, was overvalued in its peg to the British pound, its balance of payments was marked with chronic foreign exchange shortages. The Irish economy experienced slow growth through the 1950s, by which time Irish GDP per capita was only a quarter of the U.S. level. Population declined to 2.8 million by 1960 due to emigration.

Ireland began to turn the economy around with educational reforms in the 1960s, making a large public investment in education and establishing a virtually free secondary and university education system. The government also began to take on an outward orientation and reduced protectionism on imports from Britain and elsewhere. Ireland joined the European Community in the early 1970s, along with Britain, and devalued the punt.

Even though Ireland's population finally stopped declining at this time, the decade or so after these reforms was not easy. In addition to relatively high inflation in the 1970s and early 1980s, a problem shared with most of its major trading partners, Ireland's government faced chronic budget deficits, and government debt reached 130% of GDP. To turn this around, the government began negotiating a series of political agreements called social partnerships between business, labor unions, farmers, and government agencies. One policy that emerged from this was an increase in personal taxes, especially for higher incomes, combined with a reduced corporate tax rate. The result led to a substantial increase in revenues, and within a decade, public debt dropped below 30% of GDP. In addition to lower taxes on corporate profits, the government began to actively promote foreign direct investment, and this included a tax holiday for foreign-invested earnings. More money was spent for public investment in infrastructure, and more was allocated for improving education.

Ireland integrated into the European Union, which responded with subsidies for Ireland's infrastructure. Ireland was an early adopter of the euro, and foreign direct investment from both the United States and the European Union grew rapidly. One important factor in attracting investment was the Good Friday Accord, which finally brought peace to the northern six counties and reduced foreign investor worries about the violence affecting their economic interests.

However, even more important was the growing recognition of the quality of Ireland's workforce, the result of more than two decades of investment in education, and the fact that Irish wages in the 1990s were still relatively low. This is, perhaps, one of the lessons Ireland holds for Nevada. Significant public investment in education was essential to Ireland's reinvention, but it was an investment that took a decade or two to start paying off. Without major changes to its tax structure, Nevada has yet to make such an investment. Low corporate tax rates may help attract outside investment, but tax revenues need to be adequate to fund education, public investment in infrastructure, and social services.

With all of this investment, Ireland made a rapid shift from agriculture to manufacturing, especially in chemicals, pharmaceuticals, and engineering products, and Irish exports to the United States and the European Union grew dramatically. Ireland became the "Celtic Tiger," one of the fastest-growing economies in Europe, and its GDP per capita became one of highest in the European Union, as figure 1.4 illustrates. At official exchange rates, Ireland even topped the United States by 2005, though purchasing power parity adjustments reduced this. Even though its population also began to grow at a significant rate for the first time in 150 years, Ireland's population still only made up approximately 1% of the European Union population as a whole.

Figure 1.4. Per capita GDP of Ireland compared to the US, UK, and Spain, in constant 2005 PPP dollars. Source: http://appsso.eurostat. ec.europa.eu.

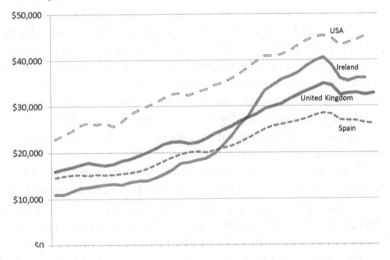

The factors that led to Ireland's impressive long-term performance did not prevent it from being damaged by the Great Recession and may have even encouraged the hubris that led to financial troubles. Like many other nations, Ireland's government deregulated its financial sector in the 1980s and 1990s. As the Central Bank of Ireland gave up responsibility for managing the punt, it also reduced its regulatory oversight of Irish banks. This bank deregulation allowed Irish banks to borrow short-term at low European Central Bank (ECB) rates in order to finance long-term investments. It also led to more consumer credit, enabling households to borrow more and save less. Personal savings fell from an average of 19% of GDP in the 1970s to 14% in the 1980s, and then to 10% by the end of the 1990s.

By the early 2000s, real estate bubbles began to form in Ireland, as well as in Spain and other areas peripheral to the European Union. Some of this was driven by foreigners and newly rich Irish seeking coastal vacation homes, and Ireland's housing stock rose to more than one home for every 2.5 people. Home prices quadrupled in less than a decade, as figure 1.5 illustrates, even adjusting for inflation, and almost a quarter of Ireland's GDP was related to the construction sector.

Figure 1.5. Irelands average housing price, in inflation adjusted euros. Source: www.cso.ie/en/databases/.

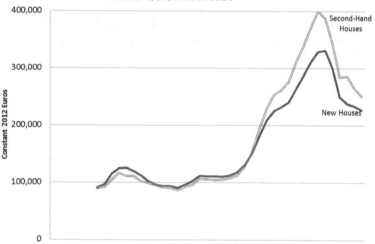

While membership in the euro area had advantages for Ireland, it also came with disadvantages. Ireland had price inflation higher than the rest of the euro zone, but the euro also appreciated significantly against the dollar. Ireland lost its advantage of low wages relative to productivity. For countries like Ireland that did most of their trade outside the European Union, the rising euro began to price out exports to other countries that did not use the euro, and export growth slowed.

Housing prices peaked in 2006, and then fell. As in Nevada, the construction sector withered, and this accounted for most of the resulting increase in the unemployment rate. Unlike Nevada, which left its financial troubles to the federal government, Ireland's government needed to step in when Irish banks became insolvent, and the resulting bailout was several times the annual budget. Ireland was able to borrow abroad to finance this bailout, but this action effectively constrained all other borrowing afterward.

Ireland's fiscal structure was less sensitive to the recession than Nevada's, but revenue declined nonetheless. Figure 1.6 shows tax revenues in comparison to the United States, the United Kingdom, and Spain (neither Nevada nor the Basque Country are included on this graph, because their tax structures are not comparable). The personal income tax, with rates of 20% and 41%, brought in over 40% of the annual state revenue. A value-added tax of 23% on most goods and services brought in over a third of revenue. Excise duties on petroleum, alcohol, and tobacco brought in about 13% of revenue, and the low corporate tax rate of 12.5% brought in about 12% of revenue. All other taxes accounted for only 7% of tax revenue.

Figure 1.6. Total tax revenue for Ireland compared to US, UK, and Spain. Share of GDP. Source: http://appsso.eurostat.ec.europa.eu.

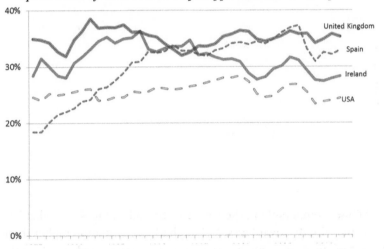

Even with a more stable tax structure and national sovereignty, Ireland's need to bail out its banks constrained its ability to use fiscal stimulus. As a result, Ireland's government was forced to impose austerity prematurely, when a fiscal stimulus might have eased the shortfall in demand. Ireland's unemployment rate matched Nevada's through the peak, but the rate took much longer before it began to come down because Ireland did not benefit from a federal structure, and the overall European economy continued to face daunting problems. Ireland's experience relative to Nevada does suggest the benefits of being part of a larger economy that helps out in bad times, especially if the larger economy is not being dragged down by other weak economies.

Comparison to the Basque Economy

The Basque Country is an autonomous community in Spain known as Euskadi or País Vasco, and is the heart of Euskal Herria, the greater Basque homelands on both sides of the French-Spanish border. Euskadi contains roughly 2.1 million people, and the greater Euskal Herria a million more. Altogether, Euskal Herria is home to around 1% of the population of the euro area.

One does not have to look far for connections between the Basque Country and the two other economies described in this Chapter. After Boise, Idaho, Reno has one of the largest concentrations of Basque emigrants in the United States, and the University of Nevada, Reno, is affectionately termed the fifth university of the Basque Country due to its efforts to preserve Basque heritage. Euskal Herria has a population comparable to Nevada's. Like Ireland, the Basque Country has struggled over centuries to maintain its identity, its language, and its autonomy, and the northern Irish experience with the Irish Republican Army may be comparable in some ways to that of Euskadi with the group Euskadi Ta Askatasuna (ETA). Like both Ireland and Nevada, the Basque Country is part of a larger economy and a common currency. Like Nevada relative to the United States, and Ireland relative to the European Union, at least before 2008, Basque incomes are significantly higher than those in the rest of Spain. Like Ireland, the economy of the Basque Country is more dependent on manufacturing and international trade, while Nevada is much more dependent on tourism.

The Basque Country has been given relatively more autonomy than most other regions of Spain, and thus its level of fiscal autonomy lies somewhere between Nevada's, as a state within a federal system, and Ireland's, as a nation within the European Union. The economic agreement of 1981 effectively recognized the Basque Country as a political and cultural unit, giving its regional government control over economic policy, tax collections, and public spending (Uriarte 2014). The Basque Country is relatively more industrial than the rest of Spain, and on average, it exports twice as much.

Until recently, the Basque Country's economy was considered a success story (Cooper 2012). Figure 1.7 shows the impressive growth in its GDP per capita between 1980 and 2010. GDP per capita in the Basque Country rose to a level roughly a third above the rest of Spain. With higher income and budgetary autonomy, the region was able to maintain a public debt ratio much lower than in the rest of Spain. Furthermore, the decline in GDP after 2008 was less than that experienced in the rest of Spain, but unfortunately, the Basque economy has not shown many signs of recovery since.

Figure 1.7. Real GDP per capita in the Basque Country, constant 2010 euros. Source: www.eustat.es.

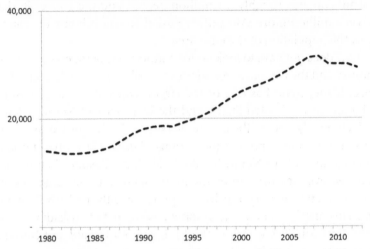

The Basque Country did not experience as dramatic a housing bubble as either Nevada or Ireland, and construction did not become one of its largest sectors, perhaps because the Basque coastline is less ideal for building vacation homes than Spain's Mediterranean coast, or perhaps because fear of ETA prior to the 2011 cessation of hostilities may have dampened potential homeowners' enthusiasm. Because the Basque Country was not the epicenter of a financial crisis, it felt the impact of the Great Recession less than did the rest of Spain, although the Basque Country was nonetheless affected by the declining economies of its trading partners. The Basque Country's BBVA, Spain's second-largest bank, did not require assistance when Spain was bailing out its banks in 2012, largely because it focused on financing international trade rather than the construction sector. Nonetheless, its credit rating was still downgraded because of Spain's economic troubles (*Wall Street Journal* 2012).

Figure 1.8 compares unemployment rates in Nevada and Ireland with those in the Basque Country. It is clear that the financial crisis led to a much sharper economic deterioration in Nevada and Ireland, but the gradual deterioration of the Spanish and European economies nonetheless took a toll on the Basque Country. While unemployment rates in Nevada and Ireland have begun to come down, the unemployment rate in the Basque Country has continued to rise slowly.

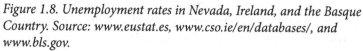

Figure 1.8. Unemployment rates in Nevada, Ireland, and the Basque Country. Source: www.eustat.es, www.cso.ie/en/databases/, and www.bls.gov.

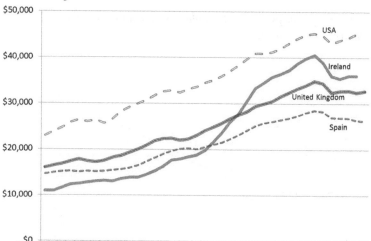

Revenues for the public sector in the Basque Country are relatively more stable than in either Nevada or Ireland, in part because they are more varied. There is a tax of 32.5% on corporate profits, a progressive personal income tax—with rates rising from 15% to 48% on marginal income—and a value-added tax of 21% that matches Spain's rates. The Basque Country also collects taxes on wealth, gifts, and inheritance (Churiaque 2008), as well as property transfer taxes and a variety of miscellaneous taxes. Figure 1.9 shows that the recession has also taken its toll on the public budget in the Basque Country, with rising demand for public expenditures. Tax revenues, however, have remained relatively stable, though this may be overstated somewhat due to the effect of falling GDP on the ratio's denominator.

Conclusion

What lessons do Nevada and Ireland hold for other small states during times of big crises? Unfortunately, policies that promote faster growth over the long term do not prevent downturns in the short run, and policies that reduce an individual economy's susceptibility to downturns do not inoculate a small economy from the effects of recession in the broader economy in which it participates. For good or bad, interdependence comes with consequences.

Countries with housing bubbles, especially if they have deregulated banks, are likely to experience longer and deeper recessions. Small economies that are part of a common currency area may be forced into prolonged declines if their wages, goods, and services become overpriced along with their assets, especially if the core economies of the common currency are unwilling to tolerate price inflation.

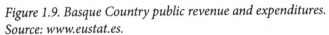

Figure 1.9. Basque Country public revenue and expenditures. Source: www.eustat.es.

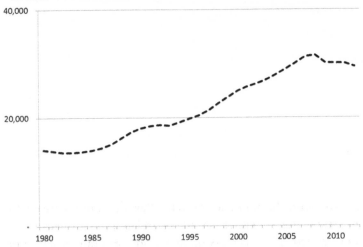

Recessions often lead to a significant decline in tax revenues, and when small economies are constrained in their ability to borrow—Nevada for constitutional reasons, Ireland because it borrowed so heavily to cover its bank bailouts—public sector austerity is likely to be counterproductive. Sovereign debt before the recession was not correlated with the depth of recession. Ireland, like Spain and the Basque Country, had much less public debt than countries like Italy or Greece, but this did not matter. If sovereign debt is high, then it is better to pay it down when the economy is growing, and public spending is not as important for maintaining private spending. With access to credit, the time for austerity is in the boom, not the bust.

However, the Basque experience tells us that it is not enough to avoid a balance-sheet recession if your major trading partners do not avoid it, or if they are forced by a common currency into a gradual deflation. As its exports slowed, consumer price inflation in the Basque Country slowed, and through the first six months of 2014, the Basque Country began to experience price deflation along with the rest of Spain. The recession grew worse for this part of Europe, and recovery had yet to gain a foothold because of continuing events elsewhere.

References

Cargill, T. F., and E. Parker. 2003. "Why Deflation Is Different." *Central Banking* 14 (1): 35–42.

Churiaque, J. I. M. 2008. "The Economic Situation in the Basque Country: A Powerful Financial Tool." *Guide to the Basque Labyrinth*. Fundación para La Libertad, 2008. Available at http://paralalibertad.org/wp-content/uploads/M_Churiaque_Ingles.pdf.

Cooper, A. 2012. "Analysis: Basque Economy Has Lessons for Spain," *Reuters*, June 28.

Guerrero, F., and E. Parker. 2006. "Deflation and Recession: Finding the Empirical Link." *Economics Letters* 93(1): 12–17.

Koo, R. C. 2009. *The Holy Grail of Macroeconomics: Lessons from Japan's Great Recession*. Singapore: Wiley Press.

Krugman, P. R. 2008. "Fifty Herbert Hoovers." *New York Times*, Dec. 28.

Minsky, H. P. 1986. *Stabilizing an Unstable Economy*. New York: Mc-Graw-Hill.

Parker, E. 2011. "Will History Repeat Itself? Nevada's Economy after the Crash." *The Nevada Review* 3(1): 4–17.

Reinhart, C. M., and K. S. Rogoff. 2009. *This Time Is Different: Eight Centuries of Financial Folly*. Princeton, NJ: Princeton University Press.

Uriarte, P. L. 2014. "The Economic Agreement of 1981." In *Basque Fiscal Systems: History, Current Status, and Future Perspectivesm*, edited by J. Agirreazkuenaga and E. A. Olea. Reno: Center for Basque Studies.

Wall Street Journal. 2012. "Fitch Downgrades Spain's Santander, BBVA," Available at www.marketwatch.com, June 11.

2

Resilience of Cooperatives in Times of Crisis: Are Mondragon's Strategies for Coping with Crisis Still a Competitive Advantage?

Jon Landeta, Imanol Basterretxea, and Eneka Albizu

The key question that this work seeks to answer is to what extent the interrelation among the Mondragon cooperatives' training policy, its management tools for organizational flexibility, and its financial intercooperation policy contributes to coping with economic crises.

To this end, the paper first offers some basic information and figures, to give a general idea of the Mondragon experience. It then goes on to examine the instruments that make the corporation different in times of economic crisis. There follows an analysis of the results in terms of Mondragon's employment and sales figures during the 2008 crisis, as compared to the overall average among industrial firms in the Basque Country, and it offers an interpretation of the failure of the leading industrial cooperative in the group, Fagor. The main conclusion is that, although the cooperatives managed to slightly ameliorate the effects of the crisis on employment, the duration and depth of the crisis counts against them, because it tends to reduce their relative advantage in terms of flexibility, and to increase their disadvantages (Bradley and Gelb 1985, 1987; Gorroño 1988; Logan 1988; ILSR 1992). Albizu and Basterretxea (1998) and Elorza et al. (2012) have concluded that the cooperatives of Mondragon were more successful than ordinary companies in dealing with the crises of the 1970s, 1980s, and early 1990s. Many studies have also highlighted the low failure rate of businesses in the group over decades. Nonetheless, during the 2008 crisis, the vulnerability of Mondragon cooperatives to market forces was greater, as shown by the failure of Fagor Electrodomésticos, the Mondragon domestic appliances manufacturer employing nearly six thousand people. Fagor, founded more than sixty years ago, was the first cooperative in the group. In October 2013, the company announced that it was obliged to default on payments; the other Mondragon cooperatives decided not to offer it a bailout.

The key question we intend to answer in this work is: To what extent does the interrelation among Mondragon's training policy, its management tools for organizational flexibility, and its financial intercooperation policy contribute to coping with economic crises?

With this objective in mind, we first offer some basic information and figures to give a general idea of the Mondragon experience. We then go on to examine the instruments that make the corporation different in times of economic crisis. There follows an analysis of the results in terms of Mondragon's employment and sales figures during the 2008 crisis, as compared to the overall average among industrial firms in the Basque Country, and we offer an interpretation of the failure of the leading industrial cooperative in the group, Fagor. Finally, we set out our conclusions.

The Mondragon Experience Today

The Mondragon cooperative experience first began in the Basque town of Mondragon in 1943, in the immediate aftermath of the Spanish Civil War. It was developed at the initiative of local priest José Maria Arizmendiarreta, who had advanced social ideas, great leadership skills, and a tremendous work ethic. Together with a group of young men from the town, this priest founded the first cooperative, which would later become FAGOR (derived from the initials of the five young founders). The cooperative was based on the values of education and training, cooperation, responsibility, and egalitarian enterprise development.

Mondragon Cooperative Corporation (MCC) is now the tenth-largest business group in Spain and the largest in the Basque Country, comprising 110 cooperatives working in four different lines of business. It employs over eighty thousand people (by sector, 46% in industry; 49.6% in retail; 3.1% in finance; and 1.3% in knowledge) in 289 centers, and has a multilevel network of training institutions and fifteen research centers (including its own university). In 2012, it had total assets of €35.9 billion; a net worth of €3.9 billion; total revenue of €14.1 billion; and an EBITDA of €1.3 billion. (MCC 2012).

The group's origins are in industry, the sector that generates most direct—and especially indirect—employment. Together with construction, industry was also the worst hit by the 2008 financial crisis.

We shall therefore center our analysis particularly on the industrial sector of Mondragon Cooperative Corporation. MCC employs 39,963 people in industry (13,903 abroad), generating an added value of €1.8 billion, with total sales of €5.8 billion. Seventy percent of the group's production value (€4.0 billion) is exported. MCC operates in 28 foreign countries, with 105 productions plants and has its own delegations in another nine countries (Mondragon 2012).

Because of the need to remain competitive and to continue providing employment in the Basque Country, the group has become highly internationalized. Studies have shown that cooperatives that have internationalized the most, establishing themselves and creating employment abroad, have created the greatest number of jobs (or lost the fewest) in the Basque Country (Luzarraga and Irizar 2012; Mondragon 2012b).

Cooperative Strategies for Coping with Crisis

As discussed in the introduction, MCC has successfully overcome previous crises. There are essentially three reasons for this resilience: its training policy (mainly based on generic training), its management tools for organizational flexibility (employment policy and wage flexibility), and the financial cooperation within the group.

Training Policy

MCC places great stress on training. The corporation was founded by students from a vocational college in Mondragon and has always invested heavily in training, even creating its own corporate university. Despite a strong orientation toward practical and applied training, the emphasis has been on general training that would be valid for improving the employability of personnel in different functions and cooperatives. General training develops knowledge and skills that are transferrable across a variety of firms. General training, therefore, has become a source of competitive advantage for the organization, especially in dynamic settings and in companies with flexible production systems and quality-based strategies, as is the case with most of the industrial cooperatives.

This type of training also has a motivating effect on employees (Barret and O'Connell 1999 and 2001). It is part of the attraction of working in a cooperative: cooperatives offer a working environment of learning, participation, and continuous improvement (Autor 2001).

Throughout the crisis, MCC has kept up its major investment in training. This includes not only operational training, but also training in cooperative values (inclusive training) and in leadership training. Indeed, leadership and leaders are two of MCC's obsessions, and it has made major investments in executive coaching, for example. In 2012, €8.7 million was earmarked in the industrial area for training, distributed across a variety of technical and socio-business programs. Of particular note was the cooperative training given to 3,048 people and training in leadership and teamwork given to 422 managers (Mondragon 2012).

However, most capital-driven companies are reluctant to support this type of training, fearing possible opportunistic behavior by employees who may take their training and depart for other companies, as Human Capital Theory predicts (Becker 1964).

Management Tools for Organizational Flexibility

Functional Flexibility

There is a very high rate of functional flexibility (ability to employ multiskilled workers who can occupy different positions when necessary) in the cooperatives, thanks to general training and the fact that the workers are essentially company members and are not bound by collective agreements with rigid demarcation of categories and jobs controlled by trade unions. Each cooperative may internally use functional mobility of its members in emergencies or for technological or economic reasons (Albizu and Basterretxea 1998).

Flexible Working Calendar

The use of flexible work schedules to offset a drop in activity has been widespread among the cooperatives in times of crisis. After informing the social council and workers, the cooperative manager may reduce working hours or the number of working days per week for members. If there is an upturn in business in the following months or years, any unworked hours are made up at that time, thus adjusting available working time to the work to be carried out. This is the first resort when cooperatives fall into periods of demand crisis (Albizu and Basterretxea 2010).

Relocations among Cooperatives

When functional flexibility and flexible working calendars are not enough to ensure work for employees, MCC has a very powerful alternative at its disposal: temporary relocation to other cooperatives. This is only possible because as members, the staff are really independent workers. Companies subject to traditional employment legislation do not have this option, since it would involve illegal re-allocation of labor among different firms within the same division or geographical area. When the unemployment situation of the cooperative with surplus staff is irreversible, the relocation becomes permanent. Such relocations have been taking place since the start of the Mondragon experience, and played an important role in the crisis of the 1970s and early 1980s, with 3.5% of all members relocated to other cooperatives in 1984 (Bradley and Gelb 1987, p. 90). In spite of the difficulties encountered in recycling part of the workforce, by the mid-1990s a monthly average of three hundred members were temporarily relocated to cooperatives other than their own, and more than five hundred of these relocations became permanent. In 2012, too, the number of temporary relocations averaged three hundred, rising by early 2014 to around five hundred, following the failure of Fagor. This process of turning temporary relocations into permanent ones may also be favored by the durability and multi-skill capability of the human resources engendered by Mondragon's training policy.

(Re)employment Assistance Fund

Through one of its cooperatives, Lagunaro, MCC operates a fund to provide pensions and benefits for leave and unemployment. The group decides how much has to be paid in; in the case of unemployment, the amount is directly related to current and forecast needs. During the boom years, the fee remained unchanged at 1% for many years, and the fund grew larger and larger; however, as the crisis has eaten into the fund, it has been necessary to raise fees to 2% in 2010 and 3% in 2013. In 2014, following the collapse of Fagor, it was again raised from 3% to 6.5%.

Early Retirement

Another instrument used by MCC is early retirement. However, this is a costly solution and tends to be one of the options of last resort. Conditions for early retirement are similar to those in place under Spain's general Social Security regime before the most recent reforms. Conditions are therefore now more favorable for cooperative worker-members than for the rest of the workforce receiving a pension from Social Security. At MCC, through Lagunaro, pensions are managed by capitalization (the amount paid out depends on the amount paid in). In the Social Security system, this amount depends on distribution (the amount paid out depends on the amount that can be distributed at the time of payment, which depends in turn on how much is being collected at that particular time).

Redundancies

Redundancies are clearly the last resort for an organization created to generate proper employment for its members. However, not all the people employed at MCC are members. In the Industry Area, for example, 85% of the total workforce in 2012 were members. The remaining 15% were non-member workers, whose contracts could not be renewed or who could be dismissed in accordance with local labor law. By various means, employment at MCC was reduced by 3.9% in 2012 (Mondragon 2012).

Wage Flexibility

Together with employment policies and instruments, the other major management instrument making cooperatives more flexible in dealing with economic crises is their greater wage flexibility. Wage policy is subordinated to the creation or maintenance of employment and to business profitability. Cooperative members can—and indeed do—decide to take a cut in their wages (or rather, their advances on profits) when necessary. In Fagor, for example, wages were progressively cut by around 20% in a series of voluntary reductions.

Financial Intercooperation within the Group

A third set of mechanisms that can be used for ameliorating the effects of the crisis is intercooperative financial aid. There are basically two types of aid. The first, which is used more exceptionally, consists of aid given by the corporation to cooperatives in difficulties through a specially created fund. All cooperatives in a position to do so contribute to this fund, and the cooperatives receiving the money make a commitment to repay it. Fagor received various payments under this scheme. The last was to a value of €70 million, which it will probably be unable to repay, at least in its entirety.

The second form of aid is more traditional and forms part of the group's inter-cooperative solidarity rules: restructuring of profits. Cooperatives are obliged to earmark between 15 and 30% of their profits to compensate the losses of the cooperatives from their reference group (if any), meaning that the latters' losses are ultimately lower.

Are Old Responses Good Enough for This Crisis?

To answer this question, we need to compare trends in domestic industrial employment in MCC with Basque industrial employment rates in general (Eustat). MCC accounts for approximately 11% of total employment in industry. This percentage appears to have increased slightly during the recession years. We can therefore conclude that the net effect is positive.

Figure 2.1. Employment in Euskadi and MCC national employment. Source: All figures in this chapter based on data from the Mondragon Annual Reports and from Eustat (Basque Statistical Office). Mondragon (2012, 2011, 2010, 2009, 2008, 2007) and Eustat (2012, 2011, 2010, 2009, 2008, 2007).

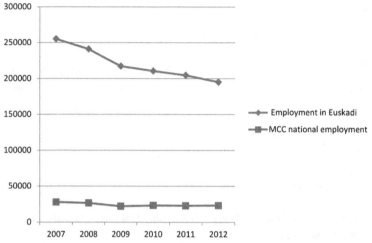

Figure 2.2. Relation between MCC national employment and employment in the Basque Country.

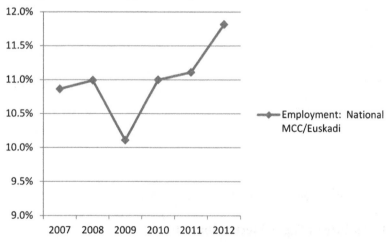

In terms of sales, we can compare Basque industrial sales in general with industrial sales by MCC (in the Basque Country—the majority—and abroad) (Mondragon reports). The results are similar to the average for industrial firms in the Basque Country. The crisis has had a similar effect on the turnover of Basque industrial firms in general and those of MCC.

Figure 2.3. Basque industrial sales and MCC industrial sales.

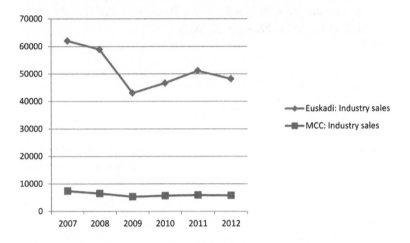

Figure 2.4. Relation between MCC industrial sales and Basque industrial sales.

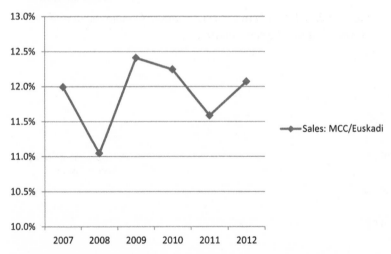

The Failure of Fagor Electrodomésticos

At the end of 2013, Fagor Electrodomésticos filed for receivership. It was MCC's first, most iconic, and most international firm and also its largest industrial firm (Eroski, in the distribution sector, is larger), accounting for approximately 8% of total MCC sales. Fagor produced household appliances for washing, cooking, heating, and cooling, as well as small domestic appliances, in sixteen production plants in six countries: the Basque Country (7), France (4), China (2), Italy (1), Poland (1), and Morocco (1). In 2007, it employed over eleven thousand people. When it closed at the end of 2013, it had approximately 5,600 employees—2,000 in the Basque Country, of whom 1,800 were worker-members.

This cooperative was hit particularly badly by the crisis for a number of reasons:

- Fagor had a mature, not technology-intensive, product.
- The product was high volume, but low price.
- It was impacted by a Europe-wide crisis in its main markets, industry, and construction.
- Before the crisis, it had acquired a large French company (Brant), of a similar size as Fagor, resulting in high debt.
- There had been a drop in consumption of medium-range (non-low-cost, nonluxury) products, which was Fagor's traditional market segment.
- Unlike its main competitors, most of Fagor's production was concentrated in countries with high wage costs (Errasti 2014).

In addition, the jobs in the Basque Country and France contributed little added value to the product, and its workers were relatively low-skilled.

The obvious answer was either to focus on innovation, developing more advanced products and/or introducing new industries, or to move the majority of production to low-cost countries.

Management at Fagor and MCC tried to apply the latter solution, but reacted too late. One former general manager had made significant efforts in this regard as early as 2007, before the recession hit. However, in those situations, the ultimate decision lies with the owners—that is, the workers—and the cooperative system does not facilitate making the sort of tough, radical decisions that harm the workers' short-term interests. The sacrifice is real and comes in the short term, whereas the benefits (or reduced losses) are conjectural and are seen in the long term. It takes great leadership to rally the support of the membership base.

Instead, Fagor opted to make other decisions and devise other solutions that would not affect employment in the Basque Country to the same extent. These aggravated the problem and affected the success of the other MCC cooperatives.

Mondragon Cooperative Corporation (MCC) is now the tenth-largest business group in Spain and the largest in the Basque Country, comprising 103 cooperatives working in four different lines of business. It employs over seventy-four thousand people (by sector, 42.8% in Industry; 52.2% in Retail; 3.6% in Finance; and 1.4% in Knowledge) in 260 centers, and has a multilevel network of training institutions and fifteen research centers (including its own university). In 2013 it had total assets of €34.0 billion; total revenue of €12.6 billion; and an EBITDA of €1.2 billion (MCC 2014).

The group's origins are in industry, the sector that generates most direct—and especially indirect—employment. Together with construction, industry was also the worst hit by the 2008 financial crisis. We shall therefore center our analysis particularly on the industrial part of MCC. MCC employs 31,736 people in industry, with total sales of €4.8 billion. Seventy-one percent of the group's production value (€3.6 billion) is exported. MCC operates in 30 foreign countries, with 125 productions plants, and has its own delegations in another 9 countries (Mondragon 2014).

Conclusions

From this general analysis and from the case of Fagor, in particular, we can draw a number of conclusions:

- In the current crisis, the cooperatives managed to slightly ameliorate the effects of the crisis on employment, due mainly to the internal flexibility provided by their general training policy, their employment policy, their wage flexibility, and the positive effects of financial cooperation among the various businesses.
- In previous crises, the cooperatives' relative capacity to reduce the effects of the crisis on employment was probably higher than during the 2008 crisis; recent legislative and social changes had notably increased the contractual, functional, and wage flexibility of other non-cooperative companies, meaning that their advantage had decreased in relative terms.
- Although maintaining employment is a priority for cooperatives, there are two clearly different degrees of commitment: that of the worker-owners, and that of non-member workers (which is evidently lower). There may even be a third category: non-member workers from outside the Basque Country.
- In the current crisis, the cooperatives do not have better (or

worse) sales results than the mean for industrial firms in their setting. The positive effects of their greater internal flexibility, intercooperative financial cooperation, and, in general, greater financial solidity (due to their obligation to self-finance/reinvest) are offset by greater contractual rigidity and greater difficulty in making the necessary radical decisions that will harm the interests of worker-owners.

- In this regard, the duration and depth of the crisis counts against the cooperatives, because it tends to reduce their relative advantage (other companies have caught up in terms of flexibility) and to increase their disadvantages (their difficulty in making drastic job cuts and changing business and location).

References

Albizu, E., and I. Basterretxea. 2010. "¿Es posible resistir la crisis? Un análisis desde la gestión de las políticas de formación y empleo en Mondragon." *Ciriec-España. Revista de Economía Pública, Social y Cooperativa*, no. 67: 75–96.

————.1998. "Flexibilidad laboral y generación de empleo en tiempos de crisis: El caso de Mondragon Corporación Cooperativa." *Revista Europea de Dirección y Economía de la Empresa*, 7 (3), (1998): 83–98.

Autor, D. H. 2001. "Why Do Temporary Help Firms Provide Free General Skills Training?" Quarterly Journal of Economics, 116(4): 1409–48.

Barrett, A., and P. J. O'Connell. 1999. "Does Training Generally Work? The Returns to In-Company Training." IZA Discussion Paper no. 51.

————. 2001. "Does Training Generally Work?" *Industrial and Labor Relations Review* 54(3): 647–62.

Becker, G. S. 1964. *Human Capital*. Princeton, NJ: Princeton University Press.

Bradley, K., and A. Gelb. 1985. *Cooperation at Work: The Mondragon Experience*. London: Heinemann.

————. 1987. "Cooperative Labor Relations: Mondragon Response to Recession." *British Journal of Industrial Relations* 25 (1): 77–97.

Elorza, N., I. Alzola, and U. López. 2012. "La gestión de la crisis en la Corporación Mondragón." *Ekonomiaz* 79 (1): 58–81.

Errasti, A. M. 2014. "Tensiones y oportunidades en las multinacionales coopitalistas de Mondragon: El caso de Fagor Electrodomésticos, Sdad. Coop." *Revesco* 113: 30–60

Eustat. 2012, 2011, 2010, 2009, 2008, 2007. Personnel Employed in the Basque Country by Province and District, and Net Industry Sales in the Basque Country by Province and District . Available at www.eustat.es/estadisticas/tema_56/opt_0/ti_Industria/temas.html#axzz33BAvN7nQ.

Gorroño, I. 1988. "El cooperativismo industrial de Mondragon: Respuesta ante la crisis económica." In *Congreso sobre el cooperativismo y la economía social en el mundo. II Congreso Mundial Vasco*, 87–97. Vitoria-Gasteiz: Servicio Central de Publicaciones del Gobierno Vasco.

ILSR. 1992. The Mondragon System: Cooperation at Work. Available at www.newrules.org/resources/MondragonCo-op.pdf.

Logan, C. G. 1988. "An Experiment That Continues: The Mondragon Co-Operatives." In *Congreso sobre el cooperativismo y la economía social en el mundo. II Congreso Mundial Vasco*, 111–13. Vitoria-Gasteiz: Servicio Central de Publicaciones del Gobierno Vasco.

Luzarraga, J. M. and I. Irizar. 2012. "La estrategia de multilocalización internacional de la Corporación Mondragon." *Ekonomiaz* 79 (1): 114–45.

Mondragon. 2012, 2011, 2010, 2009, 2008, 2007. Annual reports. Available at www.mondragon-corporation.com/eng/about-us/economic-and-financial-indicators/annual-report/#introduccion.

———. 2012b. *Impacto de la internacionalización sobre la empresa doméstica. Mondragon: Fagor Electrodomésticos.*

3

Why Does the Basque Country Cope Better with Financial Crisis Than Spain?

Andrés Araujo

After joining the eurozone, Spain enjoyed strong economic growth, leading to a sharp drop in unemployment and a rise in per capita income, with incomes drawing level with the EU average. Between 2002 and the onset of the crisis in 2008, the Spanish economy grew faster than the European average, especially in the first five years of the period (figure 3.1).

Figure 3.1. GDP annual growth. Source: Eustat.

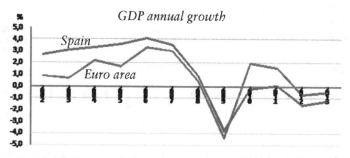

At the same time, the Spanish population grew much faster than in the eurozone as a whole. As a result, unemployment fell more slowly in Spain than in the rest of the union. In Germany, in contrast, the population remained stable, even falling slightly, and indeed, its 2013 population is still smaller than in 2002. The population of the Basque Country rose on a par with the EU average; in 2013, it was up only 5% over the 2002 figure, compared to a 15% rise in Spain as a whole.

Given that Spanish (and Basque) birthrates are among the lowest in the world, this population growth was clearly driven by immigration. However, much of the economic and population growth was based on an oversizing in the construction industry. The explosion in Spain's building industry was only outstripped by that of Poland. At its height, the industry came to account for 20% of non-financial employment and 18% of added value, when the average for EU27 was slightly above 10% (Stawinska 2010). However, compared to the eurozone average, labor productivity rates were not high. This situation becomes all the more obvious if we compare Spain to the United Kingdom, which, together with Ireland, had the highest apparent labor productivity in this sector in 2007.

In the Basque Country, too, construction was an important driver of growth, but to a much smaller extent than in Spain. Nonetheless, the crisis has also had a strong impact on employment and on added value generated by the industry from 2007 onward (figure 3.2).

Figure 3.2. Employment in construction over total employment and gross value added in construction industry. Sources: INE and Eustat..

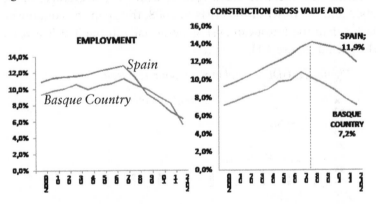

As already mentioned, that growth was made possible by Spain's membership in the eurozone. A large part of the consumption and investment was financed with foreign capital because the associated risk was underestimated; it was generally believed that the euro would result in economic convergence of member countries. Spain's risk was erroneously viewed as being similar to Germany's. Indeed, at one point the two countries had the same risk premium. Opportunities for investment were greater in Spain than in Germany, which was undergoing low growth rates at the time.

At the same time, higher inflation meant that real interest rates were lower in Spain than in other eurozone countries, especially Germany, contributing to higher consumption and investment and lower savings rates (figure 3.3).

Figure 3.3. Real eurozone interest rates. Source: Eurostat.

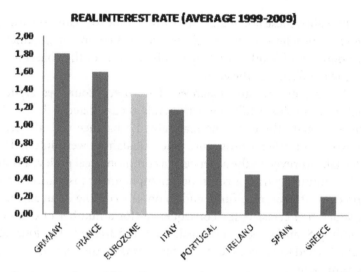

Spain was thus able to finance and maintain a substantial current account balance deficit, leading the economy to accumulate strong external imbalances (peaking in 2007 and 2008 just before the outbreak of the crisis [figure 3.4]), while gradually losing competitiveness and reaching unsustainable levels of external debt.

Figure 3.4. Spanish current account 2000–2012. Source: Instituto Nacional de Estadística INE.

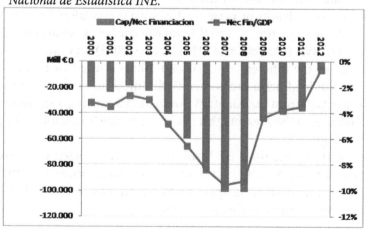

The most significant effects were:

- A high level of external debt
- High private (household and business) borrowing
- Loss of price competitiveness: inflation above eurozone average and higher unit labor costs.

In reality, these imbalances were not unique to Spain. As we know, the same problems occurred elsewhere in the eurozone, namely in the countries of southern Europe. This was one of the consequences of deficient design of the euro.

The current account balances of northern countries gradually built up a surplus, while the peripherals accumulated a deficit. As a whole, though, the eurozone maintained a balance with the rest of the world. In other words, eurozone imbalances were internal, not external. However, in the absence of a common fiscal policy; a system of debt mutualization; a common unemployment insurance; a common deposit guarantee fund, and so on, the coming of an asymmetric shock had catastrophic consequences for a number of countries, including Spain, Greece, Portugal, Italy, and Ireland. The four latter countries had to be bailed out, and Spain was on the verge of suffering the same fate.

One of the consequences of the euro crisis resulting from the asymmetric shocks was the fragmentation of the European financial system, which had serious consequences for the funding of companies. This proved to be far more serious in peripheral economies such as Spain's, but the negative effects were also being felt closer to the center.

The interbank money market is not functioning properly either. Exposure to banks of peripheral countries has fallen by 55%, and interbank exposure in central European countries has also fallen (by 42%) (BBVA research 2014; Abascal et al, 2013). In other words, the banks of the different countries no longer trusted each other and were not lending to each other. Each European economy had to finance itself from the country's own national savings, a situation that continues to the present. This has had negative implications for economic growth.

At the same time, bank risk has been transferred to sovereign risk. Here, the Spanish case is among the most obvious, with the European Union granting Spain a €40 billion loan in September 2012 to resolve the assets of its financial system

As a result, reinforcing the European banking union has become an essential task for setting the European economy back on the path of stable growth. This is a complicated undertaking and one of the most important steps to be taken in Europe since the creation of the euro.

The Situation in the Basque Country

Rapid growth led the Basque Country to climb rapidly up the ranking of European regions in terms of income levels, and by 2007 it was among the top forty. Until 2007, the Basque Country, like Spain, also performed very well in terms of employment. This was largely due to an influx of women into the workforce, a process in which the Basque economy had lagged somewhat behind the rest of Europe.

At the beginning of the crisis, Basque employment suffered less than in the rest of Spain; it, in fact, stayed in line with the EU average (figure 3.5).

Figure 3.5. Employment rate. Source: Eustat and Eurostat.

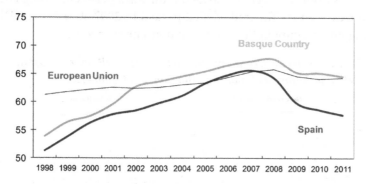

Table 3.1. Production structure of the Basque Country. (*) 2010 figures. Source: Basque Government's Economics and Planning Office with data from Eustat, INE, and Eurostat.

	Basque Country	Spain	European Union (*)
Added Value	100,0	100,0	100,0
Primary	0,7	2,6	1,7
Industrie	25,1	16,9	18,7
Construction	7,2	11,5	6,0
Services	66,9	69,0	73,6

As table 3.1 shows, industry accounts for a much larger share of the production structure in the Basque Country than in either Spain or the European Union as a whole. The figure for construction lies somewhere in between, higher than the EU average and lower than in Spain.

The industrial sector has traditionally played an important role in the Basque economy. At the beginning of the 1980s, it accounted for approximately 40% of Gross Value Added (GVA). Although the industrial crisis led to major restructuring of the sector, the momentum was not lost, and its share of GVA stabilized at around 30%. What happened in the Basque Country in the 1980s was a process of reindustrialization: greater diversification of industrial activity, recovery of the electrical and energy materials industry, together with the emergence of business services, which displaced metals and metal articles as the principal branch of the economy (Alberdi 2010).

Another major difference between the Spanish and Basque economies over the last two decades has been the performance of external demand. As figure 3.6 shows, Spain's trade balance remained negative throughout the period from 1996 to 2011, reaching a record low in the years prior to the crisis (2005–08) during a period of strong economic expansion. The trade deficit peaked in 2007 at -9.5% of GDP, taking into account both energy and non-energy goods.

Figure 3.6. Trade account balance relative to GDP. Source: Eustat, INE, and Ministry of Industry, Tourism and Commerce.

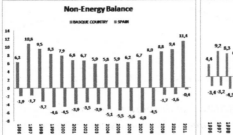 

Given that both the Spanish and Basque economies are energy-dependent, if we are to use the trade account balance as an indicator of the competitiveness of the country's business sector, it may be more helpful to exclude the energy factor from the equation. Taking only the non-energy balance into account, the situation in Spain does not change greatly; from the adoption of the euro to the outbreak of the crisis, the deficit never fell below 3.5% of GDP, peaking at 6% in 2007, although it has to be said that since the crisis it has fallen significantly, dropping to practically zero in 2011.

The Basque trade balance, on the other hand, has operated along quite different lines from the rest of Spain. Even if we take energy into consideration, the region maintained a trade surplus throughout the period from 1996 to 2011, apart from two marginally negative years in 2005 and 2006. And if we look only at the trade in non-energy goods, the figure is closer to that of Germany or the Netherlands, reaching a record 11.4% of GDP in 2011. As we shall see below, these healthy trade figures are the result of the high rates of competitiveness and productivity of Basque companies.

The growth factors in the Basque and Spanish economies have not been the same. As figure 3.11 shows, Erauskin (2010), analyzing the composition of the growth of GVA from 1995 to 2007, a period of strong economic growth, found total-factor productivity in Spain to be negative, contributing -0.36% to annual growth in GVA. The contribution in the Basque Country, on the other hand, was positive, albeit not very high, at 0.77%. In principle, this means that the Basque economy has shown a more innovative performance than that of the rest of Spain.

Figure 3.7. Average annual rate of change of gross value added and total productivity factors (1995–2007). Source: Erauskin (2010).

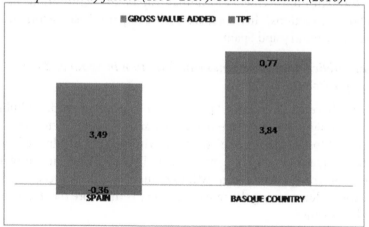

Mas and Navarro (2012) find similar results, estimating that Basque productivity between 1995 and 2007 grew at twice the annual rate of Spain's (1.28% compared to 0.66%). Nonetheless, when compared to the EU-15 average (1.63%) or the US (2.64%), these figures were still insufficient to cope securely with the financial crisis. The Basque economy was also closer to the rest of Europe in contribution of ICT capital to GVA growth; in the Basque Country, EU-15, and the U.S., ICT capital contributed more than non-ICT capital. In Spain, on the other hand, the situation was the inverse. In any case, although ICT capital grew slightly faster in the Basque Country than in Spain (0.31% and 0.25%, respectively), both figures are still well behind EU-15 levels (0.50%) and even further behind the United States (0.92%). Both the Basque Country and Spain therefore need to make considerable investments to come close to acceptable levels.

Basque Country Coping Factors

The crisis suffered by the Basque Country and Spain had a financial origin and financial causes. The crisis generated a major credit crunch and a contraction in domestic demand. Like the other economies in the eurozone, which were also in crisis, Spain and the Basque Country, in the face of austerity measures and budgetary adjustments, have concentrated growth in aggregate demand on exports. Going abroad requires companies to assume greater competition and greater risk. Reductions in salary costs, together with reform of the labor market, can help them to be more price-competitive, but improved productivity is even more important, and this can be achieved largely through improvements in human capital and innovation. In the following sections, therefore, we shall compare these factors in the Basque Country and Spain.

The Public and Private Financing Situation in Spain and the Basque Country

As we have mentioned, in Spain an unprecedented property bubble led to a high rate of private borrowing among households and businesses. Most of the accumulated borrowing was private. Indeed, both the Basque and Spanish governments had taken advantage of the years of strong economic growth to reduce their debt levels. One key factor in determining the rate of recovery is therefore the initial level of borrowing.

As figure 3.8 below shows, the rate of borrowing varied greatly among the different regions in Spain, and the crisis only served to intensify the disparity. As we can see, Basque borrowing has remained among the lowest at all times, falling to almost ridiculous levels (1% of GDP) in 2007.

The regions with the highest levels of debt (see figure 3.9: Communities of Valencia, Catalonia, Castile La Mancha, and the Balearic Islands) were among the worst affected by the property bubble and

Figure 3.8. Debt of Spanish regions as % of GDP. Source: Spanish Central Bank data.

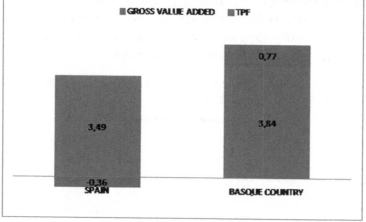

Figure 3.9. Debt and public deficit (% Regional GDP). Source: BBVA Research.

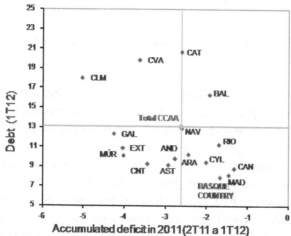

were also the areas with highest increase in population resulting from immigration. The Basque population, on the contrary, remained relatively stable throughout the decade.

Smaller imbalances in the Basque Country compared to other Spanish regions have meant that it has not had to work as hard to achieve fiscal consolidation, giving it greater room for maneuvering to implement a countercyclical fiscal policy.

Indeed, the Basque Country was the only autonomous community to reduce its debt levels during the period of growth, and is the region that increased borrowing the most during the crisis (figure

3.10). From 2000 to 2008, regional debt rose by 7.9%, whereas Basque borrowing fell by 9.1%. However, this also explains why the Basque Country's percentage of borrowing increased the most from 2009–12: it started from very low levels, which caused a significant statistical effect. After 2009, when its deficit rose sharply to more than 4%, it was among the regions with the smallest deficits.

Figure 3.10. Annual growth in debt of Spanish regions (2000–2012).
Source: Spanish Central Bank data.

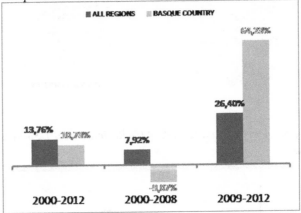

Thus, the Basque Country is the region that has seen the most countercyclical performance. Even so, it maintained one of the best debt-to-GDP ratios and, after Navarre, enjoys the best credit rating from the ratings agencies, two notches above Spain's sovereign debt.

Just as public borrowing is lower in the Basque Country, so too is private borrowing. During the financial crisis, researchers discovered a relationship between the level of borrowing and employment cutbacks, and showed that companies with higher initial levels of borrowing cut the number of workers by 11.6%, whereas in firms with lower debt levels, there was only a 9.6% reduction in workers. The study also found the same relationship in regard to company size: there have been larger job cuts in Small and Medium-sized Enterprises (SMEs) and in large companies (Menéndez and Méndez, 2013).

Compared to the rest of Spain, Basque companies tend to be larger and to have had lower leverage levels, and therefore were less affected by the credit crunch.

Internationalization

Because the Basque economy is small, it experiences major fluctuations in exports. Nonetheless, figure 3.11 shows a clear trend toward greater internationalization, especially in times of difficulty. It is also worth noting the strong growth in Basque exports after 2009, the year in which the crisis hit hardest. In 2011, exports accounted for more than 30% of GDP, a record high.

Figure 3.11. Exports of goods abroad relative to GDP. Source: Eustat, INE, and Ministry for the Economy and Competitiveness.

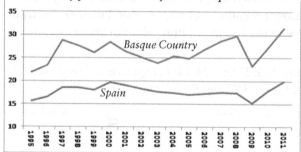

Both the Basque Country and Spain in general have been losing ground in price competitiveness, due to a greater increase in unit labor costs. In the Basque Country, salaries rose sharply during the period of growth from 1995–2007. However, as table 3.2 shows, the region managed to maintain its market share in global exports, in contrast to a fall in the share of other developed economies resulting from the strong entry of China into global markets.

Table 3.2 Share of world exports. Source: Navarro and Mas (2012).

	Per Thousand			% of change	
	1995	2007	2010	1995-2007	2007-2010
Basque Country	1,82	1,97	1,69	8,50	-14,40
Spain	19,85	19,24	17,50	-3,10	-9,00
EU-euro	390,43	343,28	306,09	-12,10	-10,80
Germany	108,84	95,52	86,28	-12,20	-9,70
USA	124,25	86,21	84,39	-30,60	-2,10

Although between 2007 and 2011 Basque market share fell more sharply than that of other advanced economies, in 2011 and 2012 it rallied well. One might conclude that Basque companies enjoy other sources of competitiveness apart from unit labor costs, such as improvements in product quality.

It is also important to look at the type of products marketed abroad and the nature of the trade balance. Naturally, the most important products are focused in the high and medium technology sectors, which provide the most added value and are least subject to price competition. As we can see in figure 3.12, both Spain and the Basque Country have improved their trade balance in this area since the onset of the crisis in 2008. The difference is that throughout the period under analysis, Spain's trade balance was negative, whereas the Basque Country enjoyed a trade surplus. Likewise, the trade coverage rose faster in the Basque Country than in Spain as a whole.

Figure 3.12. External trade in high tech and medium-high tech sectors. Source: INE and Eustat data.

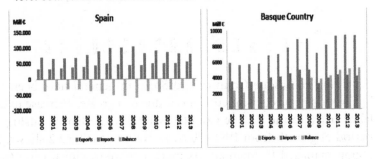

Research and Development (R&D)

The Basque Country has invested heavily in innovation as a motor of economic development. This commitment is evident in investment (R&D/GDP) and the sophisticated regional innovation system created over the last decades. Investment in R&D is already 2% of the GDP, on a par with EU-15, although it should be said that the private-sector contribution, at only 54% of the total, is still too low.

At the same time, a sophisticated science and technology network has been developed, structured around three subsystems or groups: a scientific group; a technological and innovation group; and a support group for innovation. The scientific subsystem includes the five universities in the Basque Country, cooperative research centers (CICs),[1] and Basic Research Centers of Excellence (BERCs).

---

1. There are seven CICs in all, operating in the fields of biotechnology, biomaterials, nanotechnology, high-performance machining, tourism, and energy.

The technological development and innovation subsystem comprises two large technology center corporations, Tecnalia[2] and the IK4 Research Alliance. Its mission is to provide added value to the business demand of both business clusters and sectors as well as companies in the Basque Country. Finally, the innovation support subsystem includes the technology parks and the Basque Innovation Agency (Innobasque). Its mission is to try to turn the Basque Country into a reference point for innovation.

Quality of Human Capital

In the knowledge society, the availability of well-trained human capital is key to retaining business competitiveness and high sustainable rates of economic growth. Alongside Madrid and Navarre, the Basque Country tops the scoreboard in all training and labor qualification indicators. The proportion of the Basque population aged between twenty and twenty-four with secondary education or higher is above the EU average, and 20 percentage points above Spain's; the school dropout level is below the European average and much lower than Spain's.[3] The qualification levels of the workforce are also higher than in the rest of Spain.

These advantages, combined with a lower rate of temporary employment (meaning a greater number of hours worked per employee) and the greater weight of the industrial sector (which has high productivity rates), help explain why the Basque Country has managed to keep per-employee productivity rates above Spanish and EU averages (figure 3.13).

Figure 3.13. Productivity Per Employee. Source: Eurostat and Eustat.

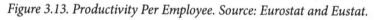
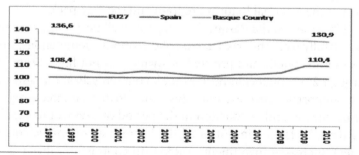

2. Tecnalia is the largest private applied research center in Spain and the fifth largest in Europe, with a staff of 1,400, turnover of €125 million, and a customer portfolio of nearly 4,000 companies

3. The percentage of 18- to 24-year-olds in the region who have completed at most the first stage of secondary education and are no longer in education or training in the Basque Country is 10.8%, as compared to 14.1% in EU-27 and 28.4% in Spain. (Eurostat and Eustat data for 2010.)

As figure 3.14 shows, labor productivity in the Basque Country is particularly high in the energy sector. It is not surprising, therefore, that the region boasts some of the world's leading players in the industry, including Iberdrola and Gamesa.

Figure 3.14. Labor productivity in the energy industry. Source: Mas and Navarro (2012).

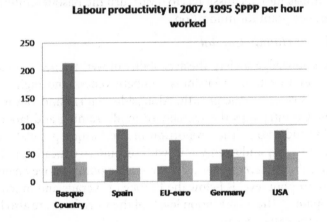

Conclusions

The Basque Country has suffered one of the worst economic crises in its recent history. This was inevitable given today's globalized economy, and its inclusion in the European Union. The region has a close exchange relationship with other European countries; the European Union fixes its monetary policy, and its fiscal policy is largely shaped through the Stability and Growth Pact, which is materialized in the form of the National Reform Program and the "Six-pack."

Nonetheless, the Basque Country was well positioned to emerge successfully from the crisis. It has solid economic foundations. In relative terms, public and private borrowing was not high. From 2009 through 2012, public authorities took countercyclical measures and lent support to business financing, with loan guarantee programs for businesses and a reduction in the period of payment to suppliers (34 days, by far the lowest of all the Spanish autonomous communities). Increased investment in R&D (in contrast to other regions) and higher labor qualifications have enabled the Basque Country to orient economic growth more toward external markets, in the face of a fall in domestic demand at times of stronger external competition. The cooperatives, too, have played a significant role during the crisis. Faced with a fall in demand, cooperatives, which account for an important part of the Basque economy, have cut salaries rather than jobs. This has contributed to some extent to the fact that the Basque unemployment rate is lower than the Spanish average.

Nonetheless, the Basque economy faces very similar challenges to those of the rest of Spain. One of the most important of these is an aging population, a factor that is beginning to create serious imbalances in the public budget, with a major impact on social spending, through healthcare, dependency, and pensions. By 2050, the largest population cohort is expected to be between the ages of 70 and 84, as compared to 1981, when the largest cohort was between 5 and 20 years old. Greater increases in productivity will be required to cope with the resulting impact on the economy. This increase can only come from technological progress, and here it will not be sufficient merely to maintain or increase investment in R&D; it will also be necessary to achieve major improvements in efficiency of spending, which is currently not very high when measured in terms of patents or new products. At the same time, reforms must be maintained that give the economy a greater degree of flexibility, thus allowing for faster adaptation to changes in the surroundings.

References

Abascal, M., T. Alonso, and S. Mayordomo. 2013. "Fragmentation in European Financial Markets: Measures, Determinants, and Policy Solutions." Working Papers 13/22. BBVA Research. Madrid, July. Available at www.bbvaresearch.com/wp-content/uploads/migrados/WP_1322_tcm348-394976.pdf.

Alberdi, A. 2010. "Economía Vasca 1980–2010: Tres crisis y una gran transformación," *Ekonomiaz* 25: 32–95.

Aranguren, M. J., E. Magro, M. Navarro, and J. M. Valdaliso. 2012. *Estrategias para la construcción de Ventajas Competitivas regionales: El caso del País Vasco.* Madrid: Marcial Pons.

Domenech, R. 2013. "La crisis en la Unión Europea." Universidad Complutense. www.bbvaresearch.com/publicaciones/la-crisis-en-la-union-europea/.

Erauskin, I. 2010. "Accounting for Growth in Spain, the Basque Country (and its Historic Territories), Madrid and Navarre since 1964." Unpublished manuscript. Available at http://paginaspersonales.deusto.es/ineraus/Files/PTF1964_2006.pdf.

Mas, M., and M. Navarro. 2012. *Un modelo de crecimiento y productividad regional: El caso del País Vasco.* Madrid: Marcial Pons.

Menéndez, A. and M. Méndez. 2013. "La evolución del endeu-
damiento de las empresas no financieras españolas desde el inicio
de la crisis. Un análisis desagregado." *Banco de España: Boletín
Económico*. Available at www.bde.es/f/webbde/SES/Secciones/
Publicaciones/InformesBoletinesRevistas/BoletinEconomi-
co/13/Ene/Fich/be1301-art3.pdf.
Stawinska, A. 2010. "The EU-27 Construction Sector: From Boom to
Gloom." *Eurostat: Statistics in Focus*. July. Available at http://epp.
eurostat.ec.europa.eu/cache/ITY_OFFPUB/KS-SF-10-007/EN/
KS-SF-10-007-EN.PDF.

4

The Crisis of Public Finances in Navarre, and the Economic Agreement

Mikel Aranburu Urtasun

From a comparative legal perspective, the historical model of the Economic Agreement (or *Convenio* in Navarre [Navarra in Spanish, Nafarroa in Basque]) provides the highest level of public financial self-government to a dependent territory of a state. In a reversal of the usual direction of financial flows, the region transfers funds to the state. The autonomous community of Navarre collects almost all taxes and contributes a share of these to the Spanish state, as payment for general expenses not assumed by the region.

In this model, the risk is unilateral for Navarre. This means that whatever tax revenues are collected, Navarre must make a financial contribution to the state according to the budget of the Spanish kingdom. In times of economic expansion and business prosperity, this method of financial and tax management can benefit Navarre. However, in times of crisis, with a significant drop in tax revenues, Navarre must continue to pay its contribution to the state as well as cover its own budget expenditures. In such periods, Navarre may fare worse than other regions or communities of the state.

Since 2011, the decline in revenues due to the economic crisis has been compounded by the effect of taxation on an important vehicle manufacturing company in Navarre: Volkswagen. The government of Navarre has been forced to negotiate with the Spanish kingdom to avoid the bankruptcy of the Foral Community. This situation illustrates the weakness of the historical model and its dependence on the political will of the Spanish government, which varies according to its political attitude toward the regional government. Thus, it exemplifies the resilience of political submission.

The Crisis of Public Finances in Navarre and the Economic Agreement

The Economic Agreement (or *Convenio* in Navarre) provides a territory dependent on a state with the maximum level of financial autonomy known in comparative law, to the extent that the usual direction of financial flow is reversed. The Economic Agreement model of financing dates back to 1841, and is the last remaining prerogative of a wider set of rights historically granted to the Basque Country and Navarre. Navarre collects almost all taxes, and in return, it pays the central government a specific sum toward the general expenses that cover the functions not assumed by the region, such as defense and foreign relations. The main areas of expenditure of the Navarrese government are education, health, social services, and transportation, roads, and highways. The municipalities (local councils) provide the usual municipal services.

Tax decentralization produces economic and political gains. Economic gains may include increased accountability and responsibility, which, combined with the risk of migration (of individuals or productive factors) in response to overtaxation, lead to more efficient regional taxation and expenditure. On the political side, tax decentralization is the natural response to self-government demands in many regions. Both the theory and the practical experience of the most advanced federations (Switzerland, Canada, and the United States) show that even decentralization of all taxes is unlikely to produce significant delocalization (of persons or businesses) or economic inefficiencies.

The Economic Agreement model is based on two principles—fiscal autonomy and the payment of a quota to the state:

Fiscal Autonomy

It is the responsibility of the Navarrese authorities to administer and, subject to some harmonization rules, regulate the following taxes: personal income tax (residents and non-residents), value-added tax (VAT), excise tax, corporation tax, inheritance tax, property taxes, and other direct and indirect taxes. The central government scarcely collects any taxes in Navarre.

In general, taxes in Navarre are not very different from taxes in the Common Territory (the rest of Spain excluding the Basque Country). The two main differences are, first, that personal income tax in Navarre is slightly lower and more progressive than in the Common

Table 4.1. GDP per capita (euros).

	2008	2009	2010	2011	2012
Navarra	29,917.00	28,676.00	28,866.00	29,640.00	29,071.00
Spain	23,858.00	22,819.00	22,766.00	23,054.00	22,772.00
EU-28	25,000.00	23,400.00	24,400.00	25,100.00	25,500.00
% Navarra/Spain	125%	126%	127%	129%	128%
% Navarra/EU-28	120%	123%	118%	118%	114%

Source: Based on Instituto Navarro de Estadística www.cfnavarra.es/estadistica.

Table 4.2. Tax collection.

	2009	2010	2011	2012	2013
Personal Income tax	1,110,226,133	1,039,601,132	1,096,506,252	1,118,359,457	1,054,885,303
Corporation tax	412,564,054	188,484,602	213,066,776	201,388,605	194,286,198
Non Residents	10,646,435	8,907,705	8,539,000	5,193,444	6,704,577
Inheritance and Gifts	37,930,796	40,463,166	36,968,666	44,851,235	92,631,607
Wealth (eliminated 2008, 2009 and 2010)	3,164,377	613,678	950,491	39,952,285	51,189,332
Other direct and indirect taxes	-	-	-	-	25,490,983
Total direct taxes	1,574,531,795	1,278,070,283	1,356,031,185	1,409,745,026	1,425,188,000
Value-added tax (VAT)	897,395,487	1,025,246,860	1,207,981,588	1,067,658,717	919,470,924
Excises	416,030,566	422,216,958	439,522,102	381,268,381	460,200,176
Capital Transfer tax	41,269,942	44,053,897	37,970,670	29,477,179	28,437,910
Stamp Duty	32,941,554	24,443,490	18,399,712	15,418,269	11,696,771
Insurance Premiums Tax	18,596,329	19,802,235	20,136,957	20,143,801	21,359,249
Tax on Hydrocarbons (retail)	21,932,722	22,416,626	23,234,284	26,766,868	10,035,657
Abolished indirect taxes	21,630	18,134	5,359	39,128	5,329
Total indirect taxes	1,428,188,230	1,558,198,200	1,747,250,672	1,540,772,343	1,451,206,016
Total taxes	3,002,720,025	2,836,268,483	3,103,281,857	2,950,517,369	2,876,394,016
Other	33,467,862	32,637,194	39,221,869	28,072,457	30,735,983
TOTAL NET COLLECTION	3,036,187,887	2,868,905,677	3,142,503,726	2,978,589,826	2,907,129,999

Source web Gobierno de Navarra http://www.navarra.es/.

Table 4.3. Collection / GDP (million euros).

	2009	2010	2011	2012
Collection	3,036.19	2,868.91	3,142.50	2,978.59
GDP	17,750.82	17,958.26	18,513.32	18,735.59
% Collection / GDP	17.1%	16.0%	17.0%	15.9%

Source: Based on data from Instituto Navarro de Estadística

Table 4.4. Evolution of the Quota (million euros) .

Year	Quota	TAX Collection	Quota/Tax Collection (%)
2009	344.6	3,036.19	11.3%
2010	485.5	2,868.91	16.9%
2011	490.0	3,142.50	15.6%
2012	546.7	2,978.59	18.4%
2013	551.1	2,907.13	19.0%

Source: Based on data from Gobierno de Navarra, www.navarra.es/.

Territory; and, second, that the Navarrese corporate tax rate is slightly lower and there are more tax incentives (for investment and job creation).

Quota Payments

Navarre pays a quota to the state toward the competences not assumed by the region and as a contribution to solidarity among all of the regions. To calculate Navarre's financial contribution to the Spanish kingdom, the model of the Economic Agreement takes into account the cost of the powers not assumed by the region, along with a number of adjustments required by the rules of tax harmonization. These settings include an adjustment for indirect taxation (VAT) that aims to approximate the theoretical consumption of the inhabitants of Navarre. These adjustments are calculated using mathematical formulas that are common in macroeconomics. However, Navarre is a very small territory within the state (comprising 1.3% of the population and 1.7% of GDP), and the formulas used for taxation issues lack sufficient flexibility to reflect the real economy of the territory.

The quota is calculated expressed in equation 4.1.

Eq. 4.1.   Quota = i × CNA

Where i = *the imputation index, and* CNA= *the total amount of the nonassumed charges covered by the state (as per the state budgets). Since 1990, the imputation index has been 1.6%.*[1]

More precisely the calculation is found in equation 4.2.

Eq. 4.2.   Quota = i × CNA – SR – D

Where SR *is the revenue obtained in Navarre by the state, and* D *is the part of the state deficit imputable to the non-assumed charges.*

In this model, the risk that Navarre assumes is unilateral, meaning that whatever tax revenues it collects, Navarre must make a financial contribution to the State according to the budget of the Spanish kingdom.

The resources that the central government obtains from Navarre (the quota) are independent of the level of tax collection in Navarre; however, the resources of Navarre depend totally on its tax collection.

---

1. For the Basque Country, the imputation index is 6.24 % (since 1981).

Table 4.5. The Quota / GPD and Quota/population.

Year	Quota (million euros)	GDP (million euros)	Quota/GDP (%)	population	Quota/population (euros)
2009	344.6	18,260.9	1.89%	619,013	556.69
2010	485.5	17,693.6	2.74%	622,125	780.39
2011	490.0	18,144.1	2.70%	624,606	784.49
2012	546.7	17,769.2	3.08%	644,477	848.28
2013	551.1	17,556.8	3.14%	640,000	861.09

Source: Data based on Gobierno de Navarra, www.navarra.es/, and Instituto Navarro de Estadística. www.cfnavarra.es/estadística

Table 4.6. VAT collection (euros).

	2009	2010	2011	2012	2013
Collection	1,308,530,224	1,422,574,625	1,483,354,922	1,218,089,287	1,147,668,455
Refunds	596,084,737	500,913,916	446,527,954	633,700,640	874,964,592
VAT direct administration	712,445,487	921,660,709	1,036,826,968	584,388,647	272,703,863
VAT adjustments	184,950,000	103,586,151	171,154,620	483,270,070	646,767,061
TOTAL VAT	897,395,487	1,025,246,860	1,207,981,588	1,067,658,717	919,470,924

Source Gobierno de Navarra http://www.navarra.es/

Table 4.7. Tax collection.

		2009	2010	2011	2012	2013
Personal Income tax	Tax deductions	1,035,586,264	1,030,783,170	1,067,793,119	1,058,532,726	1,035,271,595
	Capital gains	127,179,420	107,907,800	106,885,815	112,029,838	105,474,532
	Deferred payments	48,799,534	45,925,665	41,805,434	39,155,349	34,507,261
	Net tax liability	- 101,339,085	- 145,015,503	- 119,978,116	- 91,358,456	- 120,368,085
	Personal Income tax	1,110,226,133	1,039,601,132	1,096,506,252	1,118,359,457	1,054,885,303
Corporation tax		412,564,054	188,484,602	213,066,776	201,388,605	194,286,198
Non Residents		10,646,435	8,907,705	8,539,000	5,193,444	6,704,577
Inheritance and Gifts		37,930,796	40,463,166	36,968,666	44,851,235	92,631,607
Wealth (eliminated 2008, 2009 and 2010)		3,164,377	613,678	950,491	39,952,285	51,189,332
Other direct and indirect taxes					-	25,490,983
TOTAL CHAPTER I (Direct Taxes)		1,574,531,795	1,278,070,283	1,356,031,185	1,409,745,026	1,425,188,000
VAT	Collection	1,308,530,224	1,422,574,625	1,483,354,922	1,218,089,287	1,147,668,455
	Refunds	596,084,737	500,913,916	446,527,954	633,700,640	874,964,592
	VAT direct collection	712,445,487	921,660,709	1,036,826,968	584,388,647	272,703,863
	VAT adjustment	184,950,000	103,586,151	171,154,620	483,270,070	646,767,061
	Value-added tax (VAT)	897,395,487	1,025,246,860	1,207,981,588	1,067,658,717	919,470,924
Excises	Duty on Alcoholic Beverages	52,655,813	51,546,415	53,032,627	50,076,120	49,479,772
	Intermediary products	169,406	197,431	159,627	125,941	138,343
	Special Duty on Beer	2,146,444	165,161	216,852	179,114	201,874
	Special Duty on Tobacco Products	141,178,935	142,798,369	127,438,573	147,225,400	130,539,227
	Fuel Tax	220,635,555	229,338,190	243,528,497	202,517,583	240,366,866
	Transport	11,388,379	10,130,524	6,911,251	4,800,343	3,873,222
	Electricity	21,546,034	24,059,946	24,372,233	27,047,336	26,327,605
	Excises direct collection	449,720,566	458,236,036	455,659,660	431,971,837	450,926,909
	Excises adjustment	- 33,690,000	36,019,078	- 16,137,558	- 50,703,456	9,273,267
	Excises	416,030,566	422,216,958	439,522,102	381,268,381	460,200,176
Capital Transfer tax		41,269,942	44,053,897	37,970,670	29,477,179	28,437,910
Stamp Duty		32,941,554	24,443,490	18,399,712	15,418,269	11,696,771
Insurance Premiums Tax		18,596,329	19,802,235	20,136,957	20,143,801	21,359,249
Tax on Hydrocarbons (retail)		21,932,722	22,416,626	23,234,284	26,766,868	10,035,657
Abolished indirect taxes		21,630	18,134	5,359	39,128	5,329
TOTAL CHAPTER II (Indirect Taxes)		1,428,188,230	1,558,198,200	1,747,250,672	1,540,772,343	1,451,206,016
TOTAL TAX REVENUES CHAP I & II		3,002,720,025	2,836,268,483	3,103,281,857	2,950,517,369	2,876,394,016
Charges and other		16,954,390	18,162,035	20,983,805	9,336,338	10,499,024
Surcharges, sanctions, arrears		16,513,472	14,475,159	18,238,064	18,736,119	20,236,959
TOTAL COLLECTION TAX PAYABLE		3,036,187,887	2,868,905,677	3,142,503,726	2,978,589,826	2,907,129,999

This means that Navarre assumes all the collection risks associated with changes in the economic state of affairs, as well as the financial consequences of any tax changes.

In times of economic prosperity and dynamic managerial activity, good tax planning can favor Navarre. However, in times of crisis when the amount of taxes collected declines significantly, Navarre, notwithstanding its lower income, must disburse the payment of its contribution to the state (which is less elastic) along with its own budget expenditures. This scenario can place Navarre in a worse condition than other regions of the state. This is because the calculation of the contribution to the state under the model of the Economic Agreement takes into account not only the cost of the competences not assumed by the region, but also a series of adjustments derived from tributary harmonization.

In terms of direct taxes, Navarre has the right to tax the income of its residents and income generated within its territory. Concerning corporate taxes, the division of the tax quota is a combination of fiscal domicile (for small firms) and relative sales (for large firms). Basically, small firms with their fiscal domicile in Navarre pay taxes only in Navarre, and large firms with operations in Navarre pay taxes in Navarre in proportion to the volume of their operations in every territory.

The indirect taxes, VAT and Excise, are paid using the origin principle (location of the delivery of goods or provision of services). Navarre collects the VAT due on the production (value added) in Navarre. This gives rise to an *ex post* adjustment for the differences between what Navarre collects (VAT on the value added created in Navarre), and what it should collect (VAT on the consumption of the residents in Navarre).

When the origin principle is used, *ex post* VAT and excises adjustments are made to ensure that the final collection of Navarre is equal to the consumption taxes paid by its residents.

The VAT collected by Navarre differs from the VAT paid by the residents in Navarre for two reasons:

1. Navarre collects the VAT of the production of Navarre (but some of those goods are consumed outside of Navarre);
2. The VAT on imported goods (from outside the EU) is collected by the state (but some of those goods are consumed in Navarre).

VAT applies to the delivery of goods and provision of services supplied by businesses and professionals. Entrepreneurs and professionals are the taxpayers who are obliged to deposit their quotas in the Treasury, but the tax falls on the consumer: it is citizens, the final consumers, who bear the tax burden passed on by the taxpayers.

In Spain—a single VAT area without internal borders—the quota paid by a resident in the Common Territory could go to the Foral Treasury of Navarre, while that paid by a resident of Navarre could end up in the hands of the Spanish Treasury. In fact, this is a very frequent reality.

To correct this deviation, the Economic Agreement applies an adjustment formula to tax collection, which aims to distribute the collected amount in accordance with the consumption of the inhabitants of each territory and, at the same time, to promote good tax management in each territory. To encourage good management, the formula introduces a mechanism that aims to reward, or at least to respect, the success of the most efficient tax administration. The adjustments are calculated by means of formulas that use macromagnitudes. Given the small dimensions of Navarre, however, these are not sufficiently sensitive to changes in the taxable events.

The formulation of the VAT adjustment, as contained in the Economic Agreement, follows.

The direct collection in Navarre of value-added tax is added to the result by equation 4.3:

Eq. 4.3. $\text{Adjustment} = {}_c RR_{AD} + (c - d) H$

Where

$$H = \frac{RR_N}{d} \quad \text{if} \quad \frac{RR_N}{RR_{TC}} \leq \frac{d'}{1-d'}$$

$$H = \frac{RR_{TC}}{d} \quad \text{if} \quad \frac{RR_N}{RR_{TC}} \geq \frac{d'}{1-d'}$$

RR_{TC} = *Real annual revenue of the Common Territory.*
RR_N = *Real annual revenue of Navarre.*
RR_{AD} = *Real annual revenue from imports.*

$$c = \frac{\text{Consumption of residents of Navarre}}{\text{Consumption of residents of the State (minus Canary Islands, Ceuta, and Melilla)}}$$

$$d = \frac{v - f - e + i}{V - F - E + I}$$

v = *Gross added value of Navarre at factor cost.*
V = *Gross added value of the state (minus Canary Islands, Ceuta, and Melilla).*

f = *Gross capital formation of Navarre.*

F = *Gross capital formation of the state (minus Canary Islands, Ceuta, and Melilla).*

e = *Exports from Navarre.*

E = *Exports from the state (minus Canary Islands, Ceuta, and Melilla).*

i = *Intra-community acquisitions of goods in Navarre.*

I = Intra-community acquisitions of goods in the State (minus Canary Islands, Ceuta, and Melilla).

$$d' = \frac{v - f - e + i}{V' - F' - E' + I'}$$

V' = *Gross added value of the state (minus the Basque Country, Canary Islands, Ceuta, and Melilla).*

F' = *Gross capital formation of the state (minus the Basque Country, Canary Islands, Ceuta, and Melilla).*

E' = *Exports from the state (minus the Basque Country, Canary Islands, Ceuta, and Melilla)*

I' = *Intra-community acquisitions of goods in the state (minus the Basque Country, Canary Islands, Ceuta, and Melilla).*

$$d'' = \frac{V'' - F'' - E'' + I''}{V - F - E + I}$$

V" = *Gross added value of the state (minus Navarre, the Basque Country, Canary Islands, Ceuta, and Melilla).*

F" = *Gross capital formation of the state (minus Navarre, the Basque Country, Canary Islands, Ceuta, and Melilla).*

E" = *Exports from the state (minus Navarre, the Basque Country, Canary Islands, Ceuta, and Melilla).*

I" = *Intra-community acquisitions of goods in the state (minus Navarre, the Basque Country, Canary Islands, Ceuta, and Melilla).*

The VAT adjustment is designed to compensate for the difference between the VAT paid by the residents in Navarre (which depends on their consumption) and the tax collection in Navarre (which depends on the value-added tax created in Navarre). The VAT adjustment is the sum of two parts or elements:

1. The first part of the Adjustment (c RRAD) gives Navarre its proportional part of the VAT collection in Customs, collected by the state (RRAD), depending on the relative consumption

of the Community (c). The VAT on imports (from outside the EU) is collected by the state. Some of those goods are, however, consumed by residents in Navarre. Then, the state has to give Navarre its share of the VAT collection on imports. The coefficient c, defined as the quotient obtained by dividing the consumption of residents in Navarra by residents in the state (except territories outside application of the Tax), applies to the amount of the collection obtained by the central administration (Customs). This part of the adjustment always entails a transfer from the state to Navarre.

2. The second part of the adjustment, (c - d) H, covers the difference between the consumption in Navarre of goods and the theoretical collection corresponding to Navarre according to the rules of harmonization. This part attempts to adjust the collection obtained by Navarre according to its field of competence (the **d** parameter) defined by the criteria of harmonization, corresponding to the consumption of residents in Navarre (parameter c). By applying the rules of harmonization, Navarre collects the tax corresponding to part d, but its relative consumption corresponds to part c. The adjustment (c–d) is applied to a virtual tax collection H, which is what would be collected in Spain with the lower of two effective tax rates: the tax rate in Navarre and the tax rate in the rest of Spain. Thus, H is a theoretical state tax collection calculated based on that obtained by the least efficient administration (Navarre or Common). The reason for using the virtual tax collection is to introduce an incentive for efficient tax administration as a mechanism to safeguard the autonomy of management.

This second part of the adjustment may imply a transfer either from the state to Navarre or the other way around. These two adjustments combined serve to adjust indirect taxation (VAT, special taxes, etc.) in an attempt to bring the actual collection level near to that of the consumption of the residents of Navarre.

The main causes of the falling VAT collection are the economic crisis, the proportional increase in exports, and the taxation change in a very important company domiciled in Navarre: Volkswagen.

The economy of Navarre is very dependent on the automotive industry. Volkswagen generates 70% of the employment in automation in Navarre. It employs 8,336 workers directly and indirectly. Since 1984, Volkswagen Navarra has rolled the Polo out of the Landaben plant. Since 1998, the Company has formed part of the Group SEAT, as the dominant company. The Company invoices VAESA for all the cars sold to it depending on the "cost-bonus" agreements established by the Group at the time of sale. VAESA is the import and distribution company for the vehicles, replacement parts, and accessories for the brands Volkswagen, Audi, Skoda, and commercial Volkswagen vehicles, on the Peninsula and the Balearic Islands. The company, which belongs to the Volkswagen Group, is located in Barcelona.

Since April 1, 2012, sales to the external market have been invoiced to VW AG (Germany), but sales to the home market, to VAESA (national client). Previously, all sales were made to VAESA. Because of this change, the invoices of the cars sold to the external market issued from April 1 onwards are exempt from reverberated VAT, and therefore the total reverberated VAT of the company diminishes considerably. Consequently, the direction of VAT liquidation is reversed, since the supported VAT is higher than the reverberated VAT, and therefore the state changes from being a VAT creditor to a VAT debtor for this scenario.

In just two years (2011–13), direct VAT collection has fallen from €1,037 million to €273 million (table 4.6). And the mathematical adjustment has not been able to balance the situation. The government of Navarre now must seek to negotiate the parameters of the adjustment with the government of the state to avoid bankruptcy. This has revealed the weakness of the historical model and the political dependence of Navarre on the government of the state, which illustrates that the Economic Agreement depends on the will of the Spanish state.

Bibliography

Agirreazkuenaga, Joseba, and Eduardo Alonso, eds. 2014. *The Basque Fiscal System. History, Current Status, and Perspectives*. Reno: Center for Basques Studies.

Alli Aranguren, Juan Cruz. 2009. *Los convenios económicos entre Navarra y el Estado: De la soberanía a la autonomía armonizada*. Iruñea-Pamplona: Gobierno de Navarra.

Aranburu Urtasun, Mikel. 2005. *Provincias Exentas: Convenio-Concierto: Identidad colectiva en la Vasconia peninsular (1969–2005)*. Donostia–San Sebastián: Fundación para el Estudio del Derecho Histórico y Autonómico de Vasconia.

De la Hucha Celador, Fernando. 2014. "El IVA en Navarra: Ajustes, devoluciones y otras cuestiones de recaudación tributaria en

2013." *Navarra Confidencial,* February 17. Available at www.navarraconfidencial.com.

Martínez Bárbara, Gemma. 2014. *Armonización fiscal y poder tributario foral en la Comunidad Autónoma del País Vasco.* Bilbao: Instituto Vasco de Administración Pública.

5

Self-Government and the Economic Agreements for the Basque Autonomous Community and Navarre: The Economic Crisis, Lessons Learned, and Prospects for the Future

Juan José Ibarretxe Markuartu

This reflection aims to offer a wider vision of the Basque people than the compartmentalized one usually made of the self-governing regions of the Basque Autonomous Community and Navarre, and therefore of each region's Economic Agreement with the Spanish kingdom. This vision incorporates a variant of a cultural nature: the "K" for culture—in the Basque Language, *Kultura*; that is, our own identity as a people. Our world is a complex one. We face complex problems, far-reaching changes, and enormous transformations, so we need to find complex solutions. In the words of Edgar Morin, it is necessary to "manage complexity."[1] We are also experiencing a deep international crisis different from all those we have experienced to date, one that presents itself in many forms—legal, political, economic, sociological, environmental, cultural, and so on—and is, above all, axiological.

Today, as Eduardo Galeano writes, "development is a voyage with more shipwrecks than navigators" (1973, 171).[2] It is the first

---

1. Morin (1961), 397. He says: "I am henceforth convinced that all knowledge [Fr. *connaissance*] which simplifies is mutilated and mutilates, and is expressed by a manipulation, repression, devastation of the real as soon as it is transformed into action, and singularly into political action. *Thought which simplifies has become the barbarity of science. It is the specific barbarity of our civilization. It is the barbarity which today joins forces wilh all the historical and mythological forms of barbarity.*"
2. Galeano (1997), 224 and following pages. On page 282, he writes: "Underdevelopment isn't a stage of development, but its consequence"; on page 248, "Latin America's entry into the British orbit—which it would leave only to enter the U.S. orbit—took place within this general framework, and within it the dependence of the

lesson of this "new era": "a market without values is a flea market" or, in the recent words of Pope Francis, "… this economy kills."[3] Friedrich Hayek's concept of self-regulation has therefore been debunked (1975, 107–32). This is the first piece of evidence, but it is not the only one.

Almost everything is shrouded in uncertainty. We do not have a clear diagnosis, we do not know what is happening to us, and that is precisely what is happening to us, as Ortega y Gasset would say. In these circumstances, nothing would be more negative than returning to the "situation prior to the crisis," a view that has too many advocates in the Western world, which often impatiently yearns for "the old good days." Whatever has to happen, will happen, but it will be new and different, not inspired by nostalgia but intellectual tension and multidisciplinary reflection—nothing can escape from rational challenge—and the search for new pathways and spaces for encounter. This process will allow the dissemination of knowledge and thought, helping us to see the light in the distance as the exit from the tunnel and not as a train rushing toward us, as the genial Basque sculptor Jorge Oteiza once said.

Furthermore, and in relation to Basque self-government—and, as an essential part of it, the Economic Agreements for the Basque Autonomous Community (the Concierto) and Navarre (the Convenio)—enough time has gone by and we have traveled far enough to apply the learning of Kierkegaard (2013) to our reflection: life, if we are to *understand* it, should be observed looking backward, by analyzing the past. However, if we are to *live* life, we should be looking to the future. That is what we will do in this article: learn from the past and its crises to build the future and its crises.

The Economic Agreements for the Basque Autonomous Community and Navarre: "The Last Vestige of Our Revered

new independent countries was consolidated." In n. 23 he quotes Karl Marx, "Discourse on the New Change," in *The Poverty of Philosophy,* Moscow, undated, "It is not at all strange that the free-marketers are incapable of understanding how a country can get rich at the expense of another, because neither do those same people want to understand how one class can get rich at the expense of another within a country."

3. Pope Francis, *Evangelii Gaudium, Exhortación Apostólica,* Point 53, Vatican City, Nov. 2013: "Just as the commandment 'Thou shalt not kill' sets a clear limit in order to safeguard the value of human life, today we also have to say "thou shalt not" to an economy of exclusion and inequality. Such an economy kills." See https://w2.vatican.va/content/francesco/en/apost_exhortations/documents/papa-francesco_esortazione-ap_20131124_evangelii-gaudium.html#III.%E2%80%82From_the_heart_of_the_Gospel.

Freedoms"

What a graphic expression! The Economic Agreement is "The last vestige of our revered freedoms."[4] This is how people in the Basque Country publicly referred—following the abolition of the self-government or *Foral* Laws at the end of the nineteenth century (1876) and later—to the recently (1981) established system of the Concierto (Economic Agreement) for the Basque Autonomous Community and the Convenio (the Agreement) for Navarre (1841).

Self-government basically had three key elements: (1) the *pase foral* or veto (by the Basque Representative Assemblies or by the king) based on the "we obey, but we do not comply with" principle; (2) the *exención militar*, whereby the Basques were not obliged to do military service in Spain; and (3) the *exención fiscal* (exemption from taxation), which was applied in the Basque territories and Navarre.[5] This theory led to the removal of the political dimension of the Basque Foral Constitutional regimes in 1876, as reflected in the words of the then-Spanish Prime Minister Antonio Cánovas del Castillo in a speech to the Parliament in Madrid on July 7, 1876: "This issue of privileges is a matter of force, which ends up being solved through

---

4. Mieza y Mieg (1983), 5: "Once the power of the bourgeoisie had consolidated in the State of the Restoration and the second Carlist war had been won, Cánovas' project of imposing his personal interpretation of the 'constitutional unity of the monarchy' by force took shape. Given the enemies that his efforts created, even among the ruling classes in the three Provinces, Cánovas del Castillo put forward a lax taxation system (quotas established by mutual agreement, and their collection would be up to the provincial administrations, and also the determination of the tax concepts that could be used) if they worked on quelling the atmosphere of social tension. This would lead to public references to the recently-established system being made by always adding the qualifying term of 'the last vestige of our revered freedoms.'"

5. Agirreazkuenaga (2012). The *fuero bueno* (good charter) was considered not to have political content but maintained the economic content to keep the economic elites happy. This is reflected in Mieza y Mieg's thinking when he says: "doing without the political aspects of the Charter (capacity for self-government, the constitutional nature of the charter in that it was binding on Kings/Lords, and the possibility of applying a 'chartered territory's veto': the 'Pase' or 'Uso'), but it safeguarded the aspects of fiscal and internal administrative independence." On page 3 it states: "From the last day of the Carlist war (1839) in Euskal Herria (initially timidly but later more strongly), the appearance of an intermediate way took place that affirmed the convenience of keeping a part of the *Fueros* but doing without others. This is the theory of the *Buenos Fueros*, defended in the Spanish Parliament by the representative for Guipúzcoa, Claudio Antón de Luzuriaga, later argued by the commissioners of the Diputación Provincial of Navarre in their discussions with the Regency Ministry of Espartero. It ended up in the Law on the Charter of Navarre—the inappropriately called "Pact Law" of August 16, 1841..

violence." He then added a famous phrase: ". . . when force leads to a State, force becomes the law.[6] Basically, this was the main debate and the centralizing tendency that took place in Spain at the end of the nineteenth century. Nevertheless, what was initially supposed to be a full repeal ended with an agreement in the area of economy and taxes described by Cánovas del Castillo as a "tax approach," even though the Basque territories' capacity for political self-government was eliminated. That is how the agreement with the institutions of the fledgling State and the Basque Diputaciones or Territorial Governments took shape in the first Economic Agreement.

Political and Economic Self-Government

There is no genuine self-government if there is no political self-government—that is, the capacity to make political decisions. Obviously, real self-government is impossible without being able to manage the economy, although this does not guarantee political self-government in itself. We can affirm that Economic Agreements with the Spanish kingdom have existed in Navarre and Álava from 1841 and 1878 to today, in Gipuzkoa until 1937, and in Bizkaia from 1981 to the present. However, there was no political self-government in any of the Basque territories, except for a short period during the first Basque Government of Basque President (Lehendakari in Basque) Agirre (1936–37).

Self-government is not an exclusively economic notion: it is an overarching concept in political and cultural terms. The economy is obviously a very important dimension, but it is only one among many. We do not create a real "political personality" unless we add the "bones" (the institutions) and the "muscles" (powers and functions) to the "blood" of the system, which is what we usually associate with the Economic Agreements for the Basque Autonomous Community and Navarre. Blood (Economic Agreements), bones (Institutions), and muscles (power base) inseparably constitute authentic self-government.

An Analysis of the "Self-Government and Welfare" Tandem, 1980/2013

The period between 1980 and 2013 demonstrates that "self-govern-

---

6. A. Cánovas del Castillo, Spanish Parliament, Sessions Diary, Legislature 1876, Madrid, July 7, 1876, no. 103.

ment" means "welfare" in an empirical way. This is what I have partly dedicated my life to, and still do, initially from the Basque political institutions and now from the Agirre Lehendakaria Center for Social and Political Studies, in which the University of the Basque Country (UPV-EHU), Columbia University (New York), and George Mason University (Washington) are working together on several research projects. These universities take as their intellectual starting point *The Basque Case. A Comprehensive Model for Sustainable Human Development* a research project I led with the participation of these American academic institutions (Ibarretxe 2015).

Indeed, the direct relationship between exploring self-government in greater depth and increasing the welfare of people in Basque society is one of the subjects studied by the Agirre Lehendakaria Center. When self-government was granted in 1980, the Basque Autonomous Community had a per capita income of €3000 per year (89% of average European income), and it reached €6000 in 1986, the year of integration into the European Union. By 1998, our per capita income stood at 108%, meaning that we had achieved and surpassed the European average income figure. By 2008, we had a per capita income of €31,000, that is, 34% above the European average. According to the latest published data (Eurostat, Eustat, July 2014), the Basque Autonomous Community is currently 29% above the European average. According to Eurostat and Eustat data, in 2001 we were in eighth position in the European ranking in terms of income per capita, with 120% of average European income. We jumped to fourth place in 2005 (129%), and by 2008 we were third with 134%. In 2013, with the economic crisis fully affecting Europe, the Basque Country was third in the Top 10, with 129% of average European income.[7]

Nevertheless, we have to "look beyond GDP." I stand for sustainable human development, which means not just taking the economic agenda into account but also the cultural and social agendas and, together with them, the environmental agenda. In a nutshell, a triple agenda: economic, social, and environmental. Unfortunately, economists and international agencies have not been able to measure the welfare of people. It is well known —and accepted—that what is not measured is not improved. We are now in a new phase: what is not measured is not even part of the agenda. Joseph Stiglitz expresses this very succinctly: "What we measure affects the decisions we make."[8]

---

7. Eurostat (June 24, 2014), Eustat (July 17, 2014) and in-house data.
8. Joseph Stiglitz, Professor of Economics at the University of Columbia and Nobel Prize for Economics in 2001, presided over the Commission to Measure Economic

Indeed, "market" and "economic growth" have been the key concepts handled, together with GDP. It has become not only the main parameter but almost the only one measured. As Robert Kennedy said shortly before his assassination in 1968, GDP (or GNP) gives us excellent information about many things, but it does not tell us anything about why life is worth living:

> Yet the gross national product does not allow for the health of our children, the quality of their education, or the joy of their play. It does not include the beauty of our poetry or the strength of our marriages; the intelligence of our public debate or the integrity of our public officials. It measures neither our wit nor our courage; neither our wisdom nor our learning; neither our compassion nor our devotion to our country; it measures everything, in short, except that which makes life worthwhile.[9]

Self-Government for Peoples

This concern for the individual, not just for the economy, has made the study of the "Basque Case" appealing to leading universities around the world in the last thirty years. Basically, the Basque People have been able to position themselves at the forefront of progress in Europe, despite the internal and external difficulties experienced by the Basque Country. Progress is understood in a particular manner: not just economic progress but also social cohesion. Progress at the service of the people, of the community:[10] these aspects are reflected in figure 5.1 and figure 5.2, which show per capita GDP in the European Union and income distribution in the first years of the twenty-first century.

The experience of managing the current economic crisis and its devastating consequences for people shows us that self-government must be oriented, first and foremost, toward helping our citizens to

---

Development and Social Progress created on the initiative of French President Nicolas Sarkozy, 2009.

9. Robert F. Kennedy, address, University of Kansas, Lawrence, Kansas, March 18, 1968.

10. It is about the notion of *auzolan*: to clarify this Basque term, we can say that *auzo* means neighborhood, a physical (and above all) social and community unit. *Lan* means work, so *auzolan* is work done by everyone for the good of the neighborhood and to the benefit of the whole community. It is the basis for communal work in the farmhouses, hamlets, councils, villages, and communities in the Basque Country, and has been considered the basis for the original way of understanding work that takes the form of the Basque cooperatives.

Figure 5.1. *Per capita GDP. by country and year (EU 28 = 100.*
Source Eurostat and Eustat..

Europe top 10 ranking

2001		2005		2008		2013	
1 Luxemburgo	234	1 Luxemburgo	254	1 Luxemburgo	263	1 Luxemburgo	264
2 Países Bajos	134	2 Irlanda	144	2 Países Bajos	134	2 Austria	129
3 Irlanda	133	3 Países Bajos	131	3 C.A.de Euskadi	134	3 C.A.de Euskadi	129
4 Dinamarca	128	4 C.A.de Euskadi	129	4 Irlanda	131	4 Países Bajos	127
5 Austria	126	5 Austria	125	5 Austria	124	5 Suecia	127
6 Bélgica	124	6 Dinamarca	124	6 Dinamarca	124	6 Irlanda	126
7 Suecia	123	7 Reino Unido	124	7 Suecia	124	7 Dinamarca	125
8 Reino Unido	121	8 Suecia	122	8 Finlandia	119	8 Alemania	124
9 C.A.de Euskadi	120	9 Bélgica	120	9 Alemania	116	9 Bélgica	119
10 Italia	119	10 Alemania	116	10 Bélgica	116	10 Finlandia	112
...		...		...		...	
14 España	98	14 España	102	14 España	104	14 España	95

Figure 5.2. *Income distribution among the most egalitarian countries*
of the EU. Basque data from 2012. Source: Eurostat-SILC and EPDS.

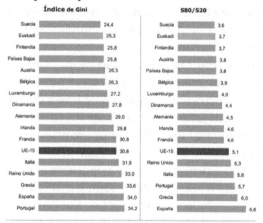

make progress. We need to debunk the neo-Liberal argument that the
welfare state is a burden for the economic performance of a country.
If that were the case, Germany should have a weaker welfare state
than Greece, but it does not. Curiously, the countries that have a
weaker welfare state (Greece, Portugal, Spain, and Italy) are the ones
that needed bailing out. Indeed, the countries that invest the most
in social services in the European Union are, according to figures
published in 2010:[11] Finland (€9,196 per person per year), Germany
(€8,804 per person per year), the Basque Autonomous Community

---

11. Eurostat June 13, 2014, Eustat July 28, 2014.

(€7,209 per person per year) and Sweden (€10,640 per person per year). They show a better economic performance than countries that invest less: Portugal (€4,069 per person per year), Greece (€4,980 per person per year) or Spain (€5,198 per person per year).

In the final decades of the twentieth century, neoliberal thinking launched an offensive on a planetary scale. The credo: the market prevails, and anything that gets in its way is pushed aside. The consequence: individuals and peoples are pushed out of the social orbit. The motto of this "ideological globalization" seems to be: Everything for individuals and peoples, but without their participation and ownership. The data show this in an increasingly harsh manner. Reports and declarations by United Nations experts to the effect that "every five seconds a child dies in the world due to avoidable causes"[12] should make us all feel ashamed. At the same time, studies such as those by the renowned North American linguist Merritt Ruhlen[13] warn that of the five thousand languages currently spoken in the world, only around five hundred will continue to exist by the end of this century. He adds that one of these will be the Basque language, and clearly explains the strategy of destruction of cultures and peoples on which "this globalization" is based.

Therefore, we can say that the idea of the "global village" is not such a pretty one after all; it is "ugly" because it abandons its children to their fate. It is increasingly unequal and leaves the most vulnerable people unprotected in an inhuman way. Recently (2014), the NGO Oxfam Intermón stated that, "Economic inequalities are growing fast in most countries. The world's wealth is divided into two: one half is in the hands of the richest 1% of the population and the other half is shared among the remaining 99%," adding that "Governments overwhelmingly serve the economic elites to the detriment of ordinary people" (OXFAM Intermón 2014). The International Labor Organization (ILO) recently published a report stating that, "Seventy-three percent of the world's population does not have social protection" (ILO 2014). It is not surprising that discontent and "indignant" social movements are gaining ground and are out on the streets in the five continents. The fight against inequality and in favor of people is the revolution of the twenty-first century. It is a revolution for "human dignity." It is not a crisis; it is the "I don't love you anymore" sentiment that appeared on a protester's poster recently. Indeed, institu-

---

12. J. Cardona, United Nations expert, Panama City, October 2014.
13. M. Ruhlen, on the origin of languages; an interview with Merritt Ruhlen, Stanford University, May 2009.

tions such as the World Economic Forum recognize that "inequality is affecting social stability within countries and represents a threat for security on a world scale" (World Economic Forum 2013). Even today, the International Monetary Fund (IMF)—which came up with "So what if people are not doing well if the economy is going well?"— recognizes "that reducing inequality helps to achieve faster and more sustainable growth" (IMF 2014). I agree with the Spanish poet Luis Garcia Montero when he recently said: "I don't believe in a theoretical project that is not based on a sentimental commitment to the happiness of others."[14]

The Reform of the Economic Agreements for the Basque Autonomous Community and Navarre: 1996–2002

The Spanish opposition to reforming the Economic Agreements aggravates the non-fulfillment of the Statute of Autonomy obtained in 1979, and, together with this, creates a great need to adjust our legal and economical status to the new policy framework of the European Union. We should not forget, moreover, that 60% of present Basque citizens did not participate in the decision to approve Basque self-government, either because they had not been born or were not of voting age. The brilliant politician Thomas Jefferson once said, "Every generation should have its own Constitution,"[15] and I am closer to that principle than the idea of not modifying the Constitution, an argument that presides the fossilized political debate in the Spanish state.

The ruling Spanish political forces argue that the current economic agreements cannot be modified due to the complexity and implications of the procedure, but in fact, the Spanish Constitution was modified in a hurry in 2011 following pressure from the Troika[16] to "rescue" Spain through the incorporation of the control of the State's fiscal deficit into the Constitution. This constitutional reform, carried out by a "fast track" procedure, completely debunks the po-

---

14. L. Garcia Montero, Agencia EFE. Madrid, February 14, 2015.
15. Thomas Jefferson, in a letter to James Madison, dated June 9, 1789: "... no society can create a perpetual constitution, not even a perpetual law. The land always belongs to the living generation. . . . Any constitution, therefore, and any law, naturally expires after nineteen years. If it is maintained for longer it becomes an act of force and not of law. . . . Each generation is independent of the previous one, just like the present one is. It has, therefore, the right to choose for itself the form of government it feels best promotes its own happiness." In Kurland and Lerner (1987), v. 1, chapter 2, document 23.
16. The World Bank, the International Monetary Fund, and the European Union.

litical argument that the Spanish Constitution is "untouchable," "unchangeable," and "immutable." The reality is that the European Union was not foreseen in the Spanish Constitution, the Statute of Gernika, or the LORAFNA[17] when they were approved, nor in the Economic Agreements for the Basque Autonomous Community and Navarre. This means that we have not been able to carry out what, in my opinion, is essential and vital for the development of our political and economic self-government in the twenty-first century.

The fact is, we are witnessing ongoing noncompliance with the Statute of Gernika, not just as a consequence of the "recentralizing trend" of the Spanish Government but also due to the sectorial laws approved by the Spanish Parliament. These new laws invade areas of competence that correspond to the Basque institutions. Furthermore, a large number of powers and functions that are extremely important for our country, such as the economic regime for Social Security, employment policy, lifelong and vocational training, and so on—all specifically stated in the Statute of Gernika—have even been declared "unconstitutional" by the official doctrine and without distinction by all the Spanish Governments of recent years, be they of the Popular Party or the Socialist Party.

The questions are very simple: Is it possible to develop new policies and actions within the European Union without having the powers to regulate official education in the areas of vocational training and lifelong training? Is there anyone who can design effective employment policies if they are disconnected from the Social Security overarching strategy? These are powers envisaged in the Statute of Autonomy but never recognized.

This same "lack of respect" toward Basque self-government by the Spanish institutions also occurs in relation to the Economic Agreements for the Basque Autonomous Community and Navarre.

I took an active part in the negotiation of the Concierto in 1996–97 as Vice-President and Treasury Minister of the Basque Government, and also in the negotiations in 2002, by which time I was lehendakari. Vice Lehendakari Idoia Zenarruzabeitia played a major role in this process, and we negotiated something that seemed to us to be fair but "almost impossible" if only it had not been for the need of the Spanish political parties to receive our parliamentary support in Spain. This negotiation process became the main driving force that

---

17. Ley Orgánica 13/1982 de Reintegración y Amejoramiento del Régimen Foral de Navarra (Organic Law on the Reincorporation and Revision of the Legal System of Navarre).

has enabled the development of Basque self-government, by adapting our Economic Agreement system in the Basque Autonomous Community. Later, the agreement for Navarre (the Convenio) was also adapted following the same criteria.

Our aim was to negotiate and achieve the capacity to carry out fiscal policy in similar terms to any other EU country before entering the third phase of economic and monetary union, knowing that monetary policy had already been transferred to the European level.

There were other issues in the negotiation, although basically we wanted to achieve three things:

1. Collect all the taxes generated in the Basque Country (income tax, corporate tax, and indirect taxes on consumption, e.g., VAT)
2. Hold legislative powers in the field of direct taxation
3. That the Basque institutions should pay a Cupo (quota) to the Spanish Treasury on an annual basis (as a result of collecting all taxes in our territory from 1997 onwards) and not the other way around, as was about to happen in 1996. The sum to be paid by the Basque Autonomous Community to Madrid went from less than €3 million in 1996—calculated on €2852 million—to more than €700 million in 1997 (on €739,875 million) and reached over €1 billion in the first years of the twenty-first century (€1,494,055 million in 2006, the last year with a definitive share, due to the fact that the sums since 2007 are awaiting approval by the "Joint Commission of the Economic Agreement"[18]). This issue has enormous strategic importance from a political and economic point of view.

However, and despite these agreements—we can actually speak of "new" Economic Agreements for the Basque Autonomous Community and Navarre from 1996 onwards—the attitude of all the Spanish governments has been highly disloyal, not only with regard to political self-government (as we have seen) but also vis-à-vis the economic self-government agreed to in the Economic Agreements for the Basque Autonomous Community and Navarre. The most serious problem we have found is that national taxation regulations are considered measures of a general nature, while ours (challenged time and time again before ordinary and European courts by the Spanish State

---

18. Órgano de Coordinación Tributaria de Euskadi, Comprehensive Annual Report on the Basque Treasury (IAI) 2012, Vitoria-Gasteiz, October 31, 2014.

and other Spanish institutions) ended up being considered "state aid." If these problems are not solved, the Economic Agreements for the Basque Autonomous Community and Navarre will not only have essential support taken away from them, they will almost be left without any support. If we do not achieve direct participation by the Basque institutions in the ECOFIN system and do not succeed in getting our legislation to be considered as measures of a general nature—just like in any other EU country—the Economic Agreements for the Basque Autonomous Community and Navarre, and their economic self-government as a result, will disappear as a consequence of their being constantly challenged at the European level.

It should also be pointed out that these systematic attacks by the Spanish government on the Economic Agreements with the Basque Autonomous Community and Navarre, and the Basque institutions' efforts to ring-fence them, go back a long way. This is not new; it is the "political game" we have had to play against our will since the end of the nineteenth century. Even during the dictatorship of Primo de Rivera (1923–30), there were attempts made to devaluate the Economic Agreement. Look at this phrase, literally taken from an encyclopedia of Espasa-Calpe, a well-known Spanish publishing house. It reads:

> In the civilian Government formed in 1925 the young Treasury Minister José Calvo Sotelo outdid himself by saying that "the State's position in the economic agreements reached with the Basque Country and Navarre improved, to the detriment of the latter."[19]

This is the doctrine that has become official in Spain in recent times. The Economic Agreements for the Basque Autonomous Community and Navarre—as they are slyly reported to Spanish public opinion—*are not a right but a privilege* for the foral territories. Any minister of a Spanish Government who negotiates against them or achieves cuts to the self-governing capacity of the Basque Country is almost considered a hero, and among his or her main virtues future Spanish encyclopedias will refer to the *"honorable"* efforts aimed at *"weakening the Basque Country and Navarre."*

Economic Agreements for the Basque Autonomous Community and Navarre: a Model for the European Union in Crisis

We need to learn from the past to build the future. As Edgar Mo-

---

19. *Diccionario enciclopédico Espasa*, p. 997.

rin said: "Europe is in crisis because there is no political unity."[20] The background is also political here, as is the case with the Economic Agreements for the Basque Autonomous Community and Navarre, and that background is none other than the lack of unity. The Program for Europe 2020 states: "Only a united Europe can get us out of the impasse we find ourselves in."[21] The Europe 2020 program provides the remedy by stating that, "We will not get out of the impasse because we are not a united European political space."

From that point of view, I believe that Europe does not know—or even worse, does not want to know—that the Economic Agreement model for the Basque Autonomous Community and Navarre is a good one for Europe in order to make progress in the realm of political union, beyond the "economic short-cut" of a single market. The Economic Agreements for the Basque Autonomous Community and Navarre constitute an innovative legal-political-economic-financial instrument that can be exported to Europe, not just something to be settled in the European Union.

The negotiation of the Economic Agreements for the Basque Autonomous Community and Navarre between 1996 and 2002 made progress in the process of harmonizing indirect taxes and their collection, with an adjustment to the level of consumption. In this respect, the transposition of the Concierto to Europe would also enable us to solve the shameful matter—which, strangely, is almost ignored—that we have had a provisional VAT system in force since 1993. More than twenty years with a provisional system, one that turns the basic objective of VAT on its head from the point of view of treasury theory: the tax should be collected at its source and not at its destination.

Second, this "new" Economic Agreement for the Basque Autonomous Community and Navarre is a model that should also be exported in relation to direct taxation. Why? Because what occurred was a recognition of the capacity of Basque institutions to not just establish direct taxes within certain ranges that ensure an effective overall tax burden equivalent to that in force in the (Spanish) state. Europe could perhaps consider the need to establish a "clearing house" that would adjust the collection of these tax concepts to income.

I sincerely believe that the Economic Agreements for the Basque Autonomous Community and Navarre are a good model for this European Union in crisis. The result? A Europe-wide monetary and

---

20. Edgar Morin, *La Vanguardia* magazine, February 17, 2012.
21. Understanding the Policies of the European Union, EUROPA 2020: The European Strategy for Growth. Brussels: European Commission, 2013.

fiscal policy with increasing harmonization of indirect taxation and the ability of Member States to collect direct and indirect taxes, regulate direct taxation within certain parameters, and develop budgetary policies on account of their capabilities as a result of the responsible management of all these factors. Basically, this means fiscal co-responsibility: if you manage well and responsibly, you will have more resources. That is precisely the philosophy behind the Economic Agreements for the Basque Autonomous Community and Navarre.

The Future of Basque Self-Government: The Economic Agreements for the Basque Autonomous Community and Navarre in 2020

Without any doubt, the new model of self-government needs to come from a new model of governance, based on the establishment of one's own and differentiated project. This is what makes a difference in the modern world: the ability to establish one's own project and to develop one's identity, not through confrontation but through cooperation with other identities nearby and in the wider world. Our experience shows that the political will to make our own (and differentiated) decisions, linked to a real ability to carry them through, have precisely been the key differentiating factors in the Basque strategy. This is a living example of the fact that, as Joseph E. Stiglitz states, the countries that take control of their own destinies are the ones benefitting most from globalization.[22]

This is the case, in my opinion, because the great paradigm change of the twenty-first century is that we have moved from "choosing" to "being chosen." Nowadays we are elected on the basis of what we offer. As a result, we will be chosen depending on the project we are able to define and carry out here—by the Basque people, and within Basque society. This leads us to a debate that is currently intensifying in the political world, in terms of "yes" or "no" to independence. As Shakespeare said: "We know what we are, but know not what we may be."

As a society, we need to hold a debate on this model of dependence, one that is becoming increasingly solid. In other words, from the point of view of the educational model of the laws produced in the Spanish Parliament, is being independent a good or a bad thing?

---

22. Stiglitz (2002), 248: "The globalization of the economy has benefited countries that took advantage of it by seeking new markets for their exports. . . . Even so, the countries that have benefited most have been those that took charge of their own destiny and recognized the role government can play in development rather than relying on the notion of a self-regulated market that would fix its own problems."

What about the Civil Service Law, or the laws on Social Security and the management of its economic system? Or those referring to taxation, budgeting and public deficit, or healthcare, industrial policy, and R&D+ i?

If the present model of dependence on Spain is perceived by a majority of Basque society as a bad one that is devastating for our self-government and stops us from walking our own path in the globalized world, well, we need to choose another model. We do not know what our ultimate fate will be, but we do know that it will have to be democratically decided here in the Basque Country. We know what we have to change and what is needed to make progress, because the basis on which the world is now being constructed lies in the following concepts: identity and innovation, in other words, roots and wings. You cannot be in the new world without roots, you need an identity to be able to present something different that is yours, and wings to innovate, to teach people skills and reach out to the rest of the world.

Pope Francis recently said that ". . . globalization that enriches is like a polyhedron. Every side is connected but each one conserves its particularity, its richness, its identity," and he added that, "Globalization understood wrongly—the present one—is like a sphere: all its points are equal, all equidistant from the center."[23] I agree. This is the real dilemma of our time: to be a sphere or a polyhedron. I have no doubts about my choice: a polyhedron.

In the global society we need, more than ever, a local response, one that is our own and differentiated—a response based on our roots, culture, way of learning things, teaching methods, ways of dealing with problems . . . and a serious response that does not mortgage the future of the generations to come. These are the things that distinguish us in a world where capital, raw materials, technology, and new devices continue to appear at an amazing pace. We need to compete using our roots. We need to innovate with our roots . . . and to do this, we need to have the necessary and sufficient capacity for self-government to make the decisions that suit us best.

This quite simply means that a Basque Country having the same level of independence–dependence that other EU countries have, would not only be very viable but, in my opinion, highly advisable. The Basque Country's main problem in its relationship with Spain is not the

---

23. Pope Francis, *La vanguardia internacional*. Interview with Henrique Cymerman, June 13, 2014.

media-driven debate on an *independence* that we do not know about, but the deeper debate on the *obligatory dependence* that we know and suffer from, in areas such as finances, government revenue, laws, education, healthcare, employment, Social Security policy, and so on. More than ever, we need our own differentiated project, one that shows solidarity with Spain, France, and Europe, but is as committed and differentiated as that of any other country in the European Union.

Economic Agreements for the Basque Autonomous Community and Navarre 2020

As a result of all this, and of the lessons learned from our experience and the new, unequal, and complicated world the European Union in crisis is operating in, we are called upon to ensure that this "new Basque self-government" should also have "New Economic Agreements for the Basque Autonomous Community and Navarre" to take on at least four main challenges by around 2020.

The Relationship between Government and Financial Markets

Models of this relationship have changed worldwide. Until recently, governments had close relationships with the people who controlled the means of production. This has changed, and the relationship—increasingly vital in the search for development at the local level—is now between governments and the financial markets. It is necessary to emphasize this because it is something we have not been able to negotiate and incorporate into our self-government practices—as all of us who have negotiated with Spanish institutions would have liked to see—first of all in our Statutes of Autonomy, and then in the changes made to the Economic Agreements for the Basque Autonomous Community and Navarre, no doubt due to systematic refusals from all the Spanish Administrations. The time has now come to redress the situation, however. A New Basque Political Statute was formally put forward and approved by an absolute majority of the Basque Parliament in December 2004; today, it remains an unresolved issue.

Channeling of Local Savings toward Local Projects

In the Basque Autonomous Community, we are currently in the middle of a process of debate and definition—one that will be a determining factor in relation to our society and its future—of a Basque model of financial design. It should be said that there are "original sins" involved from the outset, for which we all have responsibility. I sincerely believe that we did not get it right when designing the project and its alliances, probably because we did not realize the importance of channeling local savings toward local projects. This is particularly the case for a country that saves diligently, like ours; a country with one of the highest proportions of the productive sector in its economy in Europe.

The future use we make of the Economic Agreements for the Basque Autonomous Community and Navarre to achieve this objective is crucial, particularly in the Historical Territory of Navarre, where the process of the political-financial dismantling of the Caja de Ahorros de Navarra (CAN) has been scandalous. This is happening with a financial sector—including our own—that is increasingly depersonalized, shows a lesser commitment to the territory and lower involvement in local social initiatives. The process could lead us to be like a ship without sails that ends up either in port or stranded on a beach, depending on which way the wind is blowing that particular day.

In Spain, within the context of a full financial crisis, and surely to "redeem the sins" committed, it was said that if the country were bailed out by the European Union, "the blame for everything could be laid at the door of the Cajas de Ahorros" (savings banks). In truth, this argument was correct to a certain extent, in light of the abuses committed in these entities all over Spain. However, other European countries have not done the same; indeed, quite the contrary. Just look at how Germany channels local savings toward local projects, and how it protects its savings banks. They did not go for the easy option of blaming the savings banks for all the problems in the economy. Exactly the opposite happened in Spain, and the savings banks have withstood the worst of the Troika's reprimands.

We do not all behave in the same way, however. The Basque savings banks' solvency ratings are completely different from those of our southern neighbor, as seen in the recent Stress Tests on the banks organized by the ECB[24] in 2014. In order to rescue them, we wonder if it would have been possible to set up a differentiated model from the one we are told is inevitable, due to the "bad company" of irresponsibly managed Spanish savings banks and the commitments made to the European Union (naturally, without our acquiescence) by Spanish institutions. Time will show us the successes and the mistakes.

Financing: A "New" Model of Bank Intermediation

The third challenge is related to financing, and the extent to which it could facilitate the "intelligent" use of the Economic Agreements for

24. European Central Bank (ECB), Stress Test, Frankfurt, October 26, 2014.

the Basque Autonomous Community and Navarre. In a country with an industrial base, either you channel the financing of your productive structure, or you are in trouble. The present model of bank intermediation is no longer useful, nor are the systems we have to evaluate risk; we need to change them. A good example is the "financing paradox" experienced since the crisis of the subprime loans in 2007. In the past, the banks lent you money even if you did not need it, but now you have to prove to the bank that you "do not need" the money for which they are going to give you a loan.

A Serious Budgetary Policy: Relaxing the Deficit

Finally, the fourth challenge: If we carry out a serious budgetary policy, we would not need to apply a "fundamentalist" vision to the public deficit. This vision is, unfortunately, very much in vogue in Europe, which has not understood that the economic history of the world is full of examples (the United States, Japan, etc.) in which "cutbacks without incentives" end up creating "heart attacks" in the economy.

To make matters worse, as we have seen earlier in this article, those EU countries that have invested the *most* in people have had to bail out those who spend *less* on them. The pitiless cutbacks in social expenditure in the latter—especially in education, innovation, and public health care—are seriously compromising our future. What is worse, the future of young people in our countries is a much bigger problem than the debts we have accumulated. Indeed, the cost of money is not paid solely based on debt issued but not repaid, nor on the annual public deficit. You pay based on how you are using the money you borrowed—that is, whether you are able to generate public savings through a serious budgetary policy, as in any family, trying to get to the end of the month with money still in your pocket. In this respect, I agree that we should be extremely strict about the need to generate public savings, and that we should pay current expenses with current income. Nobody needs to tell us this, not even Germany or the Troika.

One finer point: if a country had to pay for sums it has borrowed but not returned, the country that would have to pay the most would probably be the United States (a country, by the way, that rejects the "sacred status" of the deficit and is making a notable effort in public investment to drive areas related to innovation). Indeed, until almost the end of 2012, Germany and other EU countries had a lower level of current debt (in terms of GDP) than Spain,[25] although Spain has paid interest at a much higher rate than those countries did during the most critical years of the crisis.

Basically, you need to be very sure that you can borrow money to buy a house or a car, although I personally would not borrow to go on holiday. However, you cannot ask for a loan every Friday to go the supermarket and buy food. Having said that, I am also convinced that we need to eliminate the sacralization of the notion of "zero deficit." It is about designating what we are going to use the borrowed money for, to try to ease the notion of "deficit" and, in my opinion, boost public healthcare and training, and in particular, anything to do with innovation. These are transcendental issues. This is particularly applicable to the Basque Autonomous Community, which, according to the latest published data, "lost its position" in the European average for R&D + i in 2013—an investment of 1.99%/GDP in the Basque Autonomous Community as opposed to 2.02% in the European Union—after reaching and surpassing the European average since 2008,[26] following a creditable effort sustained over thirty years.

We are witnessing continuous cutbacks in education/training, innovation, and the fight against inequality. Even so, these remedies do not seem to satisfy the markets (which are behaving obscenely) in order to drive economic growth and employment or to help the thousands of people out on the streets looking for a decent job. It is clearly an option for ignorance, something that the intelligent use of the Economic Agreements for the Basque Autonomous Community and Navarre—distancing ourselves (politely and affectionately) from the erratic budgetary policy of the Spanish state and walking our own path—should allow us to redress in the future.

Conclusion: R&D + i + K

The conclusion of this study is that the hopeful vision for the Basque People is enshrined in this formula: R&D + i + K (Research and Development + Innovation + Culture), keeping in mind, however, that magical recipes do not exist in our world. The bad economists are those of us who, regardless of the place and time, apply recipes

---

25. Eurostat, October 21, 2014: Public debt in percentage of GDP per country and year, 2012: Spain 84.4%, Germany 79%, United Kingdom 85.8%, and France 89.2%.
26. Eurostat and Eustat, "Technological Development and Scientific Research Statistics of the Basque Country (R&D)," press release, November 19, 2014.

when we run out of ideas. This does not usually work unless we adapt them to our culture, which is unique and makes our solutions our own.

We can learn from the successful experiences applied in other countries around the world in relation to the first part (R&D + i), although the entire polynomial will not work if we do not include the "K," the cultural element. Another reason, because there is no other way, is that if you do not incorporate your "K," your identity, your way of being and doing things, your knowledge, your ability to innovate, nobody else will do it. Reaching out to the world without forgetting your roots is the way forward.

Nowadays, in this global society, "the local element" enshrines the real hope that another world is possible. We have gone from the old paradigm of "the global cancels out the local" to a new one: "local moves the world." For some time now, people have started to not accept processes of transformation and change passively; rather, they get involved in them.[27] It is not accepted, quite rightly, that "modernity comes from outside."[28] Against the catastrophic vision of Immanuel Wallerstein regarding the individual in search of his/her

---

27. D. Osborne and T. Gaebler, *La reinvención del gobierno. La influencia del espíritu empresarial en el sector público* (Barcelona: Ed. Paidós, 1995), 62–66, reflects on the "smaller, but bigger" issue, pointing out that "communities are in good health when their families, neighbourhoods, schools, volunteer organizations and companies are in good shape, and they also know that, to achieve this, the essential function of the government is to take the helm in these institutions . . . be the catalyst that helps communities to strengthen their civil infrastructure. . . . The governments that focus on taking the helm give form to their communities, States and nations. They make *more* political decisions. They get *more* social and economic institutions moving. Some even regulate *more*. . . . There is a greater demand for *government management*, i.e. 'driving' society, convincing the different interest groups to embrace common goals and strategies."

28. A. Maalouf, *Identidades asesinas* (Madrid: Alianza, 1999), 88–91, reflects that in any corner of the world "modernization" means "westernization" and states: "This reality is experienced differently by those born in the dominant civilization people who are born within the dominant civilization and those born outside it do not experience reality in the same way. The former can transform themselves, make progress in their lives and adapt without losing their identity . . . For the rest of the world . . . modernization has always meant leaving a bit of yourself behind. Even when it has aroused enthusiasm, the process has never taken place without a certain bitterness, without a feeling of humiliation and denial. Without a painful interrogation on the risks of assimilation. Without a deep crisis of identity. . . If people find disappointment, disillusionment, or humiliation in each step they take in life, how is their personality not going to be bruised? How are they not going to feel that their identity has been bruised?"

identity, ". . . an identity embedded in an elusive concept called 'culture' or, to be more precise, 'cultures,'[29] we are now seeing, as F. J. Caballero Harriet claims, the 'return of cultures,'[30] not just from a social and political angle, but also from an economic perspective." In other words, "do what you know," but incorporate new knowledge, new technologies . . . starting over every day, innovating . . . "innovating with values," "innovating with roots"—that is, resisting the capitalist economic order, the "capitalist cosmos" of Max Weber (1992, 19), a new way of understanding progress.[31] The way forward therefore lies in innovation based on values, and we can only innovate in this way by maintaining the ethics of our roots—in other words, by knowing how to see things through to the end and fulfilling our commitments, based on the values that our culture gives us.

In this sense, the words of Pope Francis in the European Parliament in November 2014 are particularly gratifying and healing:

> The European Union's motto is 'Unity in Diversity,' but unity does not mean political, economic, or cultural uniformity, nor the uniformity of thought. In reality, any authentic unity is based on the wealth of the diversity that makes it up . . . . In this sense, I consider that Europe is a family of people that could feel the institutions of the Union close to them if they wisely combine the desired ideal of unity with the diversity inherent to each people, being aware of their history and their roots." He then addressed MEPs in the following terms: "Dear MEPs, the

---

29. I. Wallerstein, *El futuro de la civilización capitalista* (Barcelona: Icaria, 1997), 91–92: "The new geo-cultural issue has been proclaimed: it is the issue of identity. . . . We can expect explosions in all directions."

30. Caballero Harriet (2009), 196–97: "We need to accept that the return to 'cultures' does not mean a clash of civilizations . . . the return to 'cultures' cannot be understood as something tragic and regressive in the process of maturing and freeing the individual throughout history, rather a return to the axiological reservoir in which a person can rediscover the identity lost after the frustrated illusion of not achieving absolute individual freedom in a world in which universal values finally ended up being the chains of the market."

31. The Weber quote is: "The capitalistic economy of the present day is an immense cosmos into which the individual is born, and which presents itself to him, at least as an individual, as an unalterable order of things in which he must live. It forces the individual, in so far as he is involved in the system of market relationships, to conform to capitalistic rules of action." On the idea of progress, it is interesting to read Nisbet (1980).

time has come for us to build Europe together, not a Europe based on the economy but on the sacredness of the human being, of inalienable values."[32]

Finally, in the knowledge that we are living in "a new world order" that is ever more interconnected (and leads to a new form of marginalization: "unconnected" people, for whom we do not have a solution) in which the main change of paradigm is that we have gone from "choosing" to "being chosen." Nowadays, all of us (countries, universities, individuals . . .) are chosen because of what we offer.

Therefore, in the connected society the objective is not knowing, but understanding. Creativity does not consist of seeing the same thing, but thinking up something different. To be able to think up something different, it is essential to have RandD + I, but also—and above all—the "K" factor, which becomes the core element of reflection, and with it, self-government and its instruments, the Economic Agreements for the Basque Autonomous Community and Navarre among them, at the service of the people and the individuals that make up society.

Bibliography

Agirreazkuenaga, Joseba. 2012. *The Making of the Basque Question: Experiencing Self-Government, 1793–1877.* Reno: Center for Basque Studies.

Caballero, Kiko. 2009. *Algunas claves para otra mundialización.* Santo Domingo, Dominican Republic: Ediciones Funglode, Fundación Global Democracia y Desarrollo.

Galeano, Eduardo. 1997. *Open Veins of Latin America: Five Centuries of the Pillage of a Continent,* 25th Anniversary Edition. Translated by Cedric Belfrage. New York: Monthly Review Press.

Hayek, Friedrich. 1976. *Law, Legislation, and Liberty. Volume 2. The Mirage of Social Justice.* Chicago: University of Chicago Press.

Ibarretxe, Juan José. 2015. The Basque Case: A Comprehensive Model for Sustainable Human Development. Reno: Center for Basque Studies.

ILO (International Labour Organization). 2014. *World Report on Social Protection 2014–2015.* Geneva, June.

IMF (International Monetary Fund). 2014. Redistribution, Inequality, and Growth. Principal authors Jonathan D. Ostry, Andrew

---

32. Pope Francis, Speech to the European Parliament, Strasbourg, November 2014.

Berg, and Charalambos G. Tsangarides. Washington DC, February 4.

Kierkegaard, Søren. 2013. *The Seducer's Diary*. Edited and translated by Howard V. Hong and Edna H. Hong and with a foreword by John Updike. Princeton: Princeton University Press.

Kurland, Philip, and Ralph Lerner, eds. 1987. *The Founders' Constitution*. 5 volumes. Chicago: University of Chicago Press.

Maalouf, Amin. 2000. *In the Name of Identity: Violence and the Need to Belong*. Translated by Barbara Bray. New York: Arcade.

Morin, Edgar. 1961. *Method: Towards a Study of Humankind. Volume 1. The Nature of Nature*. Translated and introduced by J. L. Roland Bélanger. New York: Peter Lang.

Nisbet, Robert A. 1980. *History of the Idea of Progress*. London: Einemann.

OXFAM Intermón. 2014. *Gobernar para las élites, secuestro democrático y desigualdad económica*. Barcelona.

Stiglitz, Joseph E. 2002. *Globalization and Its Discontents*. New York: W.W. Norton.

Weber, Max. 1992. *The Protestant Ethic and the Spirit of Capitalism*. Translated by Talcott Parsons and with an introduction by Anthony Giddens. New York: Routledge.

World Economic Forum. 2013. *Perspectivas de la Agenda Mundial 2014*. Geneva, November.

6

Regional Financing System, Economic Crisis, and the Independence Movement in Catalonia

Antoni Segura

In June 1977, the first democratic elections to the Spanish Parliament after the Francoist dictatorship (1939–75) took place. The results highlighted the "Catalan difference."[1] Throughout the Spanish State, victory went to the government party, the Union of the Democratic Center (UCD), formed by the most pragmatic heirs of Francoism. In Catalonia, the Party of Catalan Socialists (PSC) won, followed by the Unified Socialist Party of Catalonia (PSUC, a Communist group), and by the Catalan nationalists of the Democratic Pact for Catalonia (PDC), which received the same percentage of votes as the UCD. In short, more than three-quarters of the votes cast went to Catalanist parties, and, in addition, more than half went to leftist parties. Thus, four decades of dictatorship could not put an end to the aspirations for self-government and recovery of the institutions (abolished first in 1714 and then in 1939) of Catalan citizens.[2]

The results in Catalonia and the Basque Country necessitated an effort to achieve a constitutional consensus on the territorial organization of the State. The Spanish Constitution of 1978 offered two ways to access autonomy. First, there was a fast track, described in article 151, that allowed a region to immediately begin the drafting of a Stat-

---

1. For a history of Catalan conflict, see Antoni Segura, *Crònica del catalanisme. De l'autonomia a la independència* (Barcelona: Angle, 2013).

2. In the Basque Country, the results also highlighted a nationalist (35.4% of the votes) and leftist (32.6%) majority, versus the government party (12.8%). Regarding the Basque elections, see Antoni Segura, *Euskadi, crónica de una desesperanza* (Madrid: Alianza, 2009), 73.

ute of Autonomy, and considered a higher level of competencies. This method, according to the second transitional provision, was initially reserved for those historic nationalities (Catalonia, the Basque Country, Galicia) that during the Second Spanish Republic (1931–39) had already been granted a Statute of Autonomy. And second, there was a slow track, through Article 143, that required a minimum period of five years to access autonomy. Finally, the first additional provision introduced protection and respect for the historical rights of the chartered territories (the Basque Country, Navarre) that allowed a different funding scheme: an Economic Agreement.

In accordance with these principles, the Statute of Autonomy of Catalonia was drawn up and approved (by 88% of the votes) in 1979. The generalitat (parliament, the president of the government, and the government) was a regional power. According to the Statute of 1979, the government funding mechanisms were their own taxes, taxes delegated to the state, a share of taxes collected by Catalonia, debt issue, surcharges on state taxes, and others.

In the first elections to the Parliament of Catalonia (March 1980), the majority was secured by Catalan nationalists, represented by the Convergence and Union party (CiU). After four years in government, in 1984 the nationalist coalition obtained an absolute majority, repeated in the following elections until 1995. Between 1995 and 2003, CiU held control of the government with the support of other parliamentary groups.

The Spanish State of Autonomies was reshaped after the coup attempt of February 23, 1981. The military leadership, one of the mainstays of the dictatorship, distrusted the State of Autonomies, fearing that it could disintegrate the unity of Spain. In addition, the Spanish government and the Socialist opposition believed that the competencies should be limited so as not to deprive the central administration of its power. In July 1982, the government and the opposition approved the Organic Law for the Coordination of the Autonomic Process (LOAPA), a law that aimed to limit the transfer of competencies and standardize the self-government levels of the different autonomies. It was a clear attempt to dilute and lower the aspirations of Catalan and Basque nationalists, which appealed the law being unconstitutional. In 1983, the Constitutional Court abrogated part of the law, but its basic concepts remained: yes to administrative decentralization; no to the transfer of political power from the State government.

Starting in the 1990s, the autonomic financing model gradually revealed its disparities, and the imbalances and inequalities that it caused. Basically, they amount to two: the State of Autonomies did not ensure a progressive leveling of living standards in the different autonomous communities, but in fact created the opposite effect. The autonomous communities with more resources are excessively taxed by a fiscal system that is not compensated by state infrastructure investments that could ensure continued economic growth (see table 6.1).

Table 6.1. Index of autonomous communities' GDP per capita, in relation with the EU-15 average (expressed in purchasing power parity UE-15 = 100).

Communities with higher GDP per capita		Communities with lower GDP per capita			
Community	Index GDP 1980	Community	Index GDP 1980		
Navarre	91	Extremadura	45		
Basque Country	90	Andalusia	57		
La Rioja	88	Canary Islands	59		
Balearic Islands	87	Castille La Mancha	61		
Catalonia	83	Galicia	61		
Madrid	82	Murcia	65		
Cantabria	79	Castille and Leon	71		
Asturias	77	C. Valencia	72		
		Aragon	76		
Average	85	Average	63	Difference	22
Community	Index GDP 2002	Community	Index GDP 2002		
Madrid	113	Andalusia	68		
Catalonia	107	Extremadura	71		
Navarre	106	Murcia	73		
Basque Country	105	Canary Islands	77		
Balearic Islands	102	Asturias	78		
Aragon	101	Galicia	79		
La Rioja	97	Castille La Mancha	80		
C. Valencia	90	Cantabria	86		
		Castille and Leon	90		
Average	103	Average	78	Difference	25

Source: Reelaboration of Julio Alcaide Inchausti and Pablo Alcaide Guindo, 2003, *Balance económico regional (Autonomías y provincias). Años 1995 a 2002* [Madrid: Fundación de las Cajas de Ahorros (FUNCAS), Departamento de Estadística Regional, 2003]; Antoni Castells, «Desequilibris regionals a Espanya i a Europa: unes notes comparatives», Revista Económica, Banca Catalana, n. 100 [June/September 1993], 16.

As we see in table 6.1, between 1980 and 2002 all the communities experienced growth nearing the European average. The communities with higher GDP per capita are virtually the same in 1980 and 2002, although in a different order and with the incorporation of Aragon and Valencia. The exceptions are Asturias, which had been badly affected by the crisis in mining, and Cantabria; in 2002, both of these figures among the communities with a lower GDP per capita. There are also some changes in the order of communities with a lower GDP. Nevertheless, the most significant aspect is that the difference between the averages of the first and the second group increased three points. In sum, we see growth and an approach to the European average, and, in 2002, an inequality among communities greater than that of 1980. The interregional compensation funds have thus not achieved their goal of equalizing the living standards of all the communities.

On the other hand, communities with a higher GDP are excessively taxed by the interregional compensation funds, without a corresponding benefit to the communities with fewer resources. Thus, Antoni Castells, the socialist minister of Economy of the Generalitat between 2003 and 2010, estimated that the fiscal deficit of Catalonia with the Spanish state (the difference between the contributions of Catalan citizens and what they receive as investments from the state) amounted, in 1994, to 10% of Catalan GDP. The Catalan economist suggested that a more just system would be for Catalan citizens to contribute according to the Catalan GDP, and to then receive investments according to the Catalan population.

Between 1980 and 2013, Catalan GDP accounted for, on average, 18.7% of Spanish GDP, without great changes; they achieved a maximum of 19.4% in 1995 and a minimum of 17.8% in 1985. In those same years, the Catalan population represented, on average, 15.8%

Figure 6.1. Fiscal debt of Catalonia, 1995–2005.

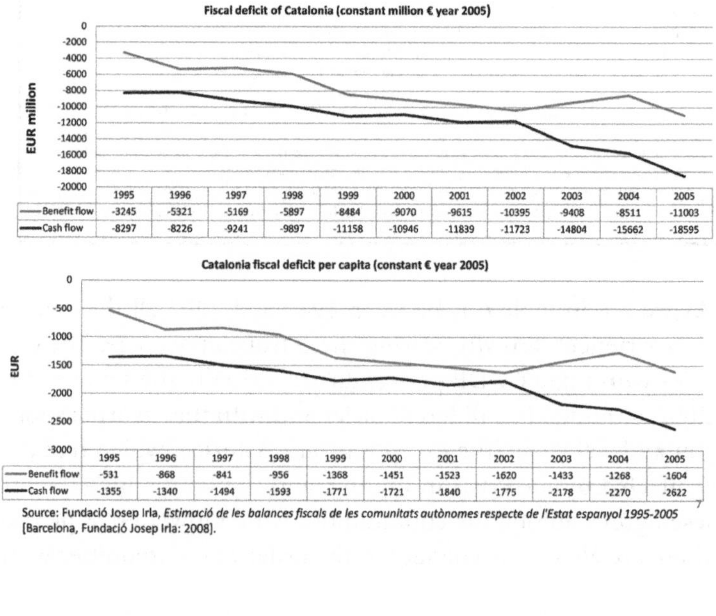

Fiscal deficit of Catalonia (constant million € year 2005)

	1995	1996	1997	1998	1999	2000	2001	2002	2003	2004	2005
Benefit flow	-3245	-5321	-5169	-5897	-8484	-9070	-9615	-10395	-9408	-8511	-11003
Cash flow	-8297	-8226	-9241	-9897	-11158	-10946	-11839	-11723	-14804	-15662	-18595

Catalonia fiscal deficit per capita (constant € year 2005)

	1995	1996	1997	1998	1999	2000	2001	2002	2003	2004	2005
Benefit flow	-531	-868	-841	-956	-1368	-1451	-1523	-1620	-1433	-1268	-1604
Cash flow	-1355	-1340	-1494	-1593	-1771	-1721	-1840	-1775	-2178	-2270	-2622

Source: Fundació Josep Irla, *Estimació de les balances fiscals de les comunitats autònomes respecte de l'Estat espanyol 1995-2005* [Barcelona, Fundació Josep Irla: 2008].

of the Spanish population, with a maximum of 16.0% in 2007 and between 2010 and 2013, and a minimum of 15.4% in 1994 and 1995.

Nevertheless, calculations and estimations of fiscal balances showed that between 1986 and 2009, the fiscal deficit of Catalonia accounted for, on average, 8% of Catalan GDP—a percentage that Catalan public opinion considered too high, even considering the contribution to interregional compensation funds or shared quota (see figure 6.1 and figure 6.2).

Figure 6.2. Fiscal balance, Catalonia/Spain.

Source: Generalitat de Catalunya, *Resultats de la balança fiscal de Catalunya amb el sector públic central 2006-2009* [Barcelona, Generalitat de Catalunya:2012].

We talk about calculations and estimations because the Spanish government never published the autonomous communities' fiscal balances with the state until 2008 (for the first and—until now—last time), with the balances for the year 2005 (see figure 6.3). According to the Report of the Ministry of Economy, a fiscal balance is "an instrument of financial information that assigns, territorially, the incomes and expenditures of public institutions over a period of time, and calculates the resulting fiscal balance in each territory"—in other words, the mentioned difference between what each community contributes to the Spanish state and the benefits that each receives from the state itself. There are two ways of calculation (with some variations in each). The *cash flow* method, which calculates the difference between contributions made by citizens of a territory to the state and what they receive as services and direct investments in the same territory from the state. In this case, only direct investments in a given ter-

Figure 6.3. Fiscal balance of the autonomous communities with the state, 2005.

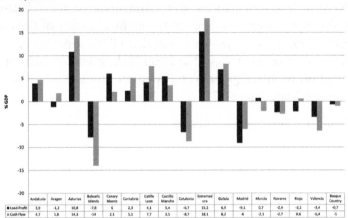

	Andalusia	Aragon	Asturias	Balearic Islands	Canary Islands	Cantabria	Catille Leon	Castille Mancha	Catalonia	Extremadura	Galicia	Madrid	Murcia	Navarre	Rioja	Valencia	Basque Country
■ Load-Profit	3,9	-1,2	10,8	-7,8	6	2,3	4,1	5,4	-6,7	15,2	6,9	-9,1	0,7	-2,4	-2,2	-3,4	-0,7
▨ Cash Flow	4,7	1,8	14,3	-14	2,1	5,1	7,7	3,5	-8,7	18,1	8,2	-6	-2,1	-2,7	0,6	-6,4	-1

Source: Ministerio de Economía y Finanzas. Secretaría de Estado de Hacienda y Presupuestos. Instituto de Estudios Fiscales, *Las balanzas fiscales de las CC.AA. españolas con las AA. públicas centrales 2005* [Madrid, Ministerio de Economía y Finanzas: 2008].

ritory—for example, Catalonia—are calculated. The *fee/profit* method does not focus on the territory where investments or expenditures are made, but rather on the supposed beneficiaries of that investment. In this case, investments realized outside the territory, considered common benefits, are also included—for example, the expenditures for Defense, or for the Prado Museum of Madrid. The results published by the Treasury did not differ substantially from the estimations made by different official and academic circles in Catalonia.

The Spanish socialist government summarized its conclusions in four points:

1. The communities with higher income per capita are those with a fiscal deficit, and those with lower income per capita contribute less—which is what you would expect from a progressive tax system and proper income redistribution through public spending.
2. The four communities with a normal fiscal system that have a higher income per capita are those who contribute more.
3. The communities with lower income per capita are the same who have a fiscal surplus.
4. The public state sector decisively contributes to a fairer distribution of the personal and territorial income.[3]

---

3. Gobierno de España, *Balanzas Fiscales de las CCAA con el sector público estatal* (Madrid: Gobierno de España, 2008), 12.

The Catalan center-left government, also led by socialists, agreed with the first three points, but disagreed with the last one. The evidence against a "fairer distribution of the personal and territorial income" belied this claim. In addition, some of the basic principles that the Catalan government tried to safeguard in the new Statute of 2006, and in the negotiation of the new autonomic financing model, were breached.

On the one hand, between 1986 and 2009 Catalonia's average contributions to the incomes of the public sector represented 19.49% of the total but, in this same period, the investments of the Spanish state in Catalonia were just 14.03% of the total amount—a difference of 5.46% that seemed excessive, especially when, in recent years, the percentage of the executed investments budgeted by the state in Catalonia remained well below the Spanish average (see figure 6.4).

Figure 6.4. Percentage of the execution budgeted investments by the state in Spain and Catalonia, 2000–2010.

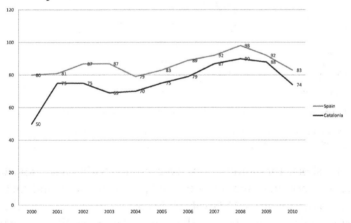

Source: Germà Bel, *Anatomia d'un desengany* (Barcelona: Destino, 2013], p. 216.

On the other hand, the principle of ordinality, by which "the State shall ensure that the application of leveling mechanisms will not alter in any case Catalonia's position in the order of income per capita among the Autonomous Communities before such application," was breached.[4] In short, after contributing to solidarity funds, the Catalan GDP per capita could not be lower than that of the communities receiving those funds. In the words of the president of the Generalitat (2006–10), it might not be that "those who receive solidarity will have

---

4. *Statute of 2006*, article 206.5.

more resources than those who give it." In fact, according to the fiscal balances developed by the Spanish Government in 2005, exactly the opposite happened—and continues to happen (see table 6.2).

Table 6.2. GDP and income per capita (Spain = 100) and ranking autonomous communities, 2005.

Table 3. GDP and Income per capita (Spain = 100) and Ranking Autonomous communities, 2005				
			Ranking	
	GDP	Income per capita[1]	GDP	Income per capita[1]
Andalusia	75,80	82,29	18	19
Aragon	109,98	111,92	5	4
Asturias	89,78	97,68	12	13
Balearic Islands	106,27	103,17	7	10
Basque Country	131,99	125,53	2	2
Canary Islands	83,96	99,47	14	12
Cantabria	100,96	105,63	8	6
Castilla - La Mancha	77,07	91,51	17	15
Castilla - Leon	95,67	107,17	11	5
Catalonia	118,97	104,26	4	9
Extremadura	69,51	89,99	19	17
Galicia	82,63	92,01	16	14
La Rioja	109,18	105,23	6	7
Madrid	133,92	120,11	1	3
Murcia	82,80	83,37	15	18
Navarra	125,86	125,75	3	1
Valencian Country	89,33	90,83	13	16
Ceuta	97,55	100,55	9	11
Melilla	97,25	104,28	10	8
Spanish State	100,00	100,00	-	-

(1) In purchasing power (after the intervention of the State: Inter-territorial compensation fund).

Source: Fundació Josep Irla, *Estimació de les Balances Fiscals de les Comunitats Autònomes respecte de l'Estat espanyol, 1995-2005* [Barcelona, Fundació Josep Irla: 2008].

In short, the autonomous community with more exportation abroad (currently more than to the Spanish market), and that adds more to the Spanish GDP in absolute terms—after satisfying the solidarity funds—descends from the fourth place in GDP ranking to the ninth in income per capita. In exchange, some receiving communities, after receiving solidarity funds, have a higher income per capita than the donors.

Without any doubt, since the end of the 1990s, the issue of fiscal balances has become a central issue in political debate for Catalan public opinion. The State of Autonomies and the Statute of 1979 could not solve the Catalan fiscal deficit and the discomfort that it caused among the population. It was therefore necessary to draft a new Statute and a new system of autonomic financing—actions included in the program of the government installed after the 2003 elections and formed by the Socialists' Party of Catalonia (Catalan socialists, center-left), the Republican Left of Catalonia (Independentist left), and the Initiative for Catalonia Greens–United and Alternative Left (Catalan left). The tripartite government repeated terms of office after the approval of the new Statute and November 2006 elections.

In March 2004, the Spanish Socialist Worker's Party won the Spanish elections. The Socialists ruled both in Spain and in Catalonia. The new statute promoted by the government of the Generalitat seemed to have everything in its favor. In the Catalan elections campaign, the future president of the Spanish government, José Luis Rodríguez Zapatero, promised that "he would support the statute that comes out of the Parliament in Catalonia."[5]

The text of the new statute was approved by 90% of members of the Parliament of Catalonia in September 2005. In January 2006, the president of the Spanish government negotiated the most controversial aspects of the new Statute with the leader of the Catalan opposition. The Constitutional Commission of the Spanish Congress of Deputies eliminated some aspects of the statute's text that could contravene the Spanish Constitution, and the Spanish Socialists presented various amendments that lowered levels of self-government. Finally, on March 30, 2006, the Spanish Parliament approved the new Statute of Autonomy of Catalonia, which was ratified in a referendum by Catalan citizens on June 18, 2006, with 73% favorable votes.

In short, the endorsed text was quite different from the text approved by the Parliament of Catalonia. The illusion of improving self-government and the financing system was lost by way of the statutory process. Without violence, with broad parliamentary support, and with figures with respect to funding below those granted to the Basques by their Statute of 1979, the two major Spanish political parties did not accept the levels of self-government that Catalan citizens required. The Popular Party went even further and appealed to the Constitutional Court against the Statute that had been approved and sanctioned by the king himself. In addition, in 2006, that same party promoted the collection of signatures in Spain against the new Statute of Catalonia, and promoted a boycott of Catalan products.

The Constitutional Court delayed the decision on the Statute for four years. The situation deteriorated rapidly and, as the new president of the Generalitat, José Montilla, warned in May 2008, there was a growing sense of "emotional disaffection of Catalonia toward Spain and toward common institutions." Montilla "complained

---

5. *La Vanguardia*, November 14, 2003.

about the negligence of investors and of the State toward Catalonia and its citizens."[6]

Finally, on June 28, 2010, the Constitutional Court pronounced its sentence. It annulled totally or partially some of the articles of the new statute concerning competences in justice, funding, and use of the Catalan language, and declared without legal value the reference to Catalonia as a nation in the preamble of the statutory text.[7] On July 10, 2010, Barcelona held a mass demonstration against the sentence of the Constitutional Court. In addition, the government of Madrid (Socialist and, later, Popular) did not respect what had been approved and had not been abolished by the Constitutional Court; nor did they respect the new funding system agreed to in 2009. Thus, with the onset of the economic crisis, the Spanish Government ceased to pay the amounts that corresponded to Catalonia by the competitiveness fund, and delayed or did not meet the approved investments in infrastructure. For the majority of Catalans, the statutory route was dead, and "disaffection" became a sentimental breakup with Spain and a claim for independence.

In any case, beyond political and institutional initiatives, the civil society organized itself once the Partido Popular denounced the new statute to the Constitutional Court in 2006. Councilors and mayors from different political parties came together in the Assembly of Municipalities for Independence (AMI) which, outside of the institutions and the parties, tried to mobilize citizens for Independence. Between September 2009 and April 2011, a series of voluntary referendums— which the Spanish Government tried to forbid—were organized in 553 municipalities of Catalonia, including the capital, Barcelona (53% of a total of 947 municipalities). With an average participation of 19%, the votes for independence reached 92%. In parallel, a group of pro-independence activists created the Catalan National Assembly with the aim of bringing together all the sensitivities of civil and social Catalanism. After the integration of the Platform for the Right to Decide (PDD), founded in 2007, and the municipal collectives that promoted the referendums, the Catalan National Assembly was formally created in Barcelona in March 2012.

In November 2010, Artur Mas and his party Convergence and Union won the elections with a program based on obtaining a "Fiscal Agreement" to achieve a result similar to the Basque "Economic Agree-

---

6. José Montilla, "Falso dilema," *El País*, May 10, 2008; and Antoni Segura, "Desafección y federalismo," *El País*, July 18, 2008.

7. Tribunal Constitucional, *Sentencia* (Madrid, June 28, 2010).

ment." On September 11, 2012, National Day of Catalonia, the Catalan National Assembly organized the largest demonstration ever seen in Catalonia (1.5 million people). The demonstration passed peacefully on the streets of Barcelona under the slogan "Catalonia, a new state of the European Union." The program of Mas and Convergence and Union for the "Fiscal Agreement" was overwhelmed in the streets of Barcelona by a huge crowd claiming independence. On September 20, 2012, the Spanish prime minister closed every door to negotiations regarding "Fiscal Agreement." A week later, Artur Mas called early elections, promising that if he obtained enough support during the next term in office, a referendum would be held under Spanish, European, or international law. Therefore, the elections of November 25, 2012 were a kind of plebiscite concerning the so-called "right to decide," that is, an election or a referendum about the future of Catalonia. The ruling party, CiU, lost twelve seats, and the socialists lost eight, but the total number of representatives whose parties explicitly defended the right to realize a referendum went from 86 to 107.

Simultaneously, polls showed that, since 2005, the percentage of the population that considers itself only Catalan has progressively increased, to the point that it now exceeds the percentage of people who feel more Catalan than Spanish. Together, the sum of these two groups, which prioritize Catalan identity, is larger than results in a February 2009 poll registering the percentage of people who feel equally Spanish and Catalan, and very broadly, the sum of the groups of people that prioritize Spanish identity (see figure 6.5).

Figure 6.5. Evolution of identity in Catalonia, 2005–13.

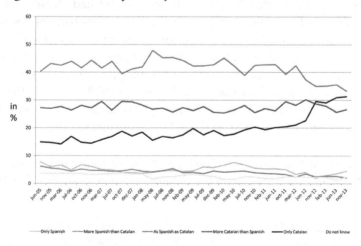

Source: Baròmetres d'Opinió Política [Generalitat de Catalunya. Centre d'Estudis d'Opinió].

Moreover, since July 2007, the percentage of people who would like Catalonia to become an independent state has also been growing. In November 2013, this was the option preferred by 49% of survey respondents, versus 21% who preferred the federal option, while the options of autonomy and region are clearly a minority with just 24%. Finally, the percentage of people who would vote "yes" in a referendum on the independence of Catalonia has continued growing: 43% in June 2011; 45% in October 2011 and March 2012; 51% in June 2012; 57% in November 2012; and 55% in November 2013. In contrast, the percentage who would vote negatively has fallen from 28% to 22% between June 2011 and November 2013.

Beyond the reliability of surveys, there is the cohesion of Catalan civil society, a society that, on September 11, 2012 was able to organize a human chain four hundred kilometers long that linked the northern Catalan border with France to the southern border with Valencia. It was an amazing effort considering its coordination, its logistics, and for the peaceful participation of more than 1.5 million citizens claiming to exercise their right to choose independence (see figure 6.13).

Conclusions

On January 23, 2013, the Parliament of Catalonia approved the "Declaration of Sovereignty and the Right of the Catalan People to Decide," obtaining the support of almost two-thirds of the representatives.[8] It was not the first time that the Catalan Parliament approved such an initiative. In fact, the discomfort with the State of Autonomies and insufficient Catalan self-government had already become evident in December 1989, when the Catalan Parliament approved a bill stating that "the observance of the existing institutional framework ... does not mean that the Catalan people renounce to the right to self-determination, as established by the principles of international organizations, and by the preamble to the 1979 Statute."[9] This was followed over the next several years by two motions (2011) and three resolutions (1998, 2010, and 2012) that reaffirmed the right of the

8. Parlament de Catalunya, "Resolució 5/X del Parlament de Catalunya, per la qual s'aprova la Declaració de sobirania i del dret a decidir del poble de Catalunya," *Butlletí Oficial del Parlament de Catalunya*, no. 13 [January 24, 2013]: 3–4.

9. Parlament de Catalunya, "Resolució 98/III del Parlament de sobre el dret d'auto-determinació de la nació catalana," *Butlletí Oficial del Parlament de Catalunya*, no. 120 [December 18, 1989], 7791–92.

Catalan nation to self-determination. There is not, therefore, a direct relationship between the increase in fiscal deficit and the independentist process, although there is an indirect one. On the one hand, other autonomous communities also show a growing fiscal deficit: coincidentally, the communities that match with those territories of the ancient Kingdom of Aragon that were defeated in the war of 1714. This is also the case of Madrid, which nevertheless receives—as the country's capital—investments in infrastructure that are counted as investments shared by all the territories of Spain when in fact they only benefit the capital. On the other hand, the context is what differentiates the Declaration of 2013. The sentence of the Constitutional Court regarding the 2006 Statute, and the breach of the agreement on the new regional financing system adopted in 2009, closed the road to autonomy for many Catalans, and left only one possible solution: the creation of their own autonomous state.

In short, a bad financing system is not enough to produce a movement for independence or for the right to decide the political future of Catalonia through a referendum. In any case, this bad financing system favors a preexistent movement that gains momentum as the public becomes disillusioned by the existing institutional framework, and tries to find accommodation in a new one. In conclusion, this preexistent movement is none other than the existence of a nation, as this issue arose in the eighteenth and nineteenth centuries: "The personality of people is based on a substrate of language, culture, collective feelings, memory and consciousness prior to political constructions" (Herder); but, at the same time, "the existence of a nation is a daily plebiscite" (Renan).[10] Catalanism, Catalan civil society, and Catalan social movements have been playing this role of daily plebiscite since the second half of the nineteenth century. The result is, today, the existence of an identity project that articulates itself from self-identification, always with cultural, historical and territorial elements . . . , and whenever there is a project to build a community."[11] In this sense, the Catalan nation has moved from a resistance identity, which characterized it during the dictatorship, to an identity project, with a vocation of hegemony and future.

---

10. Jordi Pujol, "De Herder i Renan. I del dret a decidir," *El Punt Avui*, May 27, 2014. (Translation by author.)

11. Manuel Castells, "Globalització i identitat. Una perspectiva comparada," *IDEES*, no. 21 (2004): 17–28. (Translation by author.)

7

Fiscal Consolidation and Resilient Self-Government in the Basque Country in Periods of Financial Crises from 1814 to 2007

Joseba Agirreazkuenaga and Eduardo Alonso Olea

In every crisis, public institutions aim to reduce deficits as well as to accumulate debt, in order to achieve fiscal consolidation. Capacity for self-government is in direct relation to fiscal consolidation and we cannot—and should not—attribute such capacity solely to the member states of the European Union, but also to the regions, because in Europe the tradition of small states has prevailed over the last five hundred years.

We have set out to construct a long-term historical explanation and narrative on fiscal policy and crises in the nineteenth and twentieth centuries in Bizkaia, the main area in economic terms of the Basque Country. The focal points are:

1. Survival of a self-governing institution, with fiscal and financial powers to manage the public treasury in a context of centralization of the new Spanish nation-state, 1810–1845.
2. Practices of the self-government treasuries in the period of proto-industrial crisis on the eve of the industrial revolution, 1845–1878.
3. From neutrality to public intervention during the first period of industrial capitalism, 1878–1937.
4. Recovery of the Economic Agreement (1981–1985), intervention in the final crisis of an industrial model and in the crisis of 2007. Economic crises are recurrent in capitalism. Economic cycles are always changing (short cycles or long cycles), and attempts are made to define the specific time frame of the crisis

in order to observe and analyze whether the period is really one of stagnation or whether another cycle has been entered.[1]

Based on this general framework, we analyze how, during a long-term process over two centuries, the political leaders who managed the Basque territorial Governments ("Deputations"), in particular terms the Government of Biscay, have reacted over the last two hundred years in the face of different economic crises.[2] The self-governing powers of the Basque representative institutions to manage the crises are also key. For the nineteenth century, this analysis is discussed in the book *The Making of the Basque Question: Experiencing Self-Government*.[3]

The practice of self-government by Basque public institutions preceded the organization of Basque nationalism as a political movement. The Basque Question is not a consequence of the nationalist movement, but arises instead from the historical experience of self-government and the powers of the Basque Representative Assemblies, particularly during the nineteenth century. The contrast and competition between the general will of the Basque people, expressed in the Representative Assemblies, and the Spanish national Parliament to regulate the public powers during the making of the Spanish nation-State became a "Basque question."

The Representative Assemblies managed public resources during the economic crisis.

The political institutions of Europe are the representation of its multilevel federal historical background.[4] Many nation-states of Europe date from the nineteenth century, but the majority of the twenty-eight nation-states of today's European Union date from the twentieth century. However, there are different models of nation-state organization within Europe with federal or centralized power. As Josep Maria Colomer wrote, "Flexibility is associated with resilience,

---

1. Francisco Comin Comin and Mauro Hernandez Benitez (eds.), *Crisis económicas en España. 1300–2012. Lecciones de la historia* (Madrid: Alianza, 2013).

2. Eduardo Alonso Olea, "El Concierto Económico como herramienta. Crisis económicas y políticas anticíclicas de las Diputaciones vascas. 1867–1936," *Boletín de Estudios Económicos* LXV, no. 201 (2010).

3. Joseba Agirreazkuenaga, *The Making of the Basque Question: Experiencing Self-Government, 1793–1877*. (Reno: Center for Basque Studies, University of Nevada, 2012)

4. Michael Herb, "Taxation and Representation," in *Studies in Comparative International Development (SCID)* 38, no. 3 (September 2003): 3–31.

like bamboo; while rigidity, like the stick, implies fragility."[5] And when in political society there are many institutions to manage the social reality, the level of resilience is higher in order to handle crises.

We examine the fiscal and financial policies of the Biscay government, as a case study, to address the following problems and to observe continuities and changes in their conduct. However, our gaze must also be directed at the present situation.[6]

1. Successive economic crises in the long term (twentieth through twenty-first centuries).
2. Fiscal consolidation.
3. Resilient self-government: The system of self-government needs to be considered in terms of the attributes that govern the system's dynamics in ecology: resilience, adaptability, and transformability. Resilience is the capacity of a system to absorb disturbance and reorganize while undergoing change in order to retain essentially the same function, structure, identity, and feedback.[7]

In this chapter, we set out to construct a long-term historical explanation of the Bizkaia and Basque case and its governments, a narrative beginning in 1812 when a new political liberal Constitution was approved in the Spanish empire or Composite Monarchy.

The focal points are as follows:

1. Survival of the Representative Assemblies and governments with fiscal and financial powers to manage the public treasury in a context of centralization of the Spanish nation-state, 1808–45.
2. Practices of the *foral or self-governing* treasuries in the period of proto-industrial crisis on the eve of the industrial revolution, 1845–78.
3. From neutrality to intervention of public provincial institutions during the first period of industrial capitalism, 1878–1937.
4. Recovery of the Economic Agreement (1981–85), intervention in the final crisis of an industrial model and in the crisis of 2007.

---

5. Josep Maria Colomer, http://jcolomer.blogspot.com/ January 12, 2014.
6. Gemma Martínez, "Opinions on Tax Autonomy of European Regions: From the Basque Country Case (1999) to the Gibraltar Case (2011)."
7. Brian Walker and David Salt, *Resilience Thinking: Sustaining Ecosystems and People in a Changing World.* (Washington: Island Press, 2006), XIII.

In every financial crisis, the public institutions aim to reduce defi-cits and debts in order to achieve fiscal consolidation. Self-governing capacity is in direct relation to fiscal consolidation, and we cannot—and should not—attribute such capacity solely to the Member States of the European Union but also to the regions, because in Europe the tradition of small states has prevailed for the last five hundred years.

1814–15: Agreement to Manage War Debt

The debt accumulated due to successive wars forced the public insti-tutions of Bizkaia to undertake a management and financial commit-ment. The accumulated debt of Bizkaia amounted to 35,433,470 mil-lion *reales* that generated an annual interest of 1,341,396 *reales,* and the ordinary incomes amounted to 2,418,651 *reales.* In this pre-statis-tical period, it is estimated that Bizkaia had a gross domestic income of 65 million *reales.*[8] The debt represented 50% of gross domestic in-come.

In order to address the repayment plan for the accumulated debt and on the initiative of Manuel María Aldecoa (third General Deputy during the 1814–16 period and mayor of Bilbao in 1815), an agree-ment was made among the three "communities" or important insti-tutions of Bizkaia, represented by the Deputation, the township of Bilbao, and the Maritime "Consulate" or representative institution of the merchants.

Indirect taxes were established, as well as direct taxes on property (6% of productive capacity, a type of income tax). In 1818, there was a debate on the tax system in the Representative Assembly of Biz-kaia: A majority of the members of the commission favored indirect taxation on consumer goods, with the following argument: "It has been taken into consideration that the more widespread the taxes, the more bearable they are to individual taxpayers."[9] The minority, led by two politicians with opposing ideologies—M. M. Aldecoa, a liberal, and P. Novia de Salcedo, a *fuerista* traditionalist, made a class analysis of tax efficiency, since indirect taxes were levied on ordinary people and were costly to organize: "Without being convinced that proceeding from the general mass of inhabitants they weigh down on the less wealthy classes; they are costly to exact, uncertain in their

---

8. Joseba Agirreazkuenaga, *Vizcaya en el siglo XIX: las finanzas públicas de un Estado emergente* (1812–1876) (Leioa: UPV-EHU, 1985), 383.

9. *Actas de Juntas Generales de Vizcaya* (Bilbao, 1818): "Ha tenido presente que cuanto más se generalicen las imposiciones son tanto más llevaderas individual-mente a los contribuyentes."

result and ruinous in essence."[10] As a result, they proposed to share out the quotas by localities where the tax should be applied according to the estimated wealth of each inhabitant, effectively an income tax.

The rejection and refusal of direct taxes among the political leaders was a commonly held fiscal philosophy in Bizkaia. The opposition to direct contributions was also evident in the Liberal Triennium. However, from 1823 onward, under the government of the anti-liberals—that is, the Royalists, later known as Carlists—direct taxes were established on property: a 10% property tax was demanded, specifically during the years 1823, 1824, 1825, and 1826, and 6% from 1827 to 1833. Of these direct taxes, two-thirds were paid by the property owner and one-third by the tenant.

Finally, the management of the debt served to consolidate the General Deputation or government of Biscay as a governing body. Fiscal consolidation was what fermented the new self-government of the Bizkaia, Araba, and Gipuzkoa governments and their common body, the Basque Conferences.[11]

Following the Carlist War of 1833–39, the territorial governments had to liquidate the new war debts. At the same time, the tax on "worship and clergy" was collected at the local level, and a progressive system was applied according to the income of heads of family.

On the other hand, to combat unemployment, after 1840 a policy of road building was promoted. Road construction companies were created, which issued shares at 5%, a high annual interest rate in a period of economic uncertainty, and these companies were underwritten by the territorial governments. From that time onward, the "Biscay Government" or Deputation became the largest financial organization in Bizkaia.[12] In short, the debt and the crisis served to strengthen the government of Bizkaia *in the territory of Bizkaia and in opposition to* the new government of the Composite Monarchy managed by the king and later the Constitutional Monarchy of the Spanish nation-state. In the Basque Country, the public and financial action attributed to the new liberal state was fulfilled by the governments of the Deputations in material terms. Legislation was dictated

---

10. Ibid.: *"Sin convencerse de que saliendo de la masa general de habitantes pesan sobre las clases menos pudientes; que son costosas en su exacción, inciertas en su producto y ruinosas por su esencia."*
11. Agirreazkuenaga, *The Making of the Basque Question: 1793–1919* (Reno: Center for Basques Studies, 2011).
12. Agirreazkuenaga, *Vizcaya en el siglo XIX: Las finanzas públicas de un Estado emergente (1812–1876).* (Bilbao: UPV-EHU, 1987).

by the Spanish Parliament. However, the rules for organizing activities were decided by the Representative Assemblies of Bizkaia, Araba, and Gipuzkoa.

Crisis of 1865: The Government of Bizkaia as Entrepreneur

The reaction of the government of Bizkaia to the crisis of the 1860s was necessarily different. In 1867, there was a financial and overproduction crisis; expenditure on railways in Europe had been immense, and this was the case in Spain as well—but once the main lines had been built, it became clear that the movement of travelers and goods was not as envisaged. With the ending of fiscal benefits and customs exemptions intended for the supply of railway building material, the situation of the stock market was dramatic. Business expectations had been placed on construction more than on exploitation—similar to what is happening at present with projects such as the building of nuclear power stations and toll motorways.

If we add the subsistence crisis resulting from a period of poor harvests due to the climate, we can form a general idea of the problem. The crisis provoked the collapse of the majority of the banks, except the Bank of Bilbao and the Bank of Santander. The Bank of Bilbao was saved *in extremis* from being caught up in the technical bankruptcy of the Bilbao-Tudela Railway when it was the main lender to the Foral Government of Bizkaia. Nonetheless, there was a liberal mentality so that private initiative did not immediately take recourse to public assistance, although it eventually did so.

The government of Bizkaia promoted a railway company—the mining railway of Triano—but the public institutions were not able to create economic companies.[13] However, in 1869 the law was changed. Eventually, the profits from this company served to balance the budget of the Deputation in the following decades, and the luxurious Foral Palace built in 1900 became a new symbol of a government of Bizkaia with reliable income.

The Crisis of 1890 and the Provincial Government or Deputation

In the early 1890s, there was another economic and industrial crisis due to overproduction. This had a special impact on Bilbao as it affected the emergent industrial and mining sectors. The effect of the conti-

---

13. Angel Maria Ormaechea, *Ferrocarriles en Euskadi, 1855–1936* (Bilbao: Eusko Trenbideak, 1989).

nental crisis and the industrial bourgeoisie's assault on the spheres of central power in an effort to promote protectionist policies led to the formation of several metal-transformation companies for the second smelting of iron ingots (Tubos Forjados, Aurrerá, Basconia, Talleres de Zorroza, and many others). With changes in the customs policy designed to increase importation rights, these companies faced the difficulties of exporting untransformed commercial iron; thus, they concentrated on transforming it *in situ*—with greater added value.[14]

Following the mining strike that paralyzed Bilbao and the mining and industrial zone in May 1890, the question of social order became an issue affecting the Deputation itself. The mining employers, who paid a tax on dynamite, influenced the Deputation to direct some of this income toward financing a Foral Police Corps.[15] Alongside agrarian, urban, and merchant *rentiers*, members of the industrial bourgeoisie entered the government of the Deputation, and they were concerned about having a police force available.

In fact, until 1894, the Provincial Deputation of Bizkaia did not raise new taxes. Incomes were based on consumer taxes and the profits of the mining railway of Triano. Ten years later, in 1903, there was a stock exchange panic in Bilbao that especially affected various recently created companies that had emerged due to the boom from the repatriation of colonial capital since 1899. These companies were Seguros Aurora, La Polar, and the shipbuilding companies formed by Martínez Rodas.[16]

The Crash of 1929

The First World War and Spanish neutrality brought a strong boost to the Biscayan economy. However, in 1918 the effects of overproduction began to be seen, given that as soon as the war ended the mines and industries found themselves without orders almost overnight. During the war, they had increased their production capaci-

---

14. The organization of industrial entrepreneurs La Liga Vizcaína de Productores and Víctor Chávarri were in favor of protectionism. Eduardo J. Alonso Olea, *Víctor Chávarri (1854–1900). Una biografía* (San Sebastián: Eusko Ikaskuntza-Ayuntamiento de Portugalete, 2005); Ignacio Arana Perez, *La Liga Vizcaína de Productores y la política económica de la Restauración* (Bilbao: Caja de Ahorros Vizcaína, 1988).
15. Ignacio Villota, *Vizcaya en la política minera española. Las asociaciones patronales, 1886–1914* (Bilbao: Servicio de Publicaciones de la Diputación Foral de Vizcaya, 1984), 66.
16. Manuel Montero, *La Bolsa de Bilbao y los negocios financieros. La formación del mercado de capitales en el despegue industrial de Vizcaya* (Bilbao: Universidad del País Vasco, 1996).

ties to meet the growing demand of the belligerent countries.[17] The acute crisis in the United Kingdom immediately after the war, with strikes that paralyzed its economy for months, affected basic sectors like mining.

In Bizkaia, the tax on profits was not collected until 1911, when profits from the year 1910 were taxed, but these were not exactly the same as in the common territory. Between 1910 and 1913, there was a tax on company profits shared out in the form of dividends. Besides, this only affected Limited Liability Companies, which were exempt from the Industrial Contribution.[18]

The tax rate applied by the Biscayan Deputation between 1910 and 1913 was 3% on profits given out in the form of dividends by Limited Liability Companies. In 1914, this was extended to all profits. In 1915, the rate was increased to 4%; in 1920, it rose to 5%. In 1921, following the example agreed on by the Ministry of the Treasury, a variable tax rate was set based on the profits on paid-in capital plus the reserves of the fiscal year. In 1927, due to the large increase in the concerted quota, the tax rates were raised. As well as the taxes, the companies affected also varied. Until 1923, only the activities of Limited Liability Companies were taxed, but from that date partnerships, limited partnerships, and jointly owned entities were also affected. In the 1930s, individual enterprises, book publishers, educational establishments, and so on, were affected.

On the other hand, in 1900, the Ministry of the Treasury established a tax with a variable percentage (15–0.5%) depending on the company's branch of activity, a rate raised in 1920 and now calculated on the part represented by profit over capital plus reserves.

However, the advantages did not only appear when there were profits, but also when there were none. In the case of a company that did not obtain profits, or where these did not reach 5% of its paid-in capital plus reserves, a minimum rate of 2% was set on its own funds, which in the case of the Ministry of the Treasury reached 3%. Here we find another variant of fiscal benefit; in some concrete cases the calculation of paid-in capital was altered so that companies would pay less, as was the case with the Biscayan shipbuilding companies.

---

17. Manuel Gonzalez Portilla "A.H.V. Expansión y crisis de la siderurgia española. La fractura de la Primera Guerra Mundial," en *Economía y empresa en el norte de España (Una aproximación histórica)*, ed. Pablo Martin Aceña-Montserrat Garate (San Sebastián: Diputación Foral de Gipuzkoa—U.P.V-EHU, 1994).

18. In Bizkaia, a public limited company, precisely because of its character, paid no more than the tariff on utilities and was exempt from the industrial tariff.

In 1920, in the midst of a crisis of the shipbuilding sector, the balance sheets of shipbuilding companies showed losses or small profits, so that they had to pay 2% on substantial capital and reserves. The accumulation of reserves was from the time of the First World War, and the sheer scale of their capital in shares due to business needs tended to be large (e.g., in 1919 the Sota and Aznar shipbuilding company had more than 155 million *pesetas* in shares and reserve funds). In Gipuzkoa, the shipbuilding companies paid 1.5% in the same case, which is why the Biscayan shipbuilding companies changed their tax residence to the neighboring province, with one company even establishing its tax residence in Eibar, several kilometers from the sea, in search of more favorable tax treatment. One of the variables of these tax rates depended on the capital of the companies. The companies presented balance sheets in accordance with current reality (values of shares according to average stock exchange prices, and not according to the founding documents of the company nor the calculation of the value of the ships on the assets side, updated to the value of the moment and not to the time of purchase, which was often very swollen due to the high prices of the war). The benefit for the companies subject to this updating of balances was clear: the minimum quota was applied on a reduced capital.[19]

In short, during this postwar crisis, the Deputation concerned itself with public order as well as with tax modifications that would benefit companies with problems. The relationship between provincial deputies and companies was of course not something indirect or remote; quite the contrary: Ramón de la Sota and Aburto or Luis de Echevarría were presidents of the Corporation and sons of outstanding "captains of industry," to mention only a few examples.

In February 1925, there was an acute financial crisis in Bilbao provoked by the collapse of a bank, the Crédito de la Unión Minera.[20] There were several reasons for the particular catastrophe of the Crédito de la Unión Minera: speculation in the stock market, which made a mess of the resources acquired in fixed-term deposits; the pledging of shares deposited in the Bank; and the problems of the mining sector itself at that time. In fact, for several years the bank had been falsify-

19. Foral Archive of Bizkaia: Informe de la Jefatura Superior de Hacienda de la Diputación de Vizcaya, June 10, 1929, F. Administrativo, Hacienda, Utilidades 326/1.
20. Eduardo Alonso Olea, "El Crédito de la Unión Minera. 1901–2002," *Historia contemporánea*, no. 24 (2002). Telegrama de la Sucursal del Banco de España en Bilbao al Banco de España, 10 February 1925, Archivo del Banco de España. Secretaría General, Leg. 1248.

ing its accounts and showing fictitious profits, as was revealed by the first audit in March 1925. Nonetheless, following the first "scare" of 1914, the bank enjoyed a good reputation, and its shares were well considered on the stock exchange.

Judicial measures were not long in coming; an examining magistrate opened proceedings immediately, calling a number of prominent businessmen to declare and testify, and ordered their imprisonment.[21] The stockbroker and well-known journalist and writer on Bilbao's social customs, Manuel Aranaz Castellano, shot himself in Rekalde. A new Management Board was also immediately appointed, drawn from the elite of the companies and local and provincial institutions, together with some business representatives from Burgos and its Chamber of Commerce. The latter is not surprising due to the important weight among its depositors of firms and individuals domiciled in this Castilian province. Niceto Duo was also appointed as the new director.

Some of the most significant financiers of the time, among whom the most distinguished was the republican Horacio Echevarrieta, initially called for the Deputation of Bizkaia to solve the problem. The problem posed in the Deputation was whether it should devote resources to solving the case with the financial shortage still unresolved. Other republicans, Ernesto Ercoreca in particular, argued that just as shareholders did not give money to the Deputation on receiving their dividend, neither should the public purse compensate them when they experienced a loss.

The immediate problem for the Deputation was that it was immersed in other programs requiring funds that had already been assigned. The Biscayan Deputation, after explaining the problem and its possible solution to the sister Deputations, proposed that the latter should also contribute to the financial effort, in this way providing some justification for their control of the quotas of their respective provinces.[22]

---

21. President of the Council José Mª San Martín, Councilor Agustín Iza, and employees Federico Meltzer (bookkeeper) and Ignacio Belausteguigoitia (teller). Additionally, he called the Director (Juan Núñez Anchústegui) and several councilors (Pedro Astigarraga, the Marquis of Acillona José Pablo Acillona, his brother Guillermo Acillona, and José R. Chapa).

22. Acta de la Conferencia de las Diputaciones Vascongadas, June 1, 1925; Joseba Agirreazkuenaga (ed.) *La articulación político institucional de Vasconia: Actas de las Conferencias firmadas por los representantes de Alava, Bizkaia, Gipuzkoa y eventualmente de Navarra (1775–1936)* (Bilbao: Diputación de Bizkaia, 1995), 2 vols.

On June 6, 1925, at last and not without problems, the definitive decision to renovate the Economic Agreement was reached. As a good example of how closely related this was to the problem of the Crédito de la Unión Minera, two agreements were signed at the same time: one referring to the Economic Agreement, and the other concerning the offer made by the Biscayan Deputation (the effort it would have to make with the quotas from 1927 onwards was well known), with the help of Gipuzkoa and Araba, to pay the passive credits of the Crédito de la Unión Minera in the form of repayable loans totaling 60 million pesetas.[23]

The new quota, which it was agreed would be paid from January 1, 1927, was approved by Royal Decree on June 9, 1925. The day after the agreement in Madrid, the legal representative of the Crédito de la Unión Minera presented a document in court offering a deposit to cover the deficit of 92,120,208.90 *pesetas*—fixed by the judge for May 6. This deposit totaled 60 million proceeding from the agreement of the Deputations, although the judge allowed a period until 30 June to make the deposit effective.

Until recent times, when one spoke of crisis, it was obligatory to mention the Depression of the 1930s. The stock market crash of October 1929 and the deep crisis it unleashed in the world economy also had an impact in Bizkaia.

The Great Depression struck several of the strategic sectors of the Biscayan economy, especially in 1931 and 1932 (as in other countries these were the most virulent years of the crisis). As table 7.1 shows,

Table 7.1. Iron ore and steel ingot production. Source: Data from Ricardo Miralles, "La crisis económica de los años treinta en el País Vasco." Ekonomiaz, no. 9–10, Vitoria (1988): 279 and 286.

Production and Exportation of Iron Ore From Bizkaia (Tons)			Production of Steel Ingots in Bizkaia and in Spain (Tonnes)	
YEARS	PROD.	EXPORT.	SPAIN	BIZKAIA
1929	2603	1745	1,003,459	563,766
1930	2346	1238	924,459	524,723
1931	1512	794	645,366	326,651
1932	1113	840	532,403	301,651
1933	1229	817	506,653	296,697
1934	1349	838	646,857	324,367
1935	1598	1013	594,710	354,938

23. Acta de la reunión de los Comisionados vascongados con los funcionarios del Ministerio de Hacienda, June 6, 1925, A.A.D.V. R.E.A.- C.E. 2660/2.

The metallurgical sector, and directly related to this the steel sector, were the most affected with a sharp fall in extraction and exportation:

The effect of this crisis in the mining and the iron and steel sectors can also be seen when analyzing the figures for unemployment in Bizkaia. In July 1933,[24] out of the 25,681 unemployed (both fully and partially) in the province, 14,138 were from the metallurgical and iron and steel sector. At this point, we also come to another conjuncture of events at the political level. For the first time during the Second Republic, the Deputations were managed by a majority formed of republicans and socialists.

The fiscal picture did not change significantly, although inspection work increased in order to reduce fraud, and provincial expenditure increased, above all in public works to contract unemployed people for provincial works. It is well known that these policies of expenditure can function until the institution's purse is empty, as in this case. Moreover, there was a drop in taxes collected, which in 1932 led the Deputation to ask the state for a credit of ten million *pesetas* in order to continue this program of public works, which was of course only a slight mitigation of the problem.

However, in those years the Deputations also sought to increase investment through tax exemption and relief. The clearest evidence of this was the arrival of a factory for manufacturing North American Firestone brand tires in the town of Basauri in Bizkaia. This company, established in 1932, absorbed a previous company that had distributed tires and was exempt from paying certain taxes for five years (50% of the profits and industrial taxes, as well as all of the rights and stamp duties) by an agreement of the Biscayan Deputation. It was perhaps not by chance that the manager of the tire distributor that this company absorbed was Juan Olóriz, Chief of the Treasury Office of the Biscayan Provincial Corporation. Another case at the time, also affecting Álava, was the placing of Villosa (Vidrieras de Llodio) in Llodio—among other possible locations—in 1934, due to the ten-year fiscal exemption conceded by the Deputation of Álava. One can wonder whether these fiscal incentives were really attractive to companies, or whether they simply helped in making the decision to locate in the Basque Country. The truth is that there were few tax exemption agreements (Firestone in 1932, Babcock and Wilcox in 1918, and Ascensores de Solocoeche in 1935), and they involved companies

---

24. A. Arregui, *Orientaciones generales para el desarrollo y prosperidad de la provincia de Vizcaya* (Bilbao: Caja de Ahorros Vizcaína, 1934).

that could truly have a natural localization, in this case in Bizkaia.

General company taxation was more lenient on profits than taxation in the common territory of Spain, and this might have influenced the decision on where to locate. In this respect, however, it is necessary to demystify the attractive role of lower taxation since many of the companies established in the Basque Country, although they had productive centers in the common territory, had significant investments of Basque capital. Nevertheless, one should not overlook the presence of companies with little or no relation to the Basque Country that established themselves there due, among other reasons, to the advantageous tax arrangements. This is the case of the Banco de Avila with its tax domicile in Donostia-San Sebastián.[25]

The Evolution of the Public Debt from 1877 to 1936

In 1877, the debt of the Deputation was a very heavy burden, which became even greater when in 1878 it lost the capacity to receive resources proceeding from the tax on tobacco, whose incomes served to balance the budgets.

At the margin of these sums was the debt of the Moroccan War of 1859, which was finally paid off in 1913 with annual payments of 60,000 pesetas until 1907, and from that year to 1912 with annual payments of 40,000 pesetas. In 1913, payment was completed with a single payment of 86,231.64 pesetas. In this way, the loan provided by the Bank of Bilbao in 1860 was finally returned. In total, these payments between 1877 and 1913 amounted to 2,146,231.64 pesetas, but as these were constant and expenditures rose over the years, these quantities fell in proportional terms.

Apart from this purpose-oriented debt, contracted through a credit operation with the Bank of Bilbao, the Deputation logically issued debt aimed at covering the shortfalls of its fiscal system and its incomes proceeding from the Mining Railway of Triano. In general, the debt followed a falling tendency within the section of expenditure, as shown in figure 7.1.

In this long series, although there are gaps for some years (1882–1885, 1900–1903, and 1932), it can be clearly seen that the tendency was decreasing. It rose at times of crisis, as well as in 1907, due to the increase in the quota. The increase in 1925 was due to the following factors: increase of the quota of 1927, loans incurred for the cheap

---

25. It is "a perfect and meticulous organization aimed at achieving a pronounced tax evasion for the concerted territory." December 30, 1929, Archivo General de la Administración. Alcalá de Henares, Hacienda, 16/24 no. 17112-6.

Figure 7.1. Debt in the Expenditure of the Deputation of Bizkaia, 1877–1936 (%).

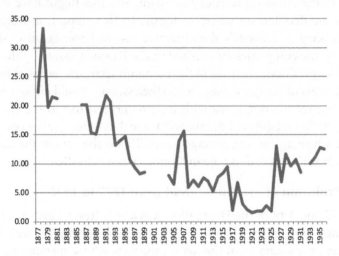

Figure 7.2. Loans as Income of the Deputation of Bizkaia, 1877–1936 (%).(Source: Foru Artxiboa–Foral Archives. Bilbao: Presupuestos and Historia de la Diputación Foral de Bizkaia 1500–2014).

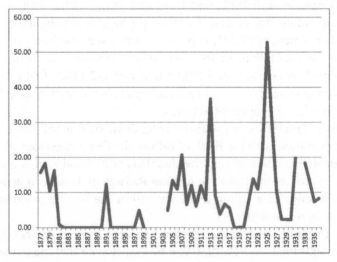

housing program, loan for resolving the bankruptcy of the Crédito de la Unión Minera, and, from 1930 onwards, the Depression.

Another perspective is clearly that of income—that is, the extent to which the Deputation financed itself through loans (see figure 7.2). This was an extraordinary resource: to the extent that ordinary incomes were not sufficient, it was necessary to have recourse to credit. The change of the Foral treasury to the "concerted" treasury in 1878 meant the loss of income from products like tobacco and the fixed increase in expenditures due to payment of the annual quota, which is why in the short term it was necessary for the Deputation to have recourse to debt in order to finance itself.

Except during crises, or an unexpected increase of need, it was exceptional for the Deputacion to request loans.

The arrival of the new century brought a clear change in the management of loans, so that they ceased to be extraordinary and became ordinary—except during the First World War, when the provincial treasury "reveled in abundance." Additionally, during crises, extraordinary loans were also taken out for programs like that aimed at financing cheap housing in 1925, as well as the operation aimed at covering the financial shortage caused by the bankruptcy of the Crédito de la Unión Minera. This was followed in 1927 by another loan, which was finally paid off in 1967, aimed at covering the increase in the quota. During the crisis of the 1930s, there was a return of recourse to credit, in this case funded by the state, to mitigate the problem of unemployment through public works programs.

Abolition of the Economic or Concerted Agreement in 1937 by General F. Franco.

We now make another leap in time. The concerted economic regime was abolished in 1937 for Bizkaia and Gipuzkoa, leaving the provincial corporations in the aftermath of the civil war. In short, their capacity of action facing the subsistence crisis was limited by the centralism of the state that concentrated the (few) resources and (all) the political capacity for trying resolve it. As we know, Franco's regime preferred to blame foreign powers and the prolonged drought for the problems.

Even without the Economic Agreement, Bizkaia and Gipuzkoa, in terms of income per capita, were at the head of the provinces of Spain, although with a clear deficit in infrastructures that did not correspond to their levels of income.

The Crisis of 1973

The crisis of 1973, which was initially an energy crisis (western support for Israel, increase of petroleum prices by OPEC), and then an economic crisis, affected the basic sectors of the Biscayan economy: iron and steel and shipbuilding. The Deputation had few mechanisms for intervention until the Economic Agreement was recovered in 1981.

During the process of reconstructing a renovated Foral Treasury,[26] the public sector had to be organized in the midst of an economy almost in free fall and with a growing rate of unemployment. In 1983, just as the new Foral Treasury started to work in an effective way, torrential rains arrived in the summer.

At that time, therefore, the Deputation had to involve itself in very significant debt operations to be able to counteract the effects of those factors in the shortest possible time. Most evident was the reconstruction of the communication routes, which had started in 1981 but was now essential if productivity was to recover. Besides these programs of public works—which were not necessarily developed to provide work for the unemployed as was done fifty years before, but rather to facilitate trade—credit operations were carried out with companies so that they would be able to resume their activities in the shortest possible time.

If the Economic Agreement served for something, it was of course so that the institutions could correct the falling tendency of economic activity. Since the tax collecting instruments were in the hands of the Foral Deputations, it was through these that different fiscal measures were mediated to favor investment. These were the first "tax holidays."

During the early 1980s, there was an attempt to cushion the "tragedies" that occurred, such as the closure of emblematic shipbuilding companies (the case of Euskalduna) or the consequences of natural disasters such as the floods of 1983, with damages estimated at 190,822 million pesetas, of which 76,228 corresponded to industry. The unemployment rates continued to rise, and it was not until the second half of the decade that there was some improvement, although unemployment remained high. While in 1981 the rate of unemployment in the Basque Country was 16.3%, in Bizkaia it reached 17.6% (versus 13.9% in Spain); in 1985 it reached 23% in the Basque Country, but 25% in Bizkaia—that is, a quarter of the active population that was prepared to work could not find jobs. From 1985 onward, the different measures put into practice by the institutions began to have a positive effect, apart from the favorable world economic conjuncture noted above, although there was another relapse in the early 1990s.

---

26. Javier Muguruza, "La creación de la Hacienda Foral de Bizkaia en 1981–1982 al recuperarse el Concierto Económico," *I Seminari Catalunya-Euskadi. la institucionalització política de les constitucions històriques als estatuts d'autonomia. I Mintegia Catalunya-Euskadi. Erakundentze politikoaz: irageneko konstituzioetatik, autonomi estatutue-tara (1808–2005)* (Barcelona: Generalitat de Catalunya, 2007).

The change in the state of affairs in the mid-1980s was achieved following ten years of disinvestment, crisis, and limited profits, which were once again reinvested from 1986 onward, with a drop in unemployment led above all by the service sector.

European integration in 1986 without question invigorated the economy. With the worst years behind them, companies found themselves in diverse situations, because while some sectors achieved profits, others (like integral steelmaking) continued to have problems. Meanwhile, they witnessed how traditional advantages disappeared, such as tax relief on exports or the drop in the level of protection of import duties. And if initially the external sector (exports were very difficult) grew with the timid economic recovery, new tendencies appeared, like the internationalization of company activities.

In this respect as well, public institutions tried to take advantage of the stimulus that might be provided by Spain's entry into the European Union, perhaps through an opening to European markets and the use of the investment possibilities of resources managed by the European Union, that is, the Community Funds. At the same time, the gradual strengthening of Community decision-making centers increasingly concentrated the powers of regional decision-making.

The structural funds have been one of the instruments of this policy. Following their reform in 1988, they made it possible to concentrate resources on concrete objectives. Three of these were especially relevant for the Basque Country: regions with a lower level of income, those affected by the loss of industrial employment in highly industrialized areas, and even aid to particular low-income rural zones (mountain agriculture). These funds made it possible to construct long-term initiatives that have proved socially profitable (e.g., the Bilbao Metro).

However, beyond these funding policies, or the policy employed by the Foral Governments under the shelter of the Economic Agreement—which established particular tax exemptions for the implantation of companies (carried out under Foral Norm 8/1988 of 5 July, in the case of Bizkaia)—it was clear to any observer that the path was participation in exterior markets, and not only in price—as in the 1960s at the cost of intensive labor—but also on the basis of competing in quality, costs, and competitiveness.

At the end of the 1980s, as a preface to other conflicts, one of the first serious problems of coexistence of the Basque tax regime with that of the state was unleashed. The problem derived from raising private funds by issuing public debt by the Foral Governments, the famous "Foral promissory notes." They were the recipients of the concerted taxes, and as in any public institution, debt issuance was proposed to rationalize their accounts and enable them to raise liquid capital for their treasuries.[27]

The Crisis of 2007

The Foral Governments or Deputations, as they were also collectors of taxes on personal property, gave a guarantee of fiscal opacity to amounts invested in foral debt, which were attractive even to foreign investors, to the detriment of the state's public debt. The Treasury and the Treasury Ministry complained and tried to limit the possibility of issuing foral debt in 1989, until an arrangement was finally made. The Deputations ceased to issue opaque debt, in exchange for the state ceasing to make claims about its issuances (at the risk of having to return the money).

In the tax sphere, the main instrument used to foment investment was the first Foral Norm on Incentives, the Norm 8/1988 of July 5. This was an incentive in the form of a tax credit offset against taxes on personal and corporate income, according to the type of entrepreneur. It consisted of a credit equivalent to a percentage of the investment (in 1988 it was 20% and in the most recent Norms, from the 1990s, it reached 45% if the investment was over 2500 million pesetas; at the moment, the percentage in force is 10% without a required minimum investment) that was offset in the fiscal year of investment and in the four subsequent fiscal years. Additionally, in other tax years there were other much less significant facilities, such as allowances in the Tax on Property Transfer, which disappeared when VAT came into use to cover all aspects of company purchases and freedom of amortization. With the upturn from the crisis at the start of the 1990s, systems of "tax holidays" were once again approved for investing companies.

In August 2007, the collapse of the North American property market—the crisis of subprime mortgages—began. This collapse affected the European financial markets by causing a fall in credit, which dragged down the Spanish property sector and then had disastrous effects on the financial network.

In this final respect, it must be made clear that the crisis in the Basque financial system has been much less dire than in the rest of

---

27. Mikel Badiola-Santiago Larrazabal-Santiago Perez Maturana, José Antonio, *Financiación y endeudamiento del Territorio Histórico de Bizkaia* (Bilbao: Universidad de Deusto y Diputación Foral de Bizkaia, 1989).

the state due to its lower exposure to the adventures of the property sector and greater credit discipline. The result is that, although the Basque savings banks have been forced to merge, this has not been due to their poor results but rather to the poor results of the sector. They have become, alongside two small savings banks and Caixabank, banking foundations linked to a new bank, Kutxabank, while all others were forced to merge and/or seek a bailout.

However, let us consider the activity of the Foral Deputation in this scenario. The problems arising from the tax holidays of the 1980s and 1990s, of which some judicial "loose ends" remain to be tidied up, mean that it is not viable to take such action nowadays. Thus the policy employed in the short term was the use of postponements—that is, giving the company a cash flow margin by postponing its tax debts. A company can have years when it suffers losses, even several consecutive ones, but cannot act without liquid assets.

The effect has been a sharp increase in the foral debt, as shown in figure 7.3.

Figure 7.3. Total expenditure and Foral Debt, Bizkaia, 1992–2012 (Euros and %). Source: Foru Artxiboa—Foral Archives. Bilbao—Presupuestos, and Historia de la Diputación Foral de Bizkaia 1500–2014).

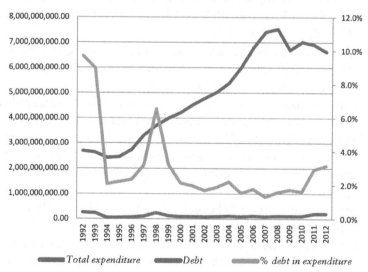

Nonetheless, although in absolute terms the debt has increased considerably, in terms relative to expenditure, it is far from reaching 10%, as happened in 1992. The recourse to debt, for the time being, has not involved a great effort for the Deputation, which is not only using the fiscal tool to combat the crisis, but also, and above all, debt issuance.

With the enactment of the latest reforms (published on December 19), which increased the tax burdens on taxpayers, one can suppose that the recourse to debt will decrease. On the other hand, recourse to debt is being increasingly restricted, since the more that is issued, the less it can be utilized.

In short, in summary fashion we have seen the options taken by the Foral governments or Deputation over two hundred years of economic crises. These crises have been of different types and degrees of gravity, but in all cases the Foral government or Deputation has employed direct intervention with the means available to it in order to mitigate them.

References:

Agirreazkuenaga, Joseba, Alonso Olea, Eduardo J., eds. *Historia de la Diputación Foral de Bizkaia. 1500–2014.* Bilbao: Diputación Foral de Bizkaia, 2014.

Agirreazkuenaga, Joseba, ed. *La articulación político-institucional de Vasconia: Actas de las "Conferencias" firmadas por los representantes de Alava, Bizkaia, Gipuzkoa y eventualmente de Navarra (1775–1936).* 2 vols. Bilbao: Diputaciones Forales de Bizkaia, Gipuzkoa y Alava, 1995.

Agirreazkuenaga, Joseba. *The Making of the Basque Question: Experiencing Self-Government, 1793–1877.* Reno: Center for Basque Studies, University of Nevada, 2012.

Agirreazkuenaga, Joseba. *Vizcaya en el siglo XIX: las finanzas públicas de un estado emergente.* Bilbao: Universidad del País Vasco, 1987.

Alonso Olea, Eduardo J. "El Concierto Económico como herramienta. Crisis económicas y políticas anticíclicas de las Diputaciones vascas. 1867–1936." *Boletín de Estudios Económicos* LXV, no. 201 (2010): 517–62.

Alonso Olea, Eduardo J. "El Crédito de la Unión Minera. 1901–2002." *Historia contemporánea* no. 24 (2002): 325–55.

Alonso Olea, Eduardo J. *Víctor Chávarri (1854–1900). Una biografía.* San Sebastián: Eusko Ikaskuntza-Ayuntamiento de Portugalete, 2005.

Arana Perez, Ignacio. *La Liga Vizcaína de Productores y la política económica de la Restauración.* Bilbao: Caja de Ahorros Vizcaína, 1988.

Arregui, A. *Orientaciones generales para el desarrollo y prosperidad de la provincia de Vizcaya.* Bilbao: Caja de Ahorros Vizcaína, 1934.

Badiola, Mikel, Santiago Larrazabal, José Antonio Perez Maturana. *Financiación y endeudamiento del Territorio Histórico de Bizkaia.* Bilbao: Universidad de Deusto, 1989.

Comin Comin, Francisco, Mauro Hernandez Benitez (eds.). *Crisis económicas en España. 1300–2012. Lecciones de la historia.* Madrid: Alianza, 2013.

Gonzalez Portilla, Manuel. "A.H.V. Expansión y crisis de la siderurgia española. La fractura de la Primera Guerra Mundial." in *Economía y empresa en el norte de España (Una aproximación histórica),* editado por Pablo Martin Aceña, Montserrat Garate Ojanguren. San Sebastián: Diputación Foral de Gipuzkoa—U.P.V., 1994.

Herb, Michael, "Taxation and Representation," *Studies in Comparative International Development (SCID)* 38, no. 3 (September 2003): 3–31.

Martinez, Gemma, "Opinions on Tax Autonomy of European Regions: From the Basque Country Case (1999) to the Gibraltar Case (2011)."

Miralles, Ricardo. "La crisis económica de los años treinta en el País Vasco." *Ekonomiaz* no. 9–10 (1988).

Montero, Manuel. *La Bolsa de Bilbao y los negocios financieros. La formación del mercado de capitales en el despegue industrial de Vizcaya.* Bilbao: Universidad del País Vasco, 1996.

Muguruza Arrese, Javier. "La creación de la Hacienda Foral de Bizkaia en 1981–82 al recuperarse el Concierto Económico." En *I Seminari Catalunya-Euskadi. la institucionalització política de les constitucions històriques als estatuts d'autonomia. I Mintegia Catalunya-Euskadi. Erakundentze politikoaz: irageneko konstituzioetatik, autonomi estatutue-tara (1808–2005).* Barcelona: Generalitat de Catalunya, 2007.

Ormaechea, Angel María. *Ferrocarriles en Euskadi. 1855–1936.* Bilbao: Eusko Trenbideak, 1989.

Villota Elejalde, Ignacio. *Vizcaya en la política minera española. Las asociaciones patronales. 1886–1914.* Bilbao: Servicio de Publicaciones de la Diputación Foral de Vizcaya, 1984.

8

Beyond the Great Crash of 1929: Fiscal Policy in Bizkaia (1929–37)

Mikel Erkoreka

Due to the Economic Agreement, the Basque Regional governments (Deputations) enjoyed a wide fiscal self-government that endowed them with important financial management instruments. This paper analyzes how and with what objectives the Government of Bizkaia made use of this fiscal autonomy in order to face the economic crisis of the 1930s.

In the 1930s, the Basque province of Bizkaia was faced with a dual crisis that battered the economy of the whole province: the international and national crises. Due to the Economic Agreement, Bizkaia, in the same way as Gipuzkoa, Araba, and Navarre (Navarra), enjoyed an economic regime that was distinct from the Common Spanish Tax System. This Agreement endowed the province with financial management instruments to respond to the crisis in its own particular way. In addition to providing statistical data, we also focus on explaining the reasons behind the decisions that were made.

The Economic Agreement Prior to 1937

The system, derived from the Economic Agreement that regulated economic relations between Bizkaia and the state until 1937, is different from that developed since 1981. In the current system, the provinces under the Agreement pay, in what is known as the quota, the equivalent of the expenses that the state spends in the provinces for non-transferred competences. Before 1937, this quota was intended to be equivalent to the income that the Spanish Treasury Ministry would have received if the territory belonged to the Common

Spanish Tax System. In order to pay these quotas, the deputations or regional governments had and have their own fiscal and tax collection powers. This power to collect taxes is the basis of the spending capacity of the provincial governments; the difference between total income and the payment of the quota is managed autonomously by the provincial government.

In Bizkaia, between 1929 and 1937, the last period of the first phase of development of the Economic Agreement (1878–1937) took place. In June 1937, only a few days after the troops that rose up against the Republic took Bilbao, the Economic Agreement was derogated, and Bizkaia reverted to the Common Spanish Tax Regime.

During the first period of the development of the Economic Agreement, sometimes in accordance with the law, and the facto, the Deputation of Bizkaia controlled a wide range of powers.[1] Of these, we will mention those powers that were most useful to the Deputation in dealing with the crisis:

- Carrying out of agreements by the president of the Deputation, rather than by the civil governor.
- Fiscal regulatory capacity and collection of direct and indirect taxes.
- Debt capacity.
- Elaboration of the provincial budget and settlements, without any external supervision.
- Censure and approval of municipal accounts.
- Public expenditure capacity: public works, education, forestry services, and so on.
- Direct election of provincial public employees.

The International Crisis of 1929

The 1929 international crisis did not have immediately visible effects on the Biscayan economy. In 1930, a decrease[2] in industrial production and in exportations became apparent; however, this decrease was not reflected in tax collection or in an increase in industrial unemployment. Thus, tax collection rose by 6% between the budget settle-

1. Eduardo Alonso, *Continuidades y discontinuidades de la Administración Provincial en el País Vasco. 1839–1978. Una "esencia" de los Derechos Históricos* (Bilbao: Basque Institut of Public Administration, 1999), 372.

2. Guillermo Ibáñez and Vicente de Vidaurrazaga, *Orientaciones generales para el desarrollo y prosperidad de la provincia de Vizcaya* (Bilbao: Caja de Ahorros Vizcaína, 1933).

ments of 1929[3] and 1930,[4] and employment[5] in the main industries was maintained at the same level in 1930 as in 1929.

1931: A New Order and Economic Depression

In April 1931, both the Spanish and Biscayan economies entered a regressive economic cycle. The establishment of the Second Spanish Republic was accompanied by an internal destabilization with negative effects on the economy. The statistics gathered by Pablo Martín Aceña[6] show the financial instability that Spain suffered after the proclamation of the Republic, mostly because of the withdrawal of private banking.

Bizkaia, as an industrial economy, experienced a double crisis in 1931: the downturn[7] caused by the international crisis, which was apparent in the decrease in exports, and in the signs of internal crisis that led to a reduction in investment and in interior consumption. Moreover, in 1931, moderation in public expenditure, which was implemented after the fall of the government of Primo de Rivera in 1930, became apparent and was not reactivated until 1932. Contemporary texts reflect the strong dependence that Biscayan production had on the interior market:

> It cannot be considered that this labor crisis is an immediate consequence of the world crisis. The latter principally affects nations that are essentially exporters, due to the current difference between world production and demand. As a consequence, it cannot be affirmed as a general thesis that the crisis in Spain, which is not an exporting country (with the exception of some specific agricultural products, the production of which satisfies their own needs), is an immediate effect of the world crisis. Rather, it is due to internal causes and consequently, it is more easily resolvable, and can be considered to be principally due to the policy known as "economic policy," which has been imposed on recent Governments . . . Vizcaya, the

---

3. The budget settlement for 1929. Foral Archive of Bizkaia (hereafter A.F.B.) / Administration of Bizkaia, Treasury and Statistics (hereafter A.B.–H.E.), PL01342.
4. The budget settlement for 1930. A.F.B. / A.B.–H.E., PL01343.
5. Ricardo Miralles, "La crisis económica de los años treinta en el País Vasco," *Ekonomiaz*, no. 9–10 (Vitoria-Gasteiz, 1988): 277–300.
6. Pablo Martín Aceña, *La cantidad de dinero en España 1900–1935* (Madrid: Bank of Spain, 1985), 54–59.
7. Charles P. Kindleberger, *La crisis económica. 1929–1939* (Madrid: Capitán Swing, 2009), 237–77.

most important zone which promotes the iron and construction industries, has to suffer more than any other the consequences of a Public Works policy which aims at the suppression of all initiated works, instead of restricting and accommodating the plan which has already been outlined, to the real capacity of the Spanish Treasury.[8]

An analysis of the evolution of the Bilbao Stock Exchange since 1929 reveals that the "Great Crash" of the Bilbao Stock Exchange did not occur in 1929, but rather in 1931, when the majority of the indicators of most industrial countries were close to hitting rock bottom (see figure 8.1).

Figure 8.1. Stock Exchange of Bilbao (1929 = 100). Source: Data from biweekly economic journal Información *during the period 1929–36.*

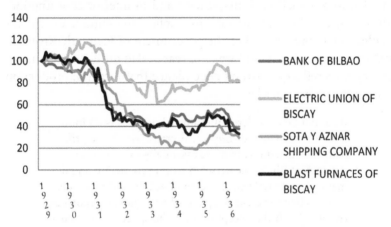

New Management Heading the Deputation of Bizkaia

The Deputations were not renewed via direct elections. Rather, the Republican Government directly elected the Managing Commissions of the Deputations via its civil governors. During the Second Spanish Republic and for the first time in history, socialists and republicans would be a majority in the Deputation of Bizkaia. The absence of direct democratic elections to choose deputies caused political instability,[9] since a large sector of the opposition, made up of both Basque

---

8. Fragment of the request delivered by Biscayan representatives to the Ministry of Treasury, Indalecio Prieto, in the meeting held in Madrid in June of 1931. Published in: *Información*, 30-VI-1931, Bilbao.

9. José Luis de la Granja, *Nacionalismo y II República en el País Vasco: estatutos de*

nationalists and Carlists—which had a strong presence in the territory—did not recognize the legitimacy of the management committees.

However, the presence of new politicians leading the Deputation of Bizkaia did not involve a substantial change in its administrative structure. Although there were new recruitments, the nucleus of the Deputation's upper administrative workforce was maintained practically intact from 1930 to 1935. Of the eighty-seven employees in 1930, seventy continued working in the Deputation in 1935.[10] Moreover, of the twenty-six employees who in 1935 received more than nine thousand pesetas per month, twenty-five were already employed there in 1930, demonstrating that the most important positions were maintained in the hands of employees who were experienced in the management of the Deputation.

The Management Committee Confronting the Crisis

The fact that the Deputation of Bizkaia managers were elected by the Spanish Government can explain the coincidences between the anti-crisis policies elaborated by the Spanish Government and by the Management Committee of Bizkaia. The first two-year period is a good example of this ideological concordance between the two administrations. Rufino Laiseca, a Bizkaian socialist leader and the new president of the Bizkaian Deputation since May 1931, maintained excellent relations,[11] both political and personal, with Indalecio Prieto. Indalecio Prieto was one of the most relevant figures in the development of Spanish anti-crisis policies during the first two years of the Republic. He had been the president, first, of the Spanish Treasury Ministry and subsequently, of the Ministry of Public Works.

The year 1931 is the *annus horribilis* of the Bizkaian economy within the Republican period. The extraction of iron and the production of steel decreased[12] by 28.5% and 37.7%, respectively. Exports[13]

---

autonomía, partidos y elecciones. 1930–1936 (Madrid: Center for Sociological Investigations, 1986), 141.

10. We have analyzed the employees in the high administration (including the Income Tax Department) of the Deputation from 1930 until 1935. In order to do this, we compared the settlements for 1930 (A.F.B. / A.B.-H.E., PL01343) and 1935 (A.F.B. / A.B.-H.E., PL01350).

11. Joseba Agirreazkuenaga (ed.), *Bilbao desde sus alcaldes: Diccionario biográfico de los alcaldes de Bilbao y gestión municipal, en tiempos de revolución democrática y social 1902–1937* (Bilbao: Bilbao City Council, 2003), 263.

12. Antonio Arregui, *Orientaciones generales para el desarrollo y prosperidad de la provincia de Vizcaya* (Bilbao: Caja de Ahorros Vizcaína, 1934), 29–31.

13. Arregui, *Orientaciones generales*, 32.

from the port of Bilbao dropped by 38.3%, and industrial production also suffered. From 1931 to 1933, unemployment rose until it stabilized at a level from which it did not drop throughout the Republican period. State statistics[14] from 1935 regarding industrial unemployment show that Bizkaia was the province with the highest industrial unemployment in the whole State: 4.5%[15] of the population experienced industrial unemployment, with Santander being the second-most affected province (2.5%).

Analysis of the 1931 budgetary settlement clearly reveals the depression of the economy. Liquidated tax income showed a -15.3% deviation[16] from that of the budget forecast. The principal cause of this drop was the corporate income tax, for which 19.3% less was collected than in 1930. Thanks to the copious increase in income due to results[17] of previous years, the Deputation was able to balance its yearly accounts.

Fiscal Reform

The Bizkaian government elaborated an important tax reform in 1931. The Republican government, perhaps due to the limitations of being a provisional government, did not implement this until 1932. Thus, the Bizkaian Deputation approved[18] the tax reform in December 1931, and began applying it in tax year 1932. There was a generalized increase in direct taxes, especially with the territorial, industrial, and commercial contributions, the property transfer tax, and corporate income tax. Among the indirect taxes, the stamp duty also was significantly increased. Consumption taxes were left unaltered.

The effects of this fiscal reform are apparent in the fiscal settlement[19] of 1932: income from the territorial, industrial, and commercial contributions increased by 27.3%; that from the property transfer tax increased by 40.5%; and that due to the stamp duty rose by 25.5%; income from corporate income tax did not significantly increase, possibly because industrial production continued to decrease during 1932. Nevertheless, this tax reform was responsible for the liquida-

---

14. Presidency of the Council of Ministers, *Proyecto de Ley Contra el Paro Obrero Forzoso* (Madrid: Sucesores de Rivad Neyra, 1935), 39.
15. Total and partial unemployment was included. The percentage is calculated over the total population, not over the active population.
16. The budget settlement for 1931. A.F.B. / A.B.-H.E., PL01344.
17. Amount still to be recovered from the settlements of previous years.
18. We have not found the original document. The details of the reform were published in *Información*, 30-XII-1931, Bilbao.
19. The budget settlement for 1932. A.F.B. / A.B.-H.E., PL01345

tion of the 1932 tax collection, being similar to that of 1930 and even higher than that of 1929. Although each year there were to be tributary changes, the 1931 reforms were those that in practice were most effective and allowed the maintenance of a balanced level of tax income throughout the entire Republican period.

Tax Exemption Policy to Encourage Industrial Activity

The Bizkaia government also used the taxation instrument to encourage the creation of companies or the development of particular activities. One of the most noteworthy cases involved the fiscal advantages offered for the establishment of the Firestone[20] company in Bizkaia: partial exemption from the stamp duty and property transfer tax for five years, and a 50% reduction in industry and corporate income taxes until 1937. From 1932 and throughout the Republican period, the construction of urban housing also enjoyed tax exemptions.

The Fight against Unemployment and Public Works

The Republican government devised three lines of action against unemployment: the creation of unemployment insurance, the development of employment offices, and the increase in public expenditure on public works. The first two measures had a limited[21] effect, whereas the public works instrument was the most significant measure against unemployment. In Bizkaia, the same pattern was found to occur.

In 1931, the new provincial government transferred the surplus from the regular budget to the extraordinary budget and started an expansive policy of public expenditure. In 1931 and 1932,[22] it used the surplus from the regular budget to provide the extraordinary budget with credit in order to invest in public spending. A comparison between 1930—a normal year without special extraordinary spending—and 1931 is revealing (see figure 8.2). In addition, in 1932, the state advanced[23] 10,000,000 pesetas to Bizkaia, interest-free, in order to fight against working-class unemployment. This advance payment was attributed to the extraordinary budget.

The decrease in public spending for 1935 correlates with the changes in the Spanish government. Following elections for the Spanish Parliament in November 1933, the Republican government

---

20. Alonso, "El Concierto Económico como herramienta," 558.
21. Sergio Espuelas, *La creación del seguro de desempleo en la II República. Un análisis de su impacto y de por qué fue voluntario* (Sevilla: Preparatory Session for the 9th AEHE Conference, 2007), 25.
22. We have not found settlements for 1933 and 1934.
23. Law for 19-VI-1932. Gaceta de Madrid, No. 171.

Figure 8.2. Public expenditure of the Bizkaia Deputation (pesetas), taking into account "public works," "investment in roads and ports," and "forestry-agricultural services" items. Source: data from settlements.

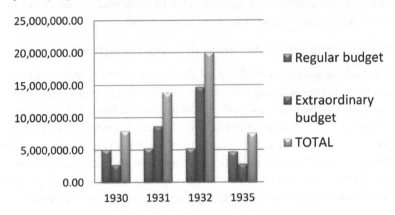

changed and veered toward the right. In January 1934, Juan Gallano, who was sympathetic to the ideological current of the new government, was elected as the president of the Bizkaia Deputation. The new government tried to adjust the budgetary accounts by means of tighter control of spending.

In the 1935 budget, the new provincial government also presented the need for greater control of the regular budget. In 1935, it decided to emit debt[24] in the value of 35,000,000 pesetas in order to return to the regular budget the money that it had "conceded" to the extraordinary budget in the previous years.

It is our belief that even today, the situation of the Treasury could have been totally normal, had it not been for the fact that since 1930, many important special works were initiated—to our mind inappropriately, as made apparent then by the Head of Treasury—thanks to the elaboration of elevated extraordinary budgets. These budgets were provided for with funds from the regular budget, instead of these actions of an extraordinary character being attended to with resources of the same nature. Thus, in order to duly re-establish the Treasury, in 1935 the Treasury Commission deemed it necessary to emit a loan that would at least serve to face the quantities made available during the 1930–35 tax years to the Extraordinary Budget.[25]

---

24. To get an idea of the relative importance of this issue, consider that the annual average of the regular budget in 1931–36 was 50,373,988 pesetas.

25. Report from the Finance Commission to the Managing Commission of Bizkaia.

Ideological Affinity, Yes—Administrative Complicity, No

We have already referred to the ideological affinity that existed throughout the Republican period between the representatives of the Spanish Republican government and the leaders of the Managing Commissions of Bizkaia. However, this affinity, which prevailed during decision-making to confront the crisis, did not extend to a relationship of complicity in administrative circles. Thus, the provincial administration maintained autonomy in the management of the Bizkaia Deputation.

One of the key themes in this regard is finance. Bizkaia financed its anti-crisis policies with its own resources.[26] The advance payment of 10,000,000 pesetas in 1932 is a good example. Bizkaia did not receive any economic subsidy, as did other regions of the Common Tax System. In contrast, it received an advance payment, which was interest-free, but that had to be repaid to the state. In 1934, the Bizkaian government asserted[27] before the Spanish Central Government that it was unjust to subsidize the rest of the regions to fight against unemployment but not subsidize Bizkaia. For this reason, it requested this advance payment, or that the Central Government delay the beginning of the repayment period. We have not found any official response to this request, but it was likely to have been negative, since the Bizkaia Deputation began to repay this payment in 1935.

In the documentation of requests to the state that we have been able to analyze, we have not found any explicit requests for credit. The majority of requests were for the state to increase public spending, since such an increase was known to have indirect repercussions that would benefit industry in Bizkaia. Beyond this, the most important example of self-financing is the debt issue of 1935. With the amount that they received from this issue, the Deputation could afford the payment for most of the public works completed in the previous years.

Another noteworthy key theme concerns the four main disputes between the Central and Provincial administrations regarding the Economic Agreement: the interpretation of stamp duty, the wine statute, as well as the implementation of the luxury tax and the income

---

Published in *Información*, Dec. 31, 1934, Bilbao.
26. The Spanish State invested money in Bizkaia, but only in those areas of power that corresponded to it. A good example of this is the 1935 "Bill against Unemployment." The State budgeted an expense of 467,543,585.70 pesetas and of this, only 5,579,815.10 pesetas (1.2%) corresponded to Bizkaia, in the category of "Ports."
27. Deputation's request to the Central Government (A.F.B. A.B.-H.E. AJ02276/024).

tax. The conflict due to the implemention of the luxury and income taxes in the Basque Provinces and Navarre persisted throughout the Republican period. Both taxes were created during the first biennium and were supposed to be applied directly by the Ministry of Finance throughout the state. The three sister provinces and Navarre joined to litigate against the State arguing that these new taxes had to be collected by the provinces who were part of the Agreement. The central government expressly ordered by decree[28] that these taxes had to be directly applied in the specified provinces. The provinces continued to avoid compliance with the decree, and the administrative conflict remained unresolved throughout the Republican period.

1936–37: The Civil War

The Spanish Civil War period is a little-known stage in the provincial administration. Following the creation of, first, the Bizkaia Defense Board and the subsequent establishment of the Basque government, the Bizkaia Deputation lost its executive power over the province. The Deputation handed over executive power, but continued to function administratively with "normality." We found no official liquidation in 1936, but we have found documents[29] showing that the Bizkaia Deputation continued to have its own income and expense accounts, at least during 1936.

In addition to its normal function, the administrative machinery of the Deputation was likely used by both the Provincial Defense Board and the Basque government in order to develop its policies. An example of this is the "Rent Decree,"[30] which was approved by the Defense Board to apply the tax on renting:

> Article 4: The said tax shall be paid by the owner of the property, who will pay it in accordance with the form and schedule established by the Most Excellent Bizkaia Deputation, to whom is entrusted the organization and collection of this tax.
> Article 5: The income produced by the tax which is created, will remain at the disposal of the Bizkaia Defense Board . . .

---

28. Decree to apply the Luxury Tax: 20/II/1933. Gaceta de Madrid, No. 51. Decree to apply the Income Tax: 08/XII/1933. Gaceta de Madrid, Num. 342.
29. Inventory ledger of the Deputation for 1936, A.F.B. / A.B.-H.E. PL01480
30. We have not found the original document. This Decree was published in *Información*, 16-IX-1936, Bilbao.

Conclusions

The effects of the 1929 international crisis were not visible in Bizkaia until 1931. From 1931 onwards, Bizkaia experienced a profound economic crisis due to both the international crisis and the internal crisis of the Spanish state. These crises induced a sharp decrease in Bizkaian industrial production and consequently led to a significant increase in unemployment.

The Deputation of Bizkaia, governed for the first time in history by socialists and Republicans, reacted from the first moment by applying anti-crisis policies:

1. The 1931 tax reform. Following a drop of more than 15% with respect to tax income forecasts in 1931, the Management Committee applied a tax reform for the 1932 tax year. This reform, prior to the 1932 tax reform of the Republican government, levied especially direct taxes. The 1931 reform, which was clearly progressive, allowed the maintenance of levels of tax income similar to those prior to the crisis.
2. The provincial government used the tax powers at its disposal to attract companies to its territory, or to promote certain industries. In 1932, it provided tax incentives to the Firestone Company to open its new factory in Bizkaia. Throughout the Republican period, the construction of urban housing also enjoyed tax incentives.
3. Application of a wide-spectrum policy of public works to fight against unemployment. The Bizkaia government, by means of its own finance, developed an expansive policy of public spending in order to alleviate the unemployment problem.

The Bizkaia Deputation used its debt capacity to finance increased spending. Thus, in 1932, it received an advance payment of 10 million pesetas from the Spanish State and in 1935 it emitted debt in the sum of 35 million pesetas. In the 1936 budget, the expenses for the provincial debt amounted to 8.87% of total spending.

Although there was a degree of ideological affinity between the Republican Government and the Management Committee, the delegation of the different functions among the administrations was clear. The state did not invest more money in Bizkaia than was strictly due to it based on its competences. On the other hand, the Bizkaia government did not allow the application of some state taxes in its province, alleging that these were incompatible with the content of the Economic Agreement.

With the onset of the Spanish Civil War, the Bizkaia Deputation began to take a backstage role. First the Bizkaia Defense Board and later the Basque government were in charge of governing Bizkaia during the war period. Nevertheless, the Bizkaia Deputation continued to function "normally," at least during 1936. Moreover, it seems that both the Defense Board and the Basque Government made use of the administrative machinery of the provincial Deputation to manage the province.

Bibliography

Agirreazkuenaga, Joseba, ed. *Bilbao desde sus alcaldes: Diccionario bibliográfico de los alcaldes de Bilbao y gestión municipal, en tiempos de revolución democrática y social 1902–1937.* Bilbao: Bilbao City Council, 2003.

Alonso, Eduardo. "El Concierto Económico como herramienta. Crisis económicas y políticas anticíclicas de las Diputaciones vascas. 1867–1936." *Boletín de Estudios Económicos*, No. 201 (2010): 517–62.

Alonso, Eduardo. *Continuidades y discontinuidades de la Administración Provincial en el País Vasco. 1839–1978. Una "esencia" de los Derechos Históricos.* Bilbao: Basque Institute of Public Administration, 1999.

Arregui, Antonio. *Orientaciones generales para el desarrollo y prosperidad de la provincia de Vizcaya.* Bilbao: Caja de Ahorros Vizcaína, 1934.

De la Granja, Jose Luis. *Nacionalismo y II República en el País Vasco: estatutos de autonomía, partidos y elecciones. 1930–1936.* Madrid: Center for Sociological Investigations, 1986.

Espuelas, Sergio. *La creación del seguro de desempleo en la II República. Un análisis de su impacto y de por qué fue voluntario.* Sevilla: Preparatory session for the 9th AEHE Conference, 2007.

Hernández, J. *Depresión económica en España, 1925–1934.* Madrid: Instituto de Estudios Fiscales, 1980.

Ibáñez, Guillermo, and Vidaurrazaga Vicente. *Orientaciones generales para el desarrollo y prosperidad de la provincia de Vizcaya.* Bilbao: Caja de Ahorros Vizcaína, 1933.

Kindleberger, Charles P. *La crisis económica. 1929–1939.* Madrid: Capitán Swing, 2009.

Martín Aceña, Pablo. *La cantidad de dinero en España 1900-1935*. Madrid: Bank of Spain, 1985.

Miralles, Ricardo. (1988). "La crisis económica de los años treinta en el País Vasco," *Ekonomiaz*, No. 9–10 (Vitoria-Gasteiz): 277–300.

Presidency of the Council of Ministers. *Proyecto de Ley Contra el Paro Obrero Forzoso*. Madrid: Sucesores de Rivad Neyra, 1935.

9

The Role of Regions with Taxation Powers in the European Union: The Basque Economic Agreement

José Rubí Cassinello

As you may know, the Economic Agreement, as the public financing model establishing the financial and fiscal relations between the Basque Country and the Spanish central government,[1] is one of the most remarkable elements of the current political and economic legal framework of the Basque Country, which dates back to the nineteenth century,[2] when it replaced the model known as the "tax exemption regime."[3] Even though the Economic Agreement was already well settled after Franco's era, over the last few decades, its integration into the new legal international order of the European Union has raised relevant questions that were successfully resolved by the European Court of Justice in 2008[4] after a long, rough fight for regions with wide and autonomous taxation powers to be acknowledged and fit into the European Union. This is why this chapter focuses on the role

---

1. A general overview of the Economic Agreement regime can be found in Ignacio Zubiri, *The Economic Agreement between the Basque Country and Spain* (Bilbao: Ad Concordiam, 2010).

2. On the historical evolution of the Economic Agreement regime, see Eduardo Alonso Olea, *El Concierto Económico (1878–1937). Orígenes y formación de un Derecho Histórico* (Oñati: IVAP, 1995).

3. About recent background of the Economic Agreement, see Joseba Agirreazkuenaga Zigorraga, *The Making of the Basque Question: Experiencing Self-Government, 1793–1877* (Basque Politics Series), Reno: Center for Basque Studies, University of Nevada, 2014.

4. ECJ, 11 September 2008, Joined Cases C-428/06 to C-434/06, *Unión General de Trabajadores de La Rioja (UGT-Rioja) and Others* v. *Juntas Generales del Territorio Histórico de Vizcaya and Others*.

of regions, such as the Basque Country, in the European construction process—regions that can either be part of a single member state or be divided into more than one state.

After a short introduction about the current role of regions in the European decision-making forums and, in particular, of the Basque Country, I will focus on the main features of the Economic Agreement, how it fits within the European Union legal order, and how it has proved to be a valuable tool for the Basque Country to overcome crises.

Regions and the European Union

Just to place the Basque Country in the European regional map, we must remember there are 272 regions that form the 28 Member States. In addition to the cultural, economic, and social differences—even linguistic differences, at times—from a political point of view, these 272 regions are granted several competences, including financial powers, in an absolutely heterogeneous way by the different national legal orders.

A wide range of strongly centralized states and federal states co-exist inside the European Union. Within the federal states, regions play a major role in different fields of public life. To start with, we can affirm that the European Union has been developed under the pre-eminence of Member States, and both federalists and Euro-skeptics criticize the current European Union for its democratic deficit, which arises when decisions are moved from the national parliaments and the electorates within the Member States to Brussels. In Brussels, civil servants make most decisions, and laws are made via agreements between all Member States.

According to the federalists, the solution would be to establish a genuine EU parliamentary democracy, in which laws would be made by the European Parliament rather than by the states' representatives in the Council of Ministers. Out of the twenty-eight Member States, only eight can be regarded as federal with diverse degrees of decentralization: Austria, Belgium, Finland, Germany, Italy, Portugal, the United Kingdom, and Spain. These states comprise seventy-four regions—including the Basque Country—with legislative powers in various areas exercised in their regional parliaments.

The Conference of European Regional Legislative Assemblies (CALRE)[5] brings together the seventy-four presidents of these re-

---

5. http://www.calrenet.eu/.

gional legislative assemblies. CALRE emerged in 1998 from the sentiment that regional parliamentary regulations did not have sufficient voice or were not taken sufficiently into account during the EU formation process.

This conference of chairmen of the regional parliaments of the European Union sees the European Union as a challenge to institutional integration; the regional legislative assemblies do not want to be forced to only watch from the sidelines.

In essence, this conference also represents many civilians from the European Union. The regional parliaments express not only a political vision but also a cultural identity, and they are well positioned to protect that cultural uniqueness from the processes of globalization and unification.

One of these 72 regions is the Basque Country. Figure 9.1 provides an overview of our region. The geographical extension of the Basque Country is 1.4 percent of the total area of Spain, with a population of 5% and a GDP of 6.3%. Its GDP per capita exceeds the Spanish average by 36%. One of the worst economic indicators in Spain, the unemployment rate, has only reached near 16% in the Basque

Figure 9.1. The Basque Country in Europe. (UE 28 = 100).

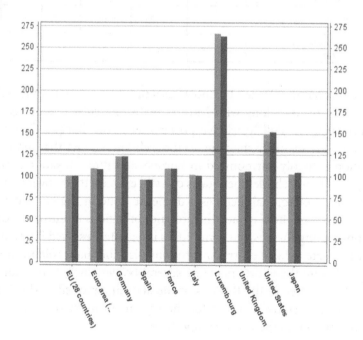

Country, far from the 26% of the whole of Spain. In addition, from an international perspective, the Basque GDP, the straight line in the chart, is 130% higher than the European average, just above the German average and 20 points lower than the American one.

One of the worst economic indicators in Spain, the unemployment rate, has only reached near 16% in the Basque Country, far from the 26% of the whole of Spain.

From an international perspective, the Basque GDP, the red line in the chart, is 130% higher than the European average, just above the German average and 20 points lower than the American one. An overview of the indicators of the size of Bizkaia in the Spanish economy is given in table 9.1.

Table 9.1. Indicators of the size of Bizkaia (labeled Biscay here) and the Basque Country in the Spanish economy.

Indicators	Unit	Spain	Basque Country	Biscay	BC / Spain	Biscay / BC
Surface	Km2	505,182	7,089	2,217	1.4%	31.3%
Population	number	47,129,783	2,191,682	1,156,447	4.7%	52.8%
GDP at current prices	million €	1,022,988	64,703	33,171	6.3%	51.3%
GDP per capita	€ p.c.	21,706	29,522	28,683	136	97
Unemployement rate	%	26.37%	15.83%	17.24%		

However, the Basque Country has a unique power: it is the only European region, along with Navarre, with full legislative power in direct taxation. Full legislative power makes the Basque Country equal to any member state due to the well-known fact that indirect taxation is highly harmonized in Europe, and direct taxation is the only field in which Member States can still exercise their sovereignty. However, the regional factor is a domestic issue in the current EU legal framework and, in fact, the presence of regions in European decision-making forums and committees is a matter resolved internally by each state, whose central institutions play the main role in most cases, despite the efforts made by several bodies, such as the European Committee of the Regions or the abovementioned CALRE, to claim a more significant role for the regions to make decisions on matters related to their own competences.

In these circumstances, no wonder the regions within Member States are widely considered to be excluded actors in the European process. Nevertheless, the miscellaneous competences attributed to the regions by the state constitutional systems pose problems of a different nature when it comes to making these regional competences compatible by virtue of the principle of institutional autonomy, which the Union must respect, with the natural tendency to legal uniformity derived from the European construction process.

The aim of my comments here today is not to get into the benefits of devolution, except to acknowledge that decentralization can be advantageous. As we all know, federalist theories support this fact with substantial empirical evidence. Nonetheless, I think we should just point out some of the benefits of a certain degree of decentralization in the political decision-making process, which always involves a more active and closer participation of citizens. Benefits are evident in:

- the level of efficiency in the provision of public services,
- the degree of satisfaction of citizens enjoying the services provided, and
- the accountability of governments to people.

Those in favor of a unitary state often assert that globalization and market interdependence in the current economic situation demand robust and highly centralized states. Nothing, however, could be further from the truth. Quite the contrary, the blurring of borders, due to globalization or to the breaking down of legal borders, leads to a decrease in the states' role and simultaneously to an increase in the regions' role. Regions are culturally, socially, and economically homogeneous units, and nowadays they are real beneficiaries of technological progress and the opening up of markets. On the other hand, differences in size among Member States in the Union make the scale less relevant, minimizing the weight that size has traditionally held in the economic field.

From an economic perspective, if regions are the real operative units, it seems essential that their public sector should play a main role and should be able to exercise their competence by themselves. Nevertheless, their legal and economic status lacks the political recognition required by the regional factor. In particular, a contradiction between the level of expenditure and income exists in most of the regional legal orders. Devolution of powers related to expenditure are increasing, while income remains largely centralized. This decentralization model contrasts with that fostered by academic fiscal federalism, which suggests that decentralization of expenditures necessarily involves a decentralization of income, so that each level of government is economically self-sufficient to finance its expenditures.[6]

Let's try to ascertain the reasons for this common regional financing model.

From the point of view of the member states—specifically Spain—the loss of the monetary and exchange rate policies, which is currently under the European Institutions' control, is the source of strong reluctance to devolve political power to infrastate units. This is due to the fear that the states' central administrations may have of losing more powers and having a lesser role to play in the European Union. Economic stabilization policies implemented in answer to the financial crisis also minimize the states' room to maneuver, as they are constrained by the need to meet the macroeconomic targets set by governments and international organizations under financial market pressure.

Tax policy has become the only economic policy area still in the hands of Member States, allowing them to design tailor-made strategies for national economies in order to implement the most adequate measures against the crisis. This explains the reluctance of the Member States' central administrations to share this policy with infrastate entities.

At the same time, the Commission itself is often unwilling to admit the existence of decentralization of taxation powers, by virtue of some Member States' constitutional order.

There is an easy explanation for this attitude: if the Commission has to supervise not only Member States but regions as well in order to guarantee the correct functioning of the internal market and establishment of a European process in line with the Treaty, its tasks and duties become more complex. The requirement of unanimity of the twenty-eight Member States to adopt decisions in direct taxation would make reaching agreements within the Union almost impossible. This would happen if the great number of regions that form the Member States had the right to vote when issues of their competence were discussed.

In my opinion, these difficulties are an explanation, but not solid grounds for the current Commission's extreme approach toward regions. In the past, the European Commission tried to deny the ca-

---

6. George Anderson, *Federalism: An Introduction*, Forum of Federations (Oxford: Oxford University Press, 2008).

pacity of some regions to play a role in certain areas, such as taxation, which their citizens naturally regard to be a regional power of their own execution by their citizens. The Basque Country is a good example. Historically, the Basque public has been very aware of taxation power as a regional competence, which is naturally exercised by Basque institutions. This regional competence has finally been acknowledged, without question, by the Spanish central administration.

During the last few years, we have faced a legal confrontation, with some ideological shades, between two positions:

- One, against any recognition of legislative taxation powers in direct taxation in the hands of infrastate entities, supported by the European Commission.
- Another, in favor of the devolution of taxation powers to infrastate units, supported by some Member States, such as the United Kingdom, Italy, Portugal, and Spain, and their regions.

The cases of the Azores[7] and Gibraltar[8] and the ruling on the Economic Agreement[9] put an end to this confrontation, which was masterfully resolved by the European Court of Justice (ECJ).

Without looking into each of the existing models, as doing so would exceed the scope of this paper, I would like to mention that the level of autonomy of the regions in Europe is absolutely diverse and based on historical, political, or even geographical foundations. In most cases, a reflexive process based on the fiscal federalist principles of assigning different responsibilities to different levels of government in the public sector was out of the question, considering that the devolution process has social and historical roots and pillars in most cases. The Spanish state, a prime example of a state involved in a devolution process, started as a fully centralized legal order and ended with a new framework whose main feature is decentralization.

The Economic Agreement Model

The most significant characteristic of the Economic Agreement model lies in the fact that it is a pact between the Basque Country and

---

7. ECJ, 6 Sept. 2006, Case C-88/03, *Portuguese Republic v. Commission of the European Communities (Azores)*.

8. ECJ, 15 Nov. 2011, Joined Cases C-106/09 and C-107/09, *European Commission* (C-106/09 P), *Kingdom of Spain* (C-107/09 P) *versus Government of Gibraltar and United Kingdom*.

9. See endnote 5.

the Spanish state, which guarantees full income from all tax figures comprising the taxation system of the Historical Territories (foral provinces) to the Basque Country. Tax income finances not only the competences of the Basque Country but also the expenditures of the Spanish central administration on behalf of the citizens of the Basque Country.

In addition, the Economic Agreement acknowledges the Historical Territories' competence to amend and update their tax system in accordance with the government plan of the ruling party and their accountability to Basque citizens. As a result, competence and accountability are the two outstanding elements of the Economic Agreement model. However, these two elements make the Basque model one of a kind among the federal systems in force in Europe today, bringing it closer to confederal unions, such as Switzerland or the United States.

Regarding the scope of the European Union, we believe the difficulties that the Economic Agreement has overcome cannot be regarded as too serious or essentially different from those suffered by the rest of the European taxation systems. The territorial or regional selectivity within the state aid concept in the Treaty was the only true European hazard of the legislative tax power acknowledged by the Economic Agreement to the Basque Country.[10]

Through the concept of territorial selectivity, I would like to point out the main features of the Economic Agreement model. Territorial selectivity questioned the capability of Basque institutions to pass tax laws that differ, even minimally, from the Spanish state's legislation. The European Commission believed that the selectivity requirement of state aid would be met without exception by the fact that a tax measure would only be applicable in a part (a region) within the state.

However, in the 2006 Azores case,[11] the European Court of Justice (ECJ) firmly rejected the Commission's interpretation of regional selectivity and set out the fundamental parameters of the new doctrine. To this end, the ECJ stated that if an infrastate unit enjoys a legal and factual status, it is sufficiently autonomous in relation to the central government of a member state; in that case, what is relevant in assessing whether a measure favors certain undertakings in comparison with others in a comparable legal and factual situation is the

---

10. Carlos Palao Taboada, *"State aid and autonomous regions: the ECJ's ruling in the Basque Country case,"* International Taxation (IBFD, 2009). [International Taxation is a tax magazine edited by IBFD whis is a foundation specialized in taxation issues placed in Amsterdam.]

11. See note 8.

area in which the infrastate unit responsible for the measure exercises its powers, and not the state as a whole. The ECJ requires three kinds of autonomy—institutional, procedural, and financial—for a region to be regarded as "sufficiently autonomous." In my opinion, the legal and financial status of the Basque Country based on the Economic Agreement smoothly fits the treble autonomy test.[12]

Institutional Autonomy

Institutional autonomy requires that a tax measure be passed by the infrastate authority with its own constitutional, political, and administrative status, separate from that of the central government.

The Basque Country's current institutions with historically based tax competences are modern versions of the 136-year-old self-government of the Foral provinces, guaranteed by the First Additional Provision of the 1978 Spanish Constitution. Moreover, article 41 of the Basque Statute of Autonomy states that the competent institutions of the Historical Territories of Bizkaia, Álava, and Gipuzkoa, among which we find the General Assemblies, may maintain, establish, and regulate, within their own territory, their tax system, subject to some limits.

Consequently, the political representatives—the members of the parliaments of the Historical Territories, or *junteros*—are the ones who pass the "laws" and stipulate the taxes in the General Assemblies, or *Juntas Generales*, under the motto "No taxation without representation."

Procedural Autonomy

Procedural autonomy means that the infrastate authority adopts tax measures according to a procedure in which the central government does not have any power to intervene directly and that carries no obligation on the part of the local authority to take into account the central state's interests when setting the tax rate.

In the Basque Country, the abovementioned provincial General Assemblies pass tax legislation without any direct or indirect intervention of the central state authority. Moreover, the scope of competence within the Economic Agreement cannot be unilaterally amended by the Basque Country or by the central state. On the one hand, the Economic Agreement is subject to consensus between the Basque

---

12. The Spanish Supreme Court has confirmed in several cases that the Basque Country meets the treble test. For illustrative purposes, see the Supreme Court Judgment of April 4, 2012.

Country and the central Spanish state and is ratified by the Spanish parliament in a single-reading legislative process. On the other hand, every committee in charge of the application of the Economic Agreement provisions is a joint body with an equal number of representatives of the Basque Country administrations and the central State administration. To understand this very unusual bilateral relationship, we might compare it to double taxation treaties in international law.

Financial Autonomy

Finally, the third autonomy required by the ECJ is the financial one, in the sense that the financial consequences of tax measures, for example a reduction of the national tax rate for undertakings in the region, must not be offset by aid or subsidies from other regions or the central government.

With regard to income, the Economic Agreement is based on the principle of fiscal autonomy, meaning that all taxes deriving from their systems belong to the Historical Territories that administer and regulate them and that, therefore, can be assigned to their taxpayers. This feature makes the Basque federal model unique. In most decentralized models, the "vertical imbalance" in favor of the central authority is a main feature. In the Economic Agreement, the imbalance is inverted, and all general taxes are collected by the Historical Territories. In short, the Basque Country is the region in the world with the highest fiscal autonomy because it is the only region in which the state central government does not collect any general tax.

In the Basque Country, there are four levels of government—plus, of course, the European Union. All of them (central government, Basque government, foral deputations, and municipalities) spend, but just one of them (foral deputations) collects most of the taxes. This leads to a complex scheme of transfers that redistributes tax revenue from the foral deputations toward the other tiers of government.

- The central government finances its expenditures in the Basque Country with the quota and Social Security contributions.
- The Basque government is financed almost exclusively by transfers (contributions) from the foral deputations.
- The foral deputations collect almost all taxes, but they transfer the largest part of what they collect to other levels of government (quota, contributions, etc.).
- The municipalities finance their expenditures with local taxes, user fees, and transfers from the foral deputations.

The payment of a quota to the state is the financial transfer that compensates the expenditures made by the state on behalf of the residents in the Basque Country and as a contribution to the solidarity among Spanish regions.[13]

The amount of quota is based on parameters within the State Annual General Budget Law and regardless of the tax collection in the Basque Country. However, the resources of the Basque Country change exactly as its tax collection does. This means that the Basque Country assumes all the collection risks associated with

- changes in the economic conjuncture,
- the financial consequences of any tax change, and
- the administration and collection of tax income.

Since the Basque Country assumes all the collection risks, the Economic Agreement implies that there is a unilateral risk entirely borne by the Basque Country.

This also makes the Basque Country financially autonomous and, therefore, it meets the three criteria of the ECJ. This newly born jurisprudence of the ECJ encourages us to foresee a clear path for European regions with taxation powers. The new status for certain regions should not result in a zero-sum game in which there can only be winners or losers among the different players: the European Institutions, the Member States, and the regions.

The experience in the practice of the Economic Agreement model confirms the fundamental role that the Basque financing system played against the industrial crisis as an essential tool in boosting competitiveness and investments in the Basque Country in the last quarter of the twentieth century. It also proved efficient in developing the Basque public sector, which effectively fostered the recovery of the economy and the increase and improvement of welfare services.

One of the most outstanding consequences of those crises was the impact on employment. Last century, during the 1970s and the beginning of the 1980s, the workforce was constantly diminished, and between 1972 and 1986, more than 140,000 jobs were destroyed—almost 20% of the total. At that moment, the unemployment rate was higher than 23%. The employment loss was greater in the Basque country than in the rest of Spain because the economic crisis mainly hit productive sectors that were the pillars of the Basque traditional

---

13. Ignacio Zubiri Oria, *The Economic Agreement between the Basque Country and Spain* (Bilbao: Ad Concordiam, 2010).

economy. The situation forced the Basque country to change from an industrial business economy to one based on technology and the provision of services. By the end of the 1970s, 45% of the workforce belonged to the industrial sector, and in 2008, only 23.5% remained. At the same time, a sharp increase in the service sector occurred, raising the percentage of the workforce in the service sector from 38% in 1977 to 65% in 2012.

For the last thirty-five years, after the reestablishment of the democratic freedoms in Spain, among which is the right of regions to self-government, the different ruling governments have made efforts to carry out certain general policies that have made the Basque Country one of the most prosperous and developed regions within the European Union. The application of any resilience indicator to the Basque Country shows good results and evolution on the scoreboard. Nevertheless, economic threats still remain, and Basque authorities have the great responsibility to strengthen and improve such indicators.

Other authors in this book address the financial crisis, its impact on the Basque Country economy, and how to face it. Even during the current difficult financial times, the Basque Country holds a top position of wealth creation in Spain. To attain this status, the Economic Agreement has proved a key element, for two main reasons. First, Basque institutions have felt the burden of fighting crises on their own. Other regions in Spain legitimately clamor for financial help or bailouts from the Spanish central government. This differs from the Economic Agreement framework, according to which the Basque Country can only obtain financial resources through its tax system or through debt. Second, the Economic Agreement provides effective tools for economic intervention—that is, wide fiscal autonomy—tools that were used in the latter decades of the last century and are also playing a main role in confronting today's crisis.

Conclusion

In sum, the Economic Agreement is a fiscal federalist model that grants the Basque Country the widest powers while requiring the greatest accountability. The Basque Country decides on the degree of fiscal pressure its taxpayers must bear and collects all the income derived from its tax system, taking the economic risk of its own decisions and being the only entity accountable to the Basque citizens. Moreover, it is a public financing model that has proved efficient and effective without causing any relevant economic distortions. Finally, the Economic Agreements grant the Basque Country outstanding powers to limit economic vulnerability and to face the negative effects of the crisis. As a result, the responsible and correct application of the Economic Agreement has brought about greater stability and efficiency in our economy.[14]

All these features encourage us to conclude that the Economic Agreement is a model that may be implemented by other regions, European or not, that legitimately long for wider self-government capacities in order to improve their citizens' welfare.

Bibliography

Agirreazkuenaga Zigorraga, Joseba. *The Making of the Basque Question: Experiencing Self-Government, 1793–1877* (Basque Politics Series). Reno: Center for Basque Studies, University of Nevada, 2014.

Alonso Olea, Eduardo. *El Concierto Económico (1878.1937). Orígenes y formación de un Derecho Histórico.* Oñati: IVAP, 1995.

Anderson, George. *Federalism: An Introduction.* Forum of Federations. Oxford: Oxford University Press, 2008.

Briguglio, Lino, Gordon Cordina, Stephanie Bugeja, Nadia Farrugia. *Conceptualizing and Measuring Economic Resilience.* CITY: Economics Department, University of Malta, YEAR.

Palao Taboada, Carlos. *State aid and autonomous regions: the ECJ's ruling in the Basque Country case,* International Taxation (IBFD, 2009).

Zubiri Oria, Ignacio. *The Economic Agreement between the Basque Country and Spain* (Bilbao: Ad Concordiam, 2010)

---

14. On the concept of economic resilience, see Lino Briguglio, Gordon Cordina, Stephanie Bujea, Nadia Farrugia, *Conceptualizing and Measuring Economic Resilience.* (University of Malta, Economics Department. Found at https://www.um.edu.mt/data/assets/pdf_file/0013/44122/resilience_index.pdf .

10

Tax Harmonization in Federal Systems: The Basque Case

Gemma Martínez Bárbara

Tax harmonization measures have proven to be an essential tool for federal systems to be effective and obtain their main targets. Some federal models, such as the Swiss one with which the Basque Country's model shares many features, are great examples. However, tax harmonization is not always an easy task due to the existing strain between the harmonizing legislation and the tax legislative powers that are to be affected and, most likely, limited. The situation with the Basque Country tax system is no exception. Multi-level tax harmonization powers are constraining in a certain way the execution of foral tax legislative powers in order to establish and administer, within their territories, their own taxation system. Harmonizing actions taken by the OECD in the tax field, different hard law and soft law measures fostered and implemented by the European institutions by virtue of the powers conferred by the Treaty, harmonizing criteria within the Economic Agreement, and the harmonizing powers of the Basque Parliament have to be taken into account by the Historical Territories of the Basque Country when drafting their tax legislative measures. No other region in the federal system is involved in so many tax harmonization levels. The Basque Country region is a rare bird among regions with wide taxation powers.

The United States and the Basque Foral System: an Ancient Link

I can't help making a brief reference to one of the founding fathers of the United States of America, John Adams, second president of the

United States. In regard to the historical ties that existed between the Basque Country and the United States, some authors stress his admiration for the Basques' historical form of government.

Adams, who on his tour of Europe visited Bizkaia, quoted the Basques as an example of "people who had preserved their ancient language, genius, laws, government, and manners, without innovation, longer than any other nation of Europe," in his book "A Defense of the Constitutions of the United States."[1] In 1780, Adams traveled to Europe to study and compare the various forms of government of the Old Continent; the first thirteen states approved the U.S. Constitution nine years later. Some of these authors, such as the Basque-American Pete T. Cenarrusa, whose memoirs are published by the Center for Basque Studies,[2] even agree on stressing the influence of the Basque Charters, or *Foruak,* on some parts of the U.S. Constitution. In Bilbao, there is now a bust at the junction of Diputación Street and Gran Via Street in remembrance of his visit, and the above-mentioned quotation is written on it in Basque, Spanish, and English.

In this paper, I review the details of one of the most outstanding elements of the foral governments: the Economic Agreement, and how it fits and interacts with other finance and fiscal models in the twenty-first century. My aim is to analyze the role tax harmonization plays in federal systems and, in particular, in the Basque case. The Basque fiscal system is subject to a complex, multi-level tax harmonization system, depending on the perspective we take. I intend to explain the main characteristics of every perspective and reach conclusions about the current state-of-the-art tax harmonization in the Basque Country, focusing mainly on the international perspective. By way of introduction, I will also discuss the effects of the 2008 financial crisis on harmonization, taking into account the main topic of this conference.

---

1. See www.constitution.org/jadams/ja1_00.htm. A Da Capo Press Reprint Edition. This Da Capo Press edition of *A Defence of the Constitutions of Government of the United States of America* is an unabridged republication of the first edition published in London in 1787–88. Library of Congress Catalog No. 69-11328, ISBN 306-71176-1. Published by Da Capo Press, a Division of Plenum Publishing Corporation, N.Y.
2. Quane Kenyon with Pete T. Cenarrusa, *Bizkaia to Boise: The Memoirs of Pete T. Cenarrusa.* (Basque Politics Series) (Reno: Center for Basque Studies, University of Nevada, 2009).

Worldwide Federations

There are roughly twenty-eight countries in the world today—together representing 40% of the world's population—regarded as federal, according to scholars. Typically, democracies with very large territories: the United States, Brazil, Australia, and Canada—and very large populations: India, Pakistan, and Nigeria—are federal. So are some small countries with very diverse populations, such as Switzerland, Germany, and Belgium, and some island states: Micronesia and Comoros. They include some of the largest and most complex democracies, and their system of government, while it can be complex, has made many federations among the most prosperous countries in the world, with high standards of government services.

Historically, most federations were the result of previously separate entities—the thirteen American colonies or the Swiss cantons—coming together to form a federal government. The entities would keep some powers to themselves, while others were pooled with the central government of the new country. In spite of the existing differences, this is also the case with the three Basque Historical Territories joined to form the Autonomous Community of the Basque Country, a new legal territorial creation set within the framework of the 1978 Spanish Constitution. We will come back to this later.

We can also find previously unitary countries, such as Spain, Belgium, and South Africa, which adopted federal structures as a way to maintain a common central government for some purposes while empowering regional governments for other purposes. In many very diverse societies, a federal system of government permits recognition of both this diversity and common interests and identity at the same time. In this setting, we can frame the federal link between the Spanish Central Administration and the Autonomous Community of the Basque Country.

No matter how different federal systems are, all of them have some common characteristics:

- At least two different orders of government: one for the whole country and the other for the constituent units of the federation. Each government has a direct electoral relationship with its citizens. There are different names to refer to these units: states, autonomous communities, regions, provinces, cantons, *länders*, and so on.
- A written constitution, some part of which cannot be amended without substantial consent of the units.

- A constitution that usually allocates legislative, including fiscal, powers to the different existing orders, ensuring some genuine autonomy for each order.
- Usually some legal provisions regarding Upper Houses, according to which the representation of constituent units for regional input in central decision-making is guaranteed.
- Different procedures, judicial or arbitration, to rule in constitutional disputes between orders.
- And finally, a set of bodies, committees, and proceedings to facilitate or conduct relations between different levels of government. For instance, the Arbitration Board of the Economic Agreement, about which there is a specific paper by Mr. Javier Muguruza, one of its arbiters, in this book.[3]

Needless to say, these requirements are not met by all federal systems in the world with the same intensity, and in some cases, even one or two of them are missing. The question is whether the lack of any of these requirements means they are not federal models. According to federal theories, as long as there is some genuine, constitutionally based autonomy at the different existing levels, the answer is negative; that is, there are at least two constitutionally established orders of government with a certain degree of real autonomy from each other, and the government at each level must be primarily accountable to its respective electorates.[4]

Fiscal Federalism[5]

In federal frameworks, the fiscal debate is as frequent as in the rest of the democratic models. However, the former have an added layer of complexity because of the existence of at least two constitutionally established tiers of government, each with its powers, responsibilities, and perspectives.

The more decentralized fiscal power is in a federation, the more autonomy the subfederal units enjoy in order to carry out their responsibilities. Therefore, fiscal federalism becomes one of the more studied and controversial aspects of federalism. The fact is that de-

---

3. Javier Muguruza Arrese, "The Arbitration Board as a strengthening element in the Institution of the Economic Agreement."

4. George Anderson, *Federalism: An Introduction*, Forum of Federations (Oxford: Oxford University Press, 2008). See note 124]

5. George Anderson, *Fiscal Federalism: A Comparative Introduction*, Forum of Federations (Oxford: Oxford University Press, 2010).

volved tax regimes open the possibility to tax competition, which may cause advantages and costs. On the one hand, the advantages are accountability, responsiveness, and self-reliance. We could say that subfederal units become more responsible because if they over-tax mobile tax bases, they will see them move away and will become more accountable because their citizens can compare their taxes with those of other jurisdictions. On the other hand, it conjures up concerns of a tax jungle, heavy administrative and compliance costs, and race-to-the-bottom situations.

There are two ways to address destructive tax competition:

- Centralizing revenue decision-making in the federal government, or
- Using tax harmonization tools, which is the real challenge for fiscal decentralized models.

The second way is the model followed by the Basque tax system.

Tax harmonization between jurisdictions can limit harmful tax competition and avoid tax jungles. In most federations, it has proved a useful tool for helping fiscal federalism to work out properly. Tax harmonization can be vertical between the federal and subfederal units or horizontal among the subfederal units. It is usually system-wide, but sometimes a central government reaches asymmetric harmonization agreements with only some constituent units. This is the case of the Spanish central government with the Autonomous Communities of the Basque Country and Navarre. According to the experience in federal models, tax harmonization is most likely to succeed in those models where the federal government plays a major role in setting and collecting taxes from a tax base.

To complete this overview of fiscal federalism, let us now discuss the EU Model. The European Union is a unique composition of confederal and federal characteristics. However, it does not have independent, central fiscal powers, as the creation of a single tax system is not among the targets of the EU Treaty, the main aim of which is the functioning of the single market. In consequence, tax harmonization has turned out to be a long and difficult task within the European Union, and competition between Member States to attract new taxpayers to their jurisdiction is a common issue that can even turn into a problem at times.

Tax Harmonization and the Crisis

A common feature of the practice of tax harmonization in federal systems is the permanent tension between the authority empowered to implement the tax harmonization measures and the entity whose power is constrained as a result. Tax harmonization is always a slow and tortuous process, full of difficulties to overcome; however, certain contexts reinforce tax harmonization, and its speed can be increased.

At this international conference we are tackling "Financial Systems and the Crisis," and tax harmonization has not been immune to crisis. In fact, I would dare say in these last few years, tax harmonization has become a trending topic thanks to the crisis.

Focusing on the EU perspective, in 2008, Member States and their economies were weaker than ever, and their struggle to reduce the causes and consequences of the global economic crisis had an on-going effect on EU-wide and national tax policies. The harmonization of tax regimes has been a goal of the EU Institutions since the beginning, and the crisis created an opportunity for Member States to align their national tax policies. Indeed, when the crisis began, many European states reacted in broadly similar ways by adjusting government spending and cutting labor taxes and, to a lesser extent, capital taxes. Moreover, Member States that were forced to call on bailout funds.

Currently, the majority of the Member States agree on the need for a higher convergence of economic policies—including tax policies—and, although the crisis has so far not brought about significant deliberate tax convergence across Europe, currently it is fairly easy to identify certain shared trends in recent national tax systems reforms.

On 24 and 25 March 2011, the Pact for Competitiveness,[6] known as the Euro-plus Pact, proposed six actions to strengthen the economic pillar of the monetary union, achieve a new quality of economic policy coordination in the euro area, and improve competitiveness, thereby leading to a higher degree of convergence. Originally, the Euro-plus pact was designed for the eurozone Member States; however, non-eurozone Member States were also invited to join. Among the actions, the development of a common corporate tax base was an important but controversial one.

According to the Pact, there are no specific commitments on tax policy initiatives other than a briefly outlined commitment by Mem-

---

6. This is the official document of the Pact by the EU Institutions. It can be quoted as EUCO 10/1/11. REV 1. CO EUR 6. CONCL 3. EUROPEAN COUNCIL 24/25. March 2011. Conclusions.

ber States to engage in discussions about it. Tax policy coordination is expected to help strengthen the sharing of best practices and the fight against tax fraud and evasion. Direct taxation remains a national competence for each Euro-plus Pact member to decide upon individually. However, the Pact states that, "developing a common corporate tax base could be a revenue-neutral way forward to ensure consistency among national tax systems while respecting national tax strategies, and to contribute to fiscal sustainability and the competitiveness of European businesses."

Just a week earlier, on March 16, 2011, the Commission had presented a legislative proposal on a common consolidated corporate tax base for calculating the tax base of businesses operating in the European Union. The proposed Common Consolidated Corporate Tax Base (CCCTB)[7] indicates that companies would benefit from a "one-stop-shop" system for filing their tax returns and would be able to consolidate all the profits and losses they incur across the European Union. Member states would maintain their full sovereign right to set their own corporate tax rate.

At the same time, France and Germany, the two leading economies of the eurozone, called jointly to have Common Corporation and Financial Transaction[8] Taxes (FTT), with the outstanding opposition of the United Kingdom, which has for years resisted moves toward tax harmonization in the twenty-seven-nation bloc. Working together beyond the supranational level, France and Germany also harmonized their domestic business tax systems on a bilateral basis in 2012.

Although the push for EU tax harmonization is highly controversial, the fact is that currently, in 2015, all Member States are still working on both tax harmonization projects (CCCTB and FTT), boosted by France and Germany, within the Economic and Financial Affairs Council of the European Union (ECOFIN), as we are about to tackle in another section of this paper.

The Basque Case: Multilevel Tax Harmonization

From the perspective of the foral territories of the Basque Country in the twenty-first century, their tax systems and their wide fiscal pow-

---

7. See http://ec.europa.eu/taxation_customs/resources/documents/taxation/company_tax/common_tax_base/com_2011_121_en.pdf. COM(2011) 121/4, Proposal for a Council Directive on a Common Consolidated Corporate Tax Base (CCCTB).
8. See http://ec.europa.eu/taxation_customs/resources/documents/taxation/com_2013_71_en.pdf COM(2013) 71 final COUNCIL DIRECTIVE implementing enhanced cooperation in the area of financial transaction tax.

ers are subject to certain limitations. Among them, I would like to point out a complex multi-level tax harmonization framework.

This complexity is due to the foral territories' multilevel integration, as well as belonging to three different legal orders: the European Union, the Spanish state, and the Autonomous Community of the Basque Country. Consequently, and in regard to the foral tax systems, the tax harmonization principle is a polysemic concept whose targets, degree of intensity, and tools differ substantially depending on the perspective we are analyzing.[9]

Fields of Tax Harmonization

The first field of tax harmonization is the European one. As mentioned at the beginning, the European Union is a unique creation bringing together confederal and federal characteristics, in the sense that Member States transfer part of their power and sovereignty to the European institutions in order to achieve common goals. According to the EU Treaty, tax harmonization is not a target of the Union itself. Needless to say, the establishment of a central and unique tax system for Member States is not among the objectives of the Treaty. Tax harmonization is just a tool at the service of the common market and its proper functioning, which is the real goal of the Treaty. Therefore, tax harmonization can be implemented only in order to prevent market distortions and double taxation.

The second field of tax harmonization impacting on the foral systems is the domestic field. The domestic level is related to the financial and tax relationships between the Basque tax systems and the central Spanish tax system within an asymmetric federal framework. The tax harmonization principle is laid out in article 41.2 of the Basque Statute of Autonomy[10] and further regulated in articles 2 and 3 of the Economic Agreement in force.[11] Since 1981, it is a principle that has

9. Gemma Martínez Bárbara, *Armonización fiscal y poder tributario foral en la CAPV.* Premio Jesús María Leizaola 2013. (Oñati: IVAP, 2014).

10. Article 41.2.a) of the Basque Statute of Autonomy reads: "2. The content of the Agreement regime shall respect and be adapted to the following principles and guidelines: a) The competent Institutions of the Historic Territories may maintain, establish and regulate, within their own territory, the tax system, bearing in mind the general tax structure of the State, the rules contained in the Economic Agreement itself for co-ordination, fiscal harmonization and collaboration with the State, and those to be issued by the Basque Parliament for the same purposes within the Autonomous Community. The Economic Agreement shall be approved by law.

11. Article 2 reads: "Article 2. General principles
One. The taxation system established by the Historical Territories shall be in accor-

proved essential for the proper integration of the foral tax systems and the Spanish central tax regime. In this context, tax harmonization aims to give consistency to financial and tax relationships among the different tax systems within the Spanish constitutional order.

The last field, and perhaps the most controversial at the moment, is the tax harmonization among the three foral tax systems within the Autonomous Community of the Basque Country. In the update of the foral rights constitutionally imposed and complied with by the Basque Statute, the tax harmonization power is assigned to the new legal entity, the Autonomous Community of the Basque Country, and, in particular, to the Basque Parliament. By means of this allocation, the foral territories freely pool part of their historically exclusive tax power with the new legal territorial entity created by the 1978 Constitution, and through this cession they self-limit their full traditional tax competence. As mentioned before, I believe there is a relevant confederal nature in the constitution of the Basque Autonomous Community.

---

dance with the following principles:

First. Respect for the principle of solidarity in the terms laid down in the Constitution and in the Statute of Autonomy.

Second. Regard for the general taxation structure of the State.

Third. Coordination, fiscal harmonization and cooperation with the State, in accordance with the rules laid down in the present Economic Agreement.

Fourth. Coordination, fiscal harmonization and mutual cooperation between the Institutions of the Historical Territories pursuant to the regulations enacted by the Basque Parliament for these purposes.

Fifth. Submission to the International Agreements or Treaties signed and ratified or adhered to by the Spanish State.

In particular, it shall comply with the provisions laid down in the International Agreements signed by Spain to avoid double taxation, as well as fiscal harmonization measures of the European Union, and shall be responsible for making the refunds called for, pursuant to application of said Agreements and rules.

Two. The rules laid down herein shall be interpreted in accordance with the provisions contained in the General Tax Law for the interpretation of tax regulations.

Article 3. Fiscal harmonization

In drafting their tax legislation, the Historical Territories shall:

a) Respect the General Tax Law in matters of terminology and concepts, without prejudice to the peculiarities established in the present Economic Agreement.

b) Maintain an overall effective fiscal pressure equivalent to that in force in the rest of the State.

c) Respect and guarantee freedom of movement and establishment of persons and the free movement of goods, capital and services throughout the territory of Spain, without giving rise to discrimination or a lessening of the possibilities of commercial competition or to distortion in the allocation of resources.

d) Use the same system for classifying livestock, mining, industrial, commercial, service, professional and artistic activities as is used in the so-called common territory, without prejudice to further itemizations that might be made."

Tax harmonization at this level is a key element in the internal model of devolution within the Basque Country, based on the principles of cohesion and mutual interdependence. This financial system is grounded on shared risk, that is, a pool of financial resources deriving from the collection of the taxes in the foral systems that is shared internally by the three different territorial orders. This model requires a reasonable degree of homogeneity of the shared resources, not only to the benefit of the Common Institutions of the Basque Country, which are the creditors of more than 90% of the resources used to pay most of the Basque public expenses, but also to the foral territories and the municipalities. From this perspective, tax harmonization plays a main role in preventing substantial differences among the three foral tax systems.

In the next section, we examine how tax harmonization affects the execution of the powers of the three Historical Territories.

European Field

Starting with the European Union field, I would like all of us to bear in mind a simple but at the same time essential idea. In spite of the lack of representation and power of regions in Europe, as already mentioned by José Rubí Cassinello,[12] no one can deny that since the integration of Spain into the European Community in 1986, Community Law has had a clear impact on the Autonomous Communities' scope of competence and, in our case, on the tax powers of the foral territories.

However, the fact that the foral territories are the only ones entitled with full faculties to establish and administer, within their territories, their own taxation system, makes the Basque region a rare bird, only comparable to Navarre, among European regions. Therefore, foral territories should play an active role, together with Member States, in the European tax harmonizing process.

Having said that, the difference in pace between indirect and direct taxes in the positive harmonization process in the European Union is well known: the first is relatively successful, and the second is slow and with very few legislative instruments adopted. Because of the Member States' reluctance to adopt positive measures, presently the real actors of the tax harmonization process have become the European Court of Justice, the European Commission, and the Coun-

---

12. José Rubí Cassinello, "The Role of regions with taxation powers in the European Union: the Basque Economic Agreement," (publication data? Year?) originally in English?

cil, through the so-called negative harmonization process.[13] In this setting, tax harmonization, which forbids Member States to adopt certain tax measures, is the side effect of a process focused on guaranteeing the four fundamental freedoms and the common market.

The Basque foral territories are subject to the results of both processes, positive and negative. Not having legislative power in indirect taxation, they have to respect and implement the results of the process when adopting tax measures in direct taxation in the exercise of their own competence. There are many examples in the Basque tax systems of the implementation of directives regarding Basque personal income tax, for instance taxation of savings income, as well as with respect to Basque corporate income tax, we have the mergers directive or parents-subsidiary directive or interests and royalties directives. Within the negative process, judicial legislation, as one of its most remarkable tools, has also had a great impact on the regulation of Basque corporate income tax and on the inheritance and gift tax.

I do not have anything else to add to what has been explained by other speakers about the effects of European state aid policy—a very powerful tool for negative harmonization in the hands of the Commission—on the foral systems, as I understand the positive impact of the current interpretation of regional selectivity on the Basque tax autonomy can be taken for granted.

The last field of negative integration tax policy relates to the methods for coordination and integration of Member States' tax systems promoted by the European institutions and, in particular, by the Council. I will end my comments on the European perspective within this field of negative integration where one of the most controversial aspects related to the Economic Agreement took place and finally found its way in 2010.

Since 1981, the Economic Agreement has had a provision within article 4, under the coordination principle, by virtue of which the Spanish central government has to establish the proceedings to facilitate the participation of the Basque Country in the international committees where issues regarding its tax competence are addressed.[14]

---

13. Michael Lang, Pasquale Pistone, Josef Schuch, and Claus Staringe. *Horizontal Tax Coordination* (Amsterdam: IBFD, 2012).
14. "Article 4 Cooperation principles. ? info seems to be missing here
... publication info.? See next note
Two. The State shall devise mechanisms for allowing the Institutions of the Basque Country to collaborate in any International Agreements affecting the application of the present Economic Agreement . . ."

Over more than twenty years, such proceedings were not implemented and, therefore, Basque institutions had to comply with whatever
decisions were adopted in those forums, but had no right to express or
defend their position. This situation was especially blatant in the EU
context. In 2001, during negotiations of the in-force Economic Agreement, this claim became the sticking point for the Basque negotiators,
to the extent that the negotiation was blocked for some months.

Finally, in 2010, the Joint Committee of the Economic Agreement
reached consensus by virtue of which the Spanish government made
a commitment to integrate Basque representatives into the Spanish
delegation within the ECOFIN working groups, in which tax issues
are managed. The first meeting attended by Basque representatives
was in April 2011. Consequently, Basque representatives[15] are currently attending the following working groups:

- D-4—Tax issues. Among them, I would like to point out the
  Financial Transaction Tax group and the Corporate Common
  Consolidated Tax Base group.
- D-5—Code of conduct, in charge of rolling back harmful tax
  measures adopted by Member States.
- D-8—Fight against fraud.

In these groups, the Basque Country is the only region with
full taxation powers in direct taxation, and attendance within these
groups allows us the same position as the rest of the participants
there, all Member States, in order to collaborate and exercise our taxation powers in line with Community Law. For instance, last week
within the Code of Conduct group (D-5), the Basque patent box was
in the agenda with the rest of the patent box regimes in force in the
Member States.

Domestic Field

As I have mentioned before, article 41.2 of the Basque Statute establishes this harmonization principle. In general, the requirement of
harmonization between the Basque foral tax systems and the Spanish
central system allows diversity and difference. Although this principle is specifically regulated in articles 2 and 3 of the Economic Agreement, we can trace it along the rest of the legal text adopting various
forms and intensities.

---

15. The author of this paper is one of the Basque representatives who attend the
ECOFIN taxation working groups.

For instance, we can find the most absolute form of tax harmonization in indirect tax figures, which are agreed to be taxes subject to the same rules in terms of substance and form as those established by the State. In this context, the tax harmonization obligation becomes so intense it turns into tax uniformity.

So at the domestic level, tax harmonization only makes sense in relation to direct taxation because this is the only field in which the foral parliaments—Juntas Generales—can adopt different tax measures from those of the rest of the state. Therefore, the personal income tax, corporate income tax, wealth tax or inheritance tax, and gift tax are subject to domestic tax harmonization principles.

In a strict sense, this principle comprises the four rules in article 3 of the Economic Agreement and they limit the foral territories in drafting their tax legislation. The rules are as follows:

- Respect the General Tax Law in matters of terminology and concepts.
- Maintain an overall effective fiscal pressure equivalent to that in force in the rest of the state.
- Respect and guarantee freedom of movement and establishment of persons and the free movement of goods, capital, and services throughout the territory of Spain.
- Use the same system for classifying economic activities as is used in the common territory.

Of these, the second and third impose genuine limits on the foral tax legislative powers, the first and the fourth being minor.

Obviously, some of these principles are, to say the least, ambiguous. For instance, it is not clear what "equivalent fiscal pressure" means. More important, the main cause of the conflicts between the state and the Basque Autonomous Community is the principle of no distortion. The principle has, however, a high degree of subjectivity. Simply put, distortion is a matter of degree, and any tax difference between the Basque Country and the rest of Spain, no matter how small, will cause some distortion. This fact introduces a high degree of subjectivity into the decision about whether a tax measure is distortional. The problem is further complicated because there is no clear method to measure the level of distortion created by a tax difference.

In consequence, these harmonization rules are overly general and quite undetermined in their application and, as a result, in many cases courts have had to interpret whether some Basque tax measures were in line with them or not. Courts have had a difficult task each time they have had to analyze the respect of these rules, in particular the maintenance of an overall effective fiscal pressure. In fact, it is quite unusual to find a sentence confirming the violation of this principle.

Therefore, there is a solid jurisprudence that requires careful weighing of the limitation of *foral* tax power deriving from the harmonizing rules in article 3, and interpretation of its intensity in a restrictive manner.

In this domestic field, the Economic Agreement also creates a specific tool in order to oversee compliance of the harmonization rules. It is the Coordination and Evaluation Committee,[16] a joint body made up of four representatives of the state administration and four representatives of the Autonomous Community appointed by the Basque government, three of which shall be at the proposal of each of the respective territorial governments.

According to article 4 of the Economic Agreement, the competent institutions of the Historical Territories shall inform the state administration with due notice prior to their coming into effect of any draft bills on tax regulations. Similarly, the State Administration shall inform the aforementioned institutions.

If, as a result of this exchange of information on draft bills, some observations should arise, any of the administrations represented may request that the Committee assemble. The Committee will make all efforts to see that the Institutions and Administrations represented reach an agreement on any discrepancies in the tax legislation. In practice, most of the discrepancies have been related to the tax harmonization rules in article 3 of the Economic Agreement. The Committee's role as a mediator and the non-binding nature of its decisions, in the sense that they do not prevent the draft from being finally adopted, minimize its harmonization impact on foral tax systems.

The Basque Country's Autonomous Community Field

Both the Statute of Autonomy, in article 41.2, and the Economic Agreement, in article 2, refer to tax harmonization between the three foral tax systems, according to the rules laid down to that effect by the Basque Parliament, as one of the general principles informing the Basque tax system.

---

16. Articles 63 and 64 of the Economic Agreement.

Another of the pillars of the Basque legal order, the 27/1983 Historical Territories Law, also includes a mandatory tax harmonization, which tends to uniformity but vanishes at the same time thanks to the transitional regime.

It was by means of the 3/1989 Tax Harmonization, Coordination, and Collaboration Law that the harmonization criteria in each tax figure of the foral systems were settled. And once again the equivalency of fiscal pressure, this time among the three Basque territories, is the parameter of tax harmonization.

It can be observed that the Basque legal order is full of references to tax harmonization. Despite this fact, nobody really knows how to interpret and apply its rules or when the foral territories are really violating this internal principle. As a result, since 2007 there has been a permanent and ongoing debate on tax harmonization within the Basque Country from each and every approach: lawyers, economists, politicians, professors, civil servants—all of us are involved in it.

Thanks to the 3/1989 Law, the Basque Country is also provided with an effective harmonization tool, the Basque Tax Coordination Committee (OCTE). The OCTE is made up of three representatives from the Basque Government and one from each of the Basque *foral* provinces. The OCTE's main mission is to promote harmonization, coordination, and collaboration between Basque foral territories in the exercise of their powers concerning taxation to improve tax management efficiency. It has proved an effective tool to prevent the foral tax systems from non-harmonization, and its functioning is mainly due to the unwritten rule of institutional loyalty and to the mostly technical nature of its debates, far from a political approach.

Latest Goals

Since Basque representatives started regularly attending the ECOF-IN working groups in April 2011, I have been wondering why we were not attending the rest of the international committees related to taxation. In regards to collaboration and participation, the Economic Agreement does not refer only to the European Union, but also to the international context.

Of course, the Organization for Economic Cooperation and Development (OECD) was the committee I had in mind. Well, out of the blue and quite naturally, last February we were called to a meeting by the Spanish Finance Ministry because the patent box regimes regulated in the corporate income tax of Bizkaia, Araba, and Gipuzkoa had been included in the agenda for information, together with some others in force in the world. One might imagine that it was easier for the Spanish central government to take us along to defend our legislation. Indeed it was! Although this was not the first time a Basque issue was on the agenda, it was the first time we were there! From my point of view, this is what really matters. It felt strange to be sitting there between the United States and Denmark explaining our legislation, and even stranger when the chairman asked us how it was possible that a region within Spain has different regulations for corporate taxation from those approved by the Spanish central government.

The Basque Country has made another step forward regarding inclusion in international tax harmonization committees.

Conclusions

To sum up, I offer some final thoughts about tax harmonization and the Basque Country at this very moment. In the European field, due to the financial crisis, the tax harmonization process is being boosted and is moving faster as the stability of the monetary union relies on an economic integrated union, and taxes are an important part of this.

After long years struggling for it, the Basque Country finally appears on the European tax harmonization scene and participates actively in tax decision-making groups. The reluctance of the Spanish central government is slowly fading away, and the mistrust or perhaps lack of awareness of Member States is vanishing, especially after the September 11, 2008 ECJ ruling that the three autonomy criteria were met by the Basque Country.

At the domestic level, tax harmonization finally rests in peace after a decade *horribilis* of central state litigation against foral tax systems during the 1990s, under the banner of tax harmonization. Settled case law of this principle allows Basque regimes room to maneuver in order to implement their own tax policies, different from those of the Spanish central government.

Tax harmonization within the Basque Country is definitely very controversial at the moment. The ongoing debate started with a corporate income tax rate difference in Gipuzkoa in 2007, was then fired up while the PSE–Basque Socialist Party was ruling the Basque government, and is at its highest now with the three foral territories being governed by three different parties. However, in my opinion, this debate is just the tip of the iceberg. I believe there is a deeper debate hiding behind it, that of the Basque internal devolution model.

Here we find the two traditionally opposed ideological positions regarding the Basque Country devolution system: one in support of a change of model by means of the reinforcement of Basque Common Institutions, in which the tax legislative power would be centralized and transferred to the Basque Parliament; and another of confederal nature backing the current maintenance of tax powers in the hands of the foral territories subject to several limits, such as the tax harmonization principle.

One thing I am convinced of: that is, tax harmonization has a major role to play in the horizontal and vertical federal relations within the Basque Country according to the current legal order, and sooner or later, some light will be shed and some consensus will be reached on the role it should play in the Basque Autonomous Community field.

Bibliography

Anderson, George. *Federalism: An Introduction.* Forum of Federations. Oxford: Oxford University Press, 2008.

Anderson, George. *Fiscal Federalism: A Comparative Introduction.* Forum of Federations Oxford: Oxford University Press, 2010.

Kenyon, Quane with Pete T. Cenarrusa. *From Bizkaia to Boise: The Memoirs of Pete T. Cenarrusa.* (Basque Politics Series) Reno: Center for Basque Studies Press, University of Nevada, 2009.

Lang, Michael, Pasquale Pistone, Josef Schuch, and Claus Staringe. *"Horizontal Tax Coordination."* (Amsterdam: IBFD, 2012)

Martínez Bárbara, Gemma. *Armonización fiscal y poder tributario foral en la CAPV.* (Premio Jesús María Leizaola 2013) Oñati: IVAP, 2014.

11

The Arbitration Board as a Strengthening Element in the Institution of the Economic Agreement

Javier Muguruza Arrese

In a model of shared tax competences within the same territory and the same target taxpayers, conflict between administrations is unavoidable when they are exercising their competences in relation to a concrete individual or a concrete business.

Even though jurisdictional resolution is utterly valid in such conflicts, it has proved to be a limited tool. This is mainly due to factors such as excessive formalism; constant blockage of the organs devoted to the resolution of conflicts between individuals; excessive cost; and, undoubtedly, the mistrust political powers feel toward ordinary court when they are concerned with the resolution of conflicts.

The model of an arbitration board formed by professionals of mutual confidence of the political powers is, in theory, a more desirable alternative. In the case of the Economic Agreement, lack of mutual trust prevented the constitution of such an organ for years. A dynamic solution was found only after this problem was overcome, and its implementation is still a difficult issue. Despite these difficulties, the doctrine developed by the Arbitration Board is definitely the best safeguard of the continuity of the regime provided by the technical tax establishment.

The Economic Agreement as a Source of Conflicts of Competence

In the Economic Agreement model, tax sovereignty is shared by different administrations, meaning that administrations share the same economic territory and have the same target collective of taxpayers.

As a result, there may be conflicts of competence between them. Conflict is unavoidable in cases where several administrations feel competent on the same taxpayer or business, or in cases of tax refunds when no administration feels competent in a given case.

Throughout history, in different Economic Agreements between the Spanish central government and the Basque Country, there were no specific procedures for conflict resolution. Traditionally, the resolution of potential conflicts was assigned to the ordinary court of law. Only very recently was the Arbitration Board deemed a peculiar instrument for the resolution of conflicts of competence originating in the Economic Agreement.

Historical Background of the Arbitration Board

In Navarre

The model of an arbitration organ for conflict resolution prior to the judicial process was born within the Economic Treaty between Navarre and the Spanish central government. The first precedent can be found in the Economic Treaty between Navarre and the central government of 1927.[1] As Simon Acosta[2] points out, up to then, the Treaty was based on real taxes that could be easily territorialized. The introduction of taxes on investment income and taxes on business complicated the delimitation of the tax jurisdiction and increased the risk of administrative conflict.

For the first time in the tradition of the successive Economic Agreements, the fifth provision of the second article of the Treaty of Navarre of 1927 established an Arbitration Board. This first Board had the following characteristics:

- Its headquarters should be located in Madrid.
- It should be renewed every three years.
- It would be constituted by
    - a state civil servant,
    - a representative of the regional government of Navarre, and

---

1. Real Decreto 15 August 1927, in José María Estecha Martínez, *Régimen Político Administrativo de las Provincias Vasco Navarras* (Bilbao: Instituto de Derecho Histórico de Euskal Herria / Diputación Foral de Bizkaia, 1935), Apéndice II, p. 242.
2. Eugenio Simón Acosta, "Sujetos y objeto del conflicto ante la Junta Arbitral del Convenio Económico entre el Estado y la Comunidad Foral de Navarra," *Revista Jurídica de Navarra*, no. 48 (2009): 75–105.

- a magistrate of the Supreme Court, who would act as the chairman.

However, no provision was made for the appointment of the chairman. From this precedent on, the subsequent Economic Treaties of Navarre have maintained the existence of an Arbitration Board. However, as Aramburu Urtasun[3] stated in 2005, the provision for the existence of an Arbitration Board was totally useless for more than seventy years. It was not until after 2000 that the Arbitration Boards were formally constituted. Until that time, they were nothing but declarations of intent.

The Treaty of Navarre of 1941 maintained the institution of the Arbitration Board, introducing two stipulations, which are important as precedents:

- the chairman would be appointed by the Government, and
- the board would be responsible for addressing *all questions related to interpretation and implementation of the Treaty.*

However, in the twenty-five years the Navarre Treaty of 1941 was in force, the Arbitration Board was never constituted. Del Burgo Tajadura[4] attributes this deficiency precisely to the fact that the regional government of Navarre did not welcome the voting privileges given to a magistrate appointed unilaterally by the government.

In the Navarre Treaty of 1969, there was a revision of the procedure for the appointment of the chairman: He or she would no longer be appointed by the central government, but rather by the Supreme Court itself. The regional government of Navarre was probably not convinced by this new provision, for the Arbitration Board did not become a reality under this Treaty, either.

It was the Navarre Treaty of 1990 that introduced a new model of the Arbitration Board, which could finally be constituted. Article 51 of this Treaty referred to an Arbitration Board for which the existence of a chairman was not even contemplated. It was to be formed by three members appointed by consensus of the Spanish Minister of Finance and the Basque Minister of Finance and Public Administration.

---

3. Mikel Aramburu Urtasun, *Provincias Exentas, Convenio-Concierto. Identidad Colectiva de la Vasconia peninsular (1969–2005)* (Donostia-San Sebastián: Fundación para el Estudio del Derecho Histórico y Autonómico de Vasconia, 2005), p. 62.
4. Jaime Ignacio Del Burgo Tajadura, *Origen y fundamento del régimen Foral de Navarra* (Pamplona: Biblioteca de Derecho Foral, vol. 12, 1968), p. 478.

As De la Hucha Celador[5] points out, the formula of parity, together with an impartial chairman with a casting vote, gave way to a formula of consensus, which was political rather than judicial.

In the Basque Country

Unlike Navarre, the Economic Agreement in the Basque Country did not constitute an Arbitration Board until 1981. Burlada Echeveste[6] has devoted himself to documenting the history of the Arbitration Board of the Economic Agreement. He cites the Joint Jury of Utilities, established in the 1925 Agreement,[7] as a precedent of the Arbitration Board. The function of this body was to set the tax for companies operating in the common territory and those operating in the Basque territory. It was constituted by a peer number of civil servants of both governments, and the chairman was a magistrate of the Supreme Court. Article 22 of the 1952 Economic Agreement between the central government and Álava established a procedure to resolve differences between administrations. This procedure did not consider an Arbitration Board, though. In a tone typical of the dictatorship, it established that conflicts were to be resolved by the Spanish Minister of Finance, following an audience with the regional government of Álava. If the Regional Government did not agree with the resolution, it would resort to judicial proceedings.

The Unborn Arbitration Board of the 1981 Agreement

For the first time in the Basque Country, the Economic Agreement of 1981 established an Arbitration Board. The first thing to catch our attention about the Arbitration Board described in the 1981 Agreement is the complexity of the procedure for the appointment of the chairman. It states that the chairman of the Arbitration Board ought to be a magistrate of the Supreme Court, appointed by the president of this tribunal, following the proposal of the State Judicial Council (Consejo General del Poder Judicial) after due hearing from the High Court of the Basque Country (Tribunal Superior de Justicia del País Vasco). It copied the inappropriate formula of Navarre that granted

---

5. Fernando De la Hucha Celador, *El régimen jurídico del Convenio Económico de la Comunidad Foral de Navarra* (Donostia-San Sebastián: Fundación para el Estudio del Derecho Histórico y Autonómico de Vasconia, 2006), p. 192.

6. José Luis Burlada Echeveste, "Génesis de la Junta Arbitral del Concierto Económico y del Convenio Económico," *Nueva Fiscalidad*, no. 2 (2007): 101–8.

7. Real Decreto 9 June 1925 and Real Decreto 24 December 1926, in Estecha, Apendice I, pp. 25 and 254.

the chairmanship to a magistrate of the Supreme Court; this was precisely the formula that had prevented Navarre from constituting its Arbitration Board since 1927. However, worse than this, the formula for the selection of the magistrate-chairman was even more complicated. Under the 1981 Agreement, the candidate was to be formally proposed by the Government Board of Judicial Power. In Spain, the Government Board of Judicial Power is a body subject to strong intervention by the political parties. Within this organ, agreements have always been very difficult to reach. A bigger complication was the compulsory previous hearing from the High Court of the Basque Country.

The consequence of this convoluted process of selecting the chairman of the Arbitration Board was that during the twenty years this regulation was in force, no chairman was ever appointed. This is why an Arbitration Board was never constituted.

Why was such a procedure elaborated for designating the chairman of the Arbitration Board, resulting in the impossibility of an appointment, in place in 1981? Moreover, why was such a procedure in place when it had already been demonstrated for more than fifty years that it led to the deadlock of the Arbitration Board? The most reasonable answer is this: Those who compelled the drafting of such language surely did not favor the creation of the Arbitration Board.

By 1981, when the Economic Agreement was negotiated, there was already complete knowledge of what had occurred with the Arbitration Board of Navarre since 1927: It had never been formally constituted. And in Navarre, the only requirement to become the chairman of the Board was to be a magistrate of the Supreme Court. So why, in the 1981 Agreement, did they make it more difficult to achieve what had already proved nearly impossible?

An Arbitration Board of Impossible Constitution

Aramburu Urtasun[8] maintained that the central administration profited from the lack of an Arbitration Board. We could not agree more with his statement, and we could ratify it with precise details. However, we cannot support the idea that the central administration was the only one to blame.

The state was not solely responsible for drafting the 1981 Agreement that made the constitution of the Arbitration Board impossible. Neither can we blame the state administration for the lack of effort to

---

8. Aramburu Urtasun, *Provincias Exentas*, p. 64.

resolve the situation between 1981 and 2000. Pedro Luis Uriarte Santamarina[9] was the president from the Basque side in the Joint Committee of the Economic Agreement. Thanks to him, we have had access to the draft papers of the negotiations, with his own manuscript annotations. We have examined the texts along with the proposals to regulate the Arbitration Board.

Negotiations started with a text that reproduced the pattern of the 1969 Navarre Treaty, in force at the time. It offered an Arbitration Board with the same number of representatives from the State and the Basque Country, presided over by a magistrate of the Supreme Court. Very soon, the Basque party attempted to change the chairmanship. They wanted to assign it to the president of the High Court of the Basque Country, but this proposal was refused by the state party.

In the course of the discussion, the Basque Party demanded the introduction of due audience from the High Court of the Basque Country. The central state accepted, but in turn demanded that the chairman be proposed by the State Judicial Council. For the designation of the chairman, each party forced the intervention of the judicial establishment they felt closest to them, which inevitably led to a protocol of appointment impossible to put into practice.

However, it is easy to understand the mutual mistrust both negotiating parties felt about the appointment of the chairman. The proposed board was composed of the same number of representatives from the state and the Basque Country. Eight members would vote on behalf of the party they represented. Four members would vote on behalf of the state, and the other four would vote on behalf of the Basque Country. In such a situation, the chairman was the sole judge to decide the disputes. Based on the documents from this negotiation, we also know that the Basque Party required the suppression of a sentence that had been borrowed from the 1941 Navarre Treaty. This sentence stated that, apart from conflict resolution, the board would be concerned with the "interpretation of the agreement." The Basque Side demanded that the Arbitration Board not be responsible for interpretation of the agreement.

This provides more evidence of the lack of confidence existing between both sides. Attribution of conflict resolution to a board, together with the prohibition of interpretation of the legal text regulating the distribution of competences, is functionally speaking an

---

9. Pedro Luis Uriarte Santamarina, *Draft papers of the negotiation of the Economic Agreement of the Basque Country of 1981.* Unpublished. Personal file of Mr. Uriarte.

absurdity. We can conclude that in the 1981 negotiation, both parties mistrusted a chairman chosen by the Judicial Power. Besides, at the time, that Judicial Power was still being updated based on the Constitution of the newly-born democracy.

Both parties were acquainted with the fact that for forty years, no agreement had been reached in Navarre to designate a magistrate of the Supreme Court as the chairman of the board. However, none of the parties dared present another alternative. Both parties introduced legal cautions that might protect them from a chairman who was insufficiently controlled; but neither was clever enough to force the selection of a chairman not chosen by the Supreme Court.

The situation was paradoxical. The Arbitration Board could not be constituted because consensus to appoint its chairman was impossible. On the other hand, in the absence of an Arbitration Board, conflicts had to be decided by professional judges. We cannot imagine that the parties were unaware of these circumstances; both sides must have behaved consciously.

In 1981, there was consensus on the need to approve the Economic Agreement at all costs. That is why they understood it was important to establish a procedure of designation of the Arbitration Board to which both parties could subscribe, even though they were certain that it would not be feasible at all. The important goal was to approve the Agreement and later, based on the practice, a way to resolve differences would be found.

From my point of view, none of the parties felt that the absence of an Arbitration Board was more convenient for themselves than for the opposite party. What they probably thought was that they had to avoid an inconvenient Board. And they preferred a blocked board rather than an inconvenient one. On the part of the Basque Party, their priority to dispose of an Agreement probably eclipsed the risks of the lack of a formally constituted Arbitration Board. And on the part of the state party, the fact that the Economic Agreement avoided the issue of constituting an inconvenient Arbitration Board was sufficient to encourage them to subscribe to its approval. Within the framework of a blocked board, the state was more eager to accept tax sovereignty shared with the Basque Country.

From 1981 Onward

As could be expected, for the duration of the 1981 Economic Agreement, up to 2001, the constitution of the Arbitration Board never became a reality. There is no evidence that the parties had formally propounded the need for its constitution. Conflicts of competence certainly arose—initially with respect to the place where certain transactions subject to taxation had been performed. However, we must emphasize that during these first twenty years of the restored Economic Agreement, the lack of an Arbitration Board was not a serious problem for anybody.

The Situation from 2002 Onward

Serious trouble emerged later, from 2002 onward. Once the 1981 Economic Agreement was no longer in force, and the succeeding text was agreed to, the question of the Arbitration Board was again solved by reproducing the Navarre formula. By then, the 1990 Treaty had already been approved in Navarre. As we have already mentioned, this Treaty introduced for the first time the formula of an Arbitration Board by consensus. The board was made up of three experts of renowned prestige appointed by mutual agreement between the two parties and without the presence of the magistrate of the Supreme Court. With no more discussion, the very same formula was brought to the 2002 Basque Economic Agreement.

In theory, after this change, the constitution of the Arbitration Board would not be a difficult issue. The only requirement was to designate three experts of recognized prestige with over fifteen years of professional experience in tax matters. The universe of candidates was infinite. However, during the next eight years, the constitution of the Board of Arbitration continued to be unsuccessful. Once again, there was no Arbitration Board, but none of the administrations actually claimed its constitution.

But the fact is that conflicts between administrations increased from 2000 on. And taxpayers started to suffer the consequences of these disputes. The central administration started taking legal action against companies that had already paid their taxes to the Basque administrations. These companies requested the establishment of an Arbitration Board to put an end to the problems affecting them. The central administration answered cynically that it had to act directly before them, arguing that, as there was no Arbitration Board, it could not decide the dispute with the Basque administration. In an absurd way, the lack of the Arbitration Board itself became an argument to levy taxes from companies that had already paid them to another administration. The Basque administration denounced such actions by the central administration before the Courts of Justice. The Court noted the absurdity of the situation, but they charged both administrations because both of them refused to reach an agreement for the appointment of the Arbitration Board.[10] The doctrine began by denouncing the absence of an Arbitration Board and the serious consequences it carried for taxpayers.[11] The pressure exerted by both professionals and taxpayers on the administrations resulted in the constitution of the first Arbitration Board in the history of the Economic Agreement.

In 2008, they reached an agreement to select the three arbitrators of the board. Three renowned university professors were appointed, and at last, the first conflicts began to be resolved. These three first arbitrators were Professors Carlos Palao Taboada, Isaac Merino Jara, and Fernando de la Hucha Celador. Immediately, the Arbitration Board was confronted with piles of cases. All the differences that had arisen in previous years were pending resolution.

The first resolutions were concerned with the fiscal domiciles of taxpayers and the place of performance of the activities.[12] One of the first interventions, dealing with Rover brand vehicles, reverberated throughout the media. The Rover firm had a depot in the Basque Country, where cars arriving in Spain from their factory in Great Britain were being checked and stored. The board decided that the consumption tax on all Rover vehicles in Spain was to be paid in the Basque Country.

The Arbitration Board: A Necessary Step Before Judicial Court

The Economic Agreement establishes that the resolutions of the Arbitration Board may be appealed to the Supreme Court. Alonso Arce[13]

---

10. Aitor Orena Domínguez, "La tutela judicial efectiva y la falta de Junta Arbitral," *Quincena Fiscal*, no. 10 (2008): 93–96; José Luis Burlada Etxebeste and Inés María Burlada Etxebeste, "El fantasma de la Junta Arbitral del Concierto Económico y su consideración como existente: el fin de un pernicioso razonamiento jurídico. Nota a la sentencia del Tribunal Supremo de 10 de julio de 2008," *Quincena Fiscal*, no. 7 (2009): 87–95.

11. Isaac Merino Jara, "Acerca de la 'inexistente' Junta Arbitral del Concierto Económico," *Aranzadi Jurisprudencia Tributaria*, no. 6 (2006): 23–27; Sofía Arana Landín, "Conflictos de competencias entre la Administración del Estado y la Diputación Foral de Bizkaia," *Aranzadi Jurisprudencia Tributaria*, no. 14 (2006): 27–40; Javier Muguruza Arrese, "Esperando a la Junta Arbitral del Concierto Económico con el País Vasco," *Actualidad Jurídica Aranzadi*, no. 604 (2004): 4–5 .

12. Gemma Martínez Bárbara, "Vías de resolución de discrepancias entre las administraciones tributarias en relación con la domiciliación de los contribuyentes en el Concierto Económico," *Zergak: Gaceta Tributaria del País Vasco*, no. 37 (2009): 89–108.

13. Iñaki Alonso Arce, "El Tribunal Supremo se pronuncia por primera vez sobre

has studied both the legal foundation and the formalism of this appeal. The appellation to the Supreme Court is surely inherited from the former institution of the chairman, who should be a magistrate of the Supreme Court. It follows logically that the decisions of a body whose chairman is a magistrate of the Supreme Court cannot be reviewed by a lower court.

Today, the appeal before the Supreme Court is nonsense, technically speaking. It gives prestige and distinction to the board but it lacks a functional explanation. Merino Jara[14] reflects on the non-"arbitrative" character of the Arbitration Board, despite its misleading name. Were it a true instance of arbitration, their resolutions would put an end to the conflicts.

In fact, it is an administrative instance of a compulsory exercise before presenting a conflict before the court. This is understandable because true arbitration would mean, in our case, the renunciation of the right to appeal to a court, which is difficult to accept in our model of separation of powers and control of the legality of public powers.

As far as I am concerned, this fact does not lessen the importance of the Arbitration Board at all. Logically, the administration has appealed many resolutions before the Supreme Court that were not granted favorable resolution. Most of the appeals have been resolved by confirming the decision made by the board.

The Arbitration Board at Work

The Arbitration Board has been operating for about four years. Even though it was constituted in 2008, a new arbitrator has had to be appointed on two occasions. In the first instance, the change was due to a resignation of one of its members, who took a political office; and in the second, one of the arbitrators retired. The need to reach a consensus for the designation of the new members has caused a stoppage of several months in each of these instances, which is why its six years of existence can be reduced to four years of effectiveness.

During this period, approximately a hundred resolutions have been issued. The Supreme Court has issued about thirty sentences resolving appellations against the decisions of the Arbitration Board. As a result, it has been possible to create a body of doctrine and a culture of interpretation and implementation of the Agreement without

---

una Resolución de la Junta Arbitral del Concierto Económico," *Forum Fiscal de Bizkaia*, (May 2010): 21–30

14. Isaac Merino Jara, "La Junta Arbitral del Concierto Económico," *Revista Vasca de Administración Pública*, no. 75 (2006): 85–104.

precedent in the 136-year history of the Economic Agreement.

One might think that delays in the constitution of the Arbitration Board, its blockages, and the number of resolutions appealed to the Supreme Court predict certain failure of the institution. I disagree. After so many years of stagnation, the constitution of the Arbitration Board is in itself an unprecedented success. Its constitution demonstrated that a valid formula of composition and appointment had eventually been found. It took a long time, but succeeded in the end. At present, consensus for the appointment of the members of the board has been reached three times—something unthinkable ten years ago.

Contribution of the Arbitration Board to the Consolidation of the Agreement

The corpus of *iurisprudentia* of the Spanish Supreme Court comprises more than forty sentences, accessible with the key phrase "Junta Arbitral del Concierto" (Arbitration Board of the Economic Agreement). At last, professionals and taxpayers have a pathway for the resolution of competence problems related to the Economic Agreement. Before the existence of the Arbitration Board, jurisdictional conflicts seemed to be problems with no solution.

Before the constitution of the Arbitration Board, the Economic Agreement was for many citizens nothing but a source of problems impossible to solve. And this was the feeling mainly of citizens from outside the Basque Country. After the Arbitration Board's implementation, problems originating in the interpretation of the Economic Agreement have become common and solvable problems.

The *iurisprudentia* of the Supreme Court and the resolutions of the Arbitration Board enrich the Economic Agreement with the doctrinal support that corresponds to such an institution. These sentences and resolutions constitute a source of inspiration for the scientific doctrine, generating considerable literature on the subject. Thanks to the Arbitration Board, conflicts, as the source of sentences and resolutions, result in consolidation of the Economic Agreement.

Bibliography

Alonso Arce, Iñaki. "El Tribunal Supremo se pronuncia por primera vez sobre una Resolución de la Junta Arbitral del Concierto Económico," *Forum Fiscal de Bizkaia*, mai 2010: 21–30. Available at: www.conciertoeconomico.org/joomdocs/FFB_2010_ALONSO_El_TS_se_pronuncia_sobre_una_resolucion_JA.pdf.

Aramburu Urtasun, Mikel. *Provincias exentas, Convenio-Concierto. Identidad colectiva de la Vasconia peninsular (1969–2005).* Donostia-San Sebastián: Fundación para el Estudio del Derecho Histórico y Autonómico de Vasconia, 2005. Available at: http:// fedhav.eu/sites/default/files/1echegaray_Aranburu.pdf.

Arana Landín, Sofía. "Conflictos de competencias entre la Administración del Estado y la Diputación Foral de Bizkaia," *Aranzadi Jurisprudencia Tributaria,* no. 14 (2006): 27–40. Available at: http://www.conciertoeconomico.org/joomdocs/autores/ JT-2006_ARANA-S_Conflictos_de%20_competencia_entre_ AGE_y_DFB.pdf.

Burlada Echeveste, José Luis. "Génesis de la Junta Arbitral del Concierto Económico y del Convenio Económico," *Nueva Fiscalidad* 2 (2007): 101–48. Available at: http:// www.conciertoeconomico. org/joomdocs/NFD_2007_BURLADA_J_Genesis_de_la_JA_ del_CE.pdf.

———. "Las relaciones entre la inexistente Junta Arbitral del Concierto Económico y el derecho de acceso a la jurisdicción," *Revista Técnica Tributaria* 83 (2008): 25–52. Available at http:// www. conciertoeconomico.org/joomdocs/RTT_2008_BURLADA_J_ Las_relaciones_entre_la_inexistente_Junt.pdf.

———. and Burlada Echeveste, Inés María. "El fantasma de la Junta Arbitral del Concierto Económico y su consideración como existente: el fin de un pernicioso razonamiento jurídico. Nota a la sentencia del Tribunal Supremo de 10 de julio de 2008," *Quincena Fiscal* 7 (2009): 87–95. Available at http:// www.conciertoeconomico.org/joomdocs/QF_2009_BURLADA_J_El_fantasma_ de_la_Junta_Arbitral.pdf.

Del Burgo Tajadura, Jaime Ignacio. *Origen y fundamento del régimen foral de Navarra,* vol. 12. Pamplona: Biblioteca de Derecho Foral, 1968.

De la Hucha Celador, Fernando. *El régimen jurídico del Convenio Económico de la Comunidad Foral de Navarra.* Donostia-San Sebastián: Fundación para el Estudio del Derecho Histórico y Autonómico de Vasconia, 2006. Available at http:// fedhav.eu/sites/ default/files/2echegaray_delaHucha.pdf.

Estecha Martínez, José María. *Régimen Político Administrativo de las Provincias Vasco Navarras: colección de leyes, decretos, reales órdenes y resoluciones del Tribunal Contencioso Administrativo relativos al País Vasconavarro.* 2nd ed. and appendices I and II. Edited by Joseba Agirreazkuenaga. Bilbao: Instituto de Derecho

Histórico de Euskal Herria / Diputación Foral de Bizkaia, 1997. Available at http:// www.conciertoeconomico.org/phocadownload/regimenprovinciasvasconavarras.pdf.

Martínez Bárbara, Gemma. "Vías de resolución de discrepancias entre las administraciones tributarias en relación con la domiciliación de los contribuyentes en el Concierto Económico," *Zergak: Gaceta Tributaria del País Vasco* 37 (2009): 89–108. Available at www.conciertoeconomico.org/joomdocs/ZERG_2009_MARTINEZ_G_Vias_de_resolucion_de_discrepancias.pdf.

Merino Jara, Isaac. "Acerca de la 'inexistente' Junta Arbitral del Concierto Económico," *Aranzadi Jurisprudencia Tributaria,* no. 6/2006: 23–27. Available at www.conciertoeconomico.org/joomdocs/JT_2006_MERINO_I_Acerca_de_la_inexistente_JA.pdf.

———. "La Junta Arbitral del Concierto Económico," *Revista Vasca de Administración Pública,* no. 75 (2006): 85–104. Available at http://www.conciertoeconomico.org/joomdocs/RVAP_2006_MERINO_I_La_Junta_Arbitral_del_CE.pdf.

Muguruza Arrese, Javier. "Esperando a la Junta Arbitral del Concierto Económico con el País Vasco," *Actualidad Jurídica Aranzadi* 604 (2004): 4–5. Available at http://www.conciertoeconomico.org/joomdocs/autores/AJA-2004_MUGURUZA-J_Esperando_a_la_Junta_Arbitral.pdf.

Orena Domínguez, Aitor. "La tutela judicial efectiva y la falta de Junta Arbitral," *Quincena Fiscal* 10 (2008): 93–96. Available at http://www.conciertoeconomico.org/joomdocs/QF_2008_ORENA_A_La_tutela_judicial_efectiva_y_la_ausencia_de.pdf.

Simón Acosta, Eugenio. "Sujetos y objeto del conflicto ante la Junta Arbitral del Convenio Económico entre el Estado y la Comunidad Foral de Navarra," *Revista Jurídica de Navarra* 48 (2009): 75–105. Available at http://www.navarra.es/home_es/Gobierno+de+Navarra/Organigrama/Los+departamentos/Presidencia+justicia+e+interior/Publicaciones/Revistas/Revista+Juridica+de+Navarra/Sumarios/sumario48.htm

Uriarte Santamarina, Pedro Luis. *Draft papers of the negotiation of the Economic Agreement of the Basque Country of 1981.* Unpublished. Personal file of Mr. Uriarte.

12

Public Policies under a Multilevel Perspective: Tax Policies in Relation to Cooperatives in the Basque Country According to EU Competition Law

Sofía Arana Landín

On the one hand, governments and public bodies have started to recognize the power of social entrepreneurship. Steps are being taken in many Member States and regions to encourage the growth of social enterprises through public policies. Public authorities should fully support the growth of social enterprises through, for example, legal frameworks, access to finance, and business startup and development support and training, as supporting these entities that benefit the general interest can be regarded as an investment in the community. Cooperatives are the main pillar of social economy; thus, public policies supporting them contribute to the community's social progress and welfare.

On the other hand, living, as we do, in a multilevel context, a wider perspective needs to be taken, keeping EU competition law in mind. State aid is a measure taken by some public body to provide, by means of state resources, directly or indirectly, an economic or financial advantage to a beneficiary undertaking that it would not have had under normal circumstances, relieving the beneficiary undertaking of the burden to which its finances would otherwise be subject.

State aid can be seen as adequate to correct market failures in certain activities, when the markets themselves are unable to develop those activities. Thus, state aid control is an essential tool to avoid distortion of competition in the internal market. However, it has evolved with time and it is continually doing so, moving from a basic prohibition to a wide set of rules and case law. This presents a consequent increase in uncertainty and difficulty, both of which become a risk and a handicap to any public policy, as certainty regarding the law and simplicity should guide all sorts of public policies.

We also have to bear in mind that this type of measure did not take into consideration the possibility of multi-territorial Member States, as exist in our case.

Even though the competition model aims only at preventing aid that could significantly distort competition, and not every state aid measure, the latest case law gives us reason to worry, as lately we have seen a significant number of cases regarding public policies in relation to cooperatives. Therefore, any public policy made in regard to this sort of entity should be questioned first in light of article 107.1 TFEU, which establishes a general prohibition of state aid.

What is more, in my opinion, state aid control is being interpreted broadly and improperly used as an indirect means of harmonization with direct taxation. We have to highlight the fact that direct taxation is not an EU competence; rather, because of the principle of subsidiarity, it is a competence belonging to each of the Member States.

Throughout this paper, we will explore the tax policies for Basque cooperatives in our multilevel system and how they can be viewed in light of EU competition law, thus trying to propose a model that cannot be questioned under competition law.[1]

Social Economy Entities in the European Union

As the Strasbourg declaration[2] very recently stated: "Europe's economic and social model needs to reinvent itself." We need growth that is fairer, greener, and anchored in local communities, valuing social cohesion as a genuine source of collective wealth. Therefore, we need to look for a kind of growth that includes not only economic indicators but, above all, social ones. It is time to seek positive social impact while achieving economic progress.

Social economy entities are forms of organization that use democratic governance or participatory principles focusing on social justice. Thus, such entities are recognized as vehicles for social and

---

1. As in the Basque case, as stated by Susana Serrano-Gaztelurrutia in "Jurisdictional...", *Basque Fiscal Systems. History, Current Status and Future Perspectives.* (Reno: Center for Basque Studies, University of Nevada: 2014), 249–87.
2. The Strasbourg declaration took place between January 16 and 17, 2014, when over two thousand social entrepreneurs, representing the rich diversity of the social economy, shared their ideas by approving a common text called "The Strasbourg Declaration."

economic cohesion across Europe, as they help build up a pluralistic and resilient social market economy by looking out for the general interest above other considerations, creating jobs locally, and investing in the community. Therefore, social economy promotes a more sustainable economy, based on values and shared principles that give it the strength to be able to endure economic crises. For example, their profits are usually reinvested with a view to achieving their social objectives so that they are ready for the bad times when they come. This does not come as a surprise, as historically such entities have been born or become particularly stronger in periods of economic crises. Regretfully, it is also at these times that we realize that all that glitters is not gold in the capitalist model.

Most social enterprises are much more concerned with measuring the achievement of their social objectives than their economic performance, and they do not usually compete only on the basis of their production chain but also on the services to the population and their impact on society—for example, reducing inequalities, improving public health, improving living conditions, protecting the environment, and achieving social innovation. According to various EU papers, such entities are as important for the achievement of the EU objectives (the European Parliament Social Economy Intergroup has existed since 1990 and has published several declarations, which are not the object of study of this paper).

What Do We Mean by Social Economy Today?

The understanding of the concept of social economy varies depending on time and space, as it has evolved with the times and will probably continue to do so. This variation in meaning has not contributed to its development but rather has been a handicap in situating and defining social economy in the context of public policies toward it.

Across Europe we have different notions of social economy. For instance, in Belgium the "Conseil Wallon de l'Économie sociale" and in France the "Charte de l'économie sociale"[3] define the term as "the group of entities that do not belong to the public sector which, being operated and managed democratically, and having equal rights and duties for the partners, operate with a special system of ownership and distribution of earnings, employing the excesses from the activity for the growth of the entity and improvement of services to the community."

---

3. Charte de l´économie sociale, *Revue des études coopératives* 9 (1983): 114.

In Spain, the 5/2011 Social Economy Bill created a legal framework that does not aim to replace the current law for each of the different entities in the sector, but instead recognizes and gives greater visibility to the social economy by providing it with greater legal security through actions to define it, and establishes the principles that should be adhered to by the various entities that are part of it. Based on common principles, it includes all those persons and enterprises making up the social economy, as many enterprises share the guiding principles of the social economy: cooperative societies in their various forms, among them those organized based on pooled work; consumption; housing; agriculture; services; maritime work; credit; education; health and transport insurance; labor societies; associations; foundations; mutual societies; special employment agencies; special employment centers; agricultural production societies; and fishermen's associations.

As Suberbiola[4] states: "All these entities are reflected directly or indirectly in article 129.2 of the Spanish Constitution. Their principles give them a specific character that sets them apart from other companies and enterprises in the business world."

The Spanish Social Economy Act not only covers the aforementioned groups and agencies, but also provides a catalog of potential entities that may join the social economy, provided that they fulfill the principles that determine the unique nature of these values and that their specific configuration is perfectly defined. Thus, Article 4 of the Social Economy Act presents the four guiding principles[5] common to all members of the social economy. These are included in Article 5, either through their direct naming in the terms of section 1, or

---

4. Irune Suberbiola, "Régimen tributario de las sociedades laborales: propuestas de reforma," *Revista Vasca de Economía Social* 10, p. 17.

5. Article 4: *Guiding Principles.* The activity of enterprises in the social economy is based on the following guiding principles:

Primacy of individuals and social purpose over capital. This is made clear in the autonomous, transparent, democratic, and participative form of management, which prioritizes a decision-making process based more on individuals and the contribution they make with their work and services to the enterprise, than in terms of their contributions to the share capital.

Distribution of the results obtained from the economic activity, mainly in accordance with the work contributed and service or activity carried out by members and, if applicable, the social purpose that is the object of the enterprise.

Promotion of solidarity within the entity and with society that favors commitment to local development, equal opportunities, social cohesion, the insertion of excluded groups, generation of stable and quality employment and sustainability.

Independence with respect to the public authorities.

through the procedure included in section 2. In this sense, there is a wide enough definition of social economy to allow entities complying with their principles and values to be considered as such.

For Social Economy Europe, social economy actors can be defined based on three markers: primacy of the person and the community objectives; democratic governance and inclusiveness; and collective ownership of the profits and surpluses that are reinvested.

As we can see, there are different definitions and understandings of what the term *social economy* means, but there is a common understanding that cooperatives are its vertebral column.

Why Are Cooperatives Particularly Strong in the Basque Country?

We are motivated to speculate on the reasons why cooperatives are stronger in the Basque Country. Has this development occurred for historical reasons or because of a stronger engagement of the community as such? Could it result from particular public policies? It is likely that a confluence of all possible factors has contributed to the strength of cooperatives in the Basque Country.

To begin with, there is a constitutional mandate, in article 129.2 of the Spanish Constitution, promoting cooperatives and other forms of social economy organizations where workers become partners. Moreover, the Basque Country's Statute of Autonomy (Organic Law 3/1979 of December 18) in article 10 recognizes the exclusive competence of this community regarding social economy: cooperatives, mutual societies, fishermen's associations, other associations, and foundations.

The mandate promoting the social economy, in particular cooperatives, that appears in both of these documents, as well as the fact that cooperatives are a matter of exclusive competence to the Basque Country, are the pillars on which the cooperative movement is anchored and has developed. The strength of the Basque Country's social economy movement comes from the cooperative movement, the greatest exponent of which is the Mondragon Humanity at Work Cooperative Group,[6] which can be regarded as a federation of a democratic nature formed by cooperatives of different types. This entrepreneurial complex is the result of the historical process of integration of the cooperatives related with the Mondragon experience, encouraged by J. M. Arizmendiarrieta. Thus, there are also historical reasons behind it all.

---

6. Previously known as MCC (Mondragón Cooperative Corporation).

The group's guiding principles are as follows:

- *Open admission:* The cooperatives do not discriminate on the basis of religion, political affiliation, ethnicity, or gender when it comes to becoming a member of the cooperative.
- *Democracy:* All authority is vested in the so-called "General Assembly," which consists of all the worker-owners of the enterprise, following the principle of "one person, one vote."
- *Labor over capital:* Labor is the main factor, and capital is only the means to achieve this end. Thus, profits are distributed in terms of the labor provided, and there is a firm commitment to the creation of new jobs. Profits are distributed among the members in proportion to their labor and not on the basis of their holdings in share capital. The pay policy of MCC's cooperatives should also be highlighted, as there must be sufficient remuneration for labor on the basis of solidarity.
- *Participatory management:* This implies the progressive development of self-management with the participation of its members in business management.
- *Solidarity and intercooperation:* These principles are key, not only among owner–workers, but also with other cooperatives, the environment, and the community.

These principles might most probably sound like a U.S. ESOP (Employee Stock Ownership Plan), but there are significant differences. For one thing, our Mondragon model is not only about distribution of profits, but also about the control of the business. For example, the workers internally elect management.

Based on these principles, Basque cooperatives have continually grown and evolved, making them a model at an international level.

Public Policies in Relation to Cooperatives in the Basque Country

First, we must bear in mind that various EU Member States have different legislation on cooperatives, depending on their growth and welfare model, which means that in the European Union, public policies are made in relation to social economy entities in several countries, above all the Mediterranean ones. Their reasons for doing so include their contribution to the general interest; their lower capacity to compete in the market because of their inherent legal obligations and characteristics; their avoidance of economic double taxation; and so on. In some countries, there is a legal recognition (sometimes at a constitutional level) of the need to have adequate legislation adapted to cooperatives. This is our case: public policies regarding cooperatives and other social economy entities where workers acquire part of the stock are required under our laws. Their contribution to the general interest has proved beneficial to the local community in which they are inserted, creating steady jobs and investing in corporate social responsibility.

With respect to the creation of new companies, we must point out that cooperatives have generally behaved in a more dynamic way over the last fifteen years than the rest of the economy in the Basque Country. This process, which generates enterprises, has a tendency of particular importance at a time of crises. However, by the year 2006, the founding of new companies had slowed down somewhat, whereas the number of employees grew in the existing companies. The number of employees in the large cooperatives also grew,[7] as pointed out by Bakaikoa[8] and others.

On the other hand, as we will see, public policies are made at five different levels: at a local level, the foral territory or provincial level, at the regional (Basque Country) level, at the state level, and at the EU level. Substantive legislation for cooperatives is a matter whose competence belongs to the Basque Country. Thus, some differences from general legislation are evident. As a whole, company law requirements for cooperatives are harder to meet under the general legislation. However, as this is a matter attributed to the different Autonomous Communities, each has its own specific law for them; the general legislation is supplementary.

Regarding the basic legislation, we have the 1/1982 Act of February 11. This Act has been updated by the 4/1993 Act of June 24, the 1/2000 Act of June 29, and the 8/2006 Act of December 1. Thus, cooperatives in the Basque Country are covered by different substantive legislation than other sorts of entities, requiring them to make greater effort and preventing them from acting as capitalist enterprises. For instance, 30% of profits are retained by the cooperative to be used to benefit the "common good" of the cooperative (research, develop-

---

7. By virtue of the latest information and in the absence of the publication of Social Economy Statistics, the report for the two-year period 2004–2006, and the Basque Government, 2008.

8. Baleren Bakaikoa, et al., "Public policies for the stimulation of Social Economy in the Basque Country," *The Emergence of Social Economy in Public Policy: An International Analysis* (Brussels: Peter Lang, 2013), 196ff.

ment, job creation, etc.), and the balance goes into capital accounts
for the owner–workers. These funds may be borrowed against at the
cooperative's bank at very low interest rates and are important parts
of the social security arrangements. The cooperatives acknowledge
a duty to contribute to the common good by reinvesting a high proportion of their profits, including regular investments in community
funds for job creation and attending to social security, unemployment, and health insurance requirements.

Thus, these higher substantive requirements impede partner–
workers from receiving the full amount of profits. Therefore, at least
10% of the net surplus must be reserved for the Education and Cooperative Promotion Fund, and at least 20% goes to the Obligatory
Reserve Funds. These funds are not distributable and, if the cooperatives were to become extinct in the Basque Country, they would be
made available to the Council of Cooperatives for the promotion and
spreading of cooperativism. Thus, a minimum of at least 30% of the
annual profits are never going to be returned to owners, and this is a
very important difference from capitalist entities.

This is why public policies, and most particularly tax policies, in
relation to cooperatives must not be considered without taking into
account the effects produced by substantive law in cooperative societies. Only with this fact in mind can we understand why there are
different tax policies.

Public Policies Concerning Cooperatives in the Basque Country

As we have said, both the Spanish Constitution and the Basque Statute of Autonomy coincide in the compulsory promotion of cooperatives. Article 129.2 of the Spanish Constitution of 1978 establishes
that the state must implement cooperative development. The Statute
of Autonomy of the Basque Country (Organic Law, 3/1979 of December 18) in article 10 includes the constitutional mandate, and it
is recognized that the Basque Country has exclusive competence in
cooperative issues. Neither text specifies how to achieve this goal.

However, it is clear that it can only be achieved through the use
of public policies. It is up to the Basque government to decide what
policies are to be used within its competences. It will also be up to the
state and the *foral* territories to do likewise within their competences,
and so will it be for local authorities. Basically, the state will be in
charge of taking measures for the promotion of these entities within
the areas of work, employment, and social security, while the *foral*

territories will be in charge of tax policies concerning entities. The Basque government also has other kinds of public policies for cooperatives, particularly measures of financial aid and technical support. Moreover, local administrations also have the competence over certain local taxes, so they can approve of tax policies concerning cooperatives.

As we can see, there are at least five levels of administration that can approve of public policies in relation to cooperatives: local entities, *foral* territories, the Basque government, the Spanish state, and the European Union. All of them need to coordinate in order to have an adequate system for promoting these cooperatives. Thus, much coordination is necessary both at a vertical and at a horizontal level.

For the purpose of this paper, we will review the public policies concerning cooperatives in the Basque country from small to large— that is, from local entities to those of the European Union—and delve deep into tax policies.

To begin with, a general distinction must be made, according to Chaves,[9] among others, between offer or supply public policies and demand public policies. Powers of offer or supply are those carried out in order to promote the creation and development of the organizations of the social economy as such. We can classify them into three categories: the juridical-financial measures, the measures of financial aid to entities, and the measures of technical support that deal with the real services supplied to the entities. Policies of demand are those that have an influence on the economic activities deployed by the organizations of the social economy. Therefore, the demand-side policies approach does not so much affect the structure itself, stimulating and strengthening the sector, but rather aims to support it in everything it does by encouraging the economic activity it performs. Thus, through public spending, public administrations are great demanders of goods and services offered by the private sector. In this context, the public authorities can promote cooperatives by facilitating their access to the condition of supplier of the public sector. We have to admit that this kind of policy has not been developed yet in the Basque Country, as Garcia Arejula recently noted.[10] However, the new Proposal of Directive for Public Procurement states the mandate

---

9. Rafael Chaves, "Public Policies and Social Economy in Spain and Europe," *CIRIEC, Revista de Economía Pública, Social y Cooperativa,* 62 (October 2008)..

10. Jesús Garcia Arejula, *Contratación pública y Economía Social en Euskadi: 2010–2012,* PhD dissertation, defended January 31, 2014 and not yet published.

of social clauses in public procurement, which leaves an open door to demand policies concerning not only cooperatives, but also other forms of social economy.

Local Policies Relating to Cooperatives

Local policy is the first level in our multilevel system. At a local level, there are a limited number of measures that can be taken for the promotion of cooperatives. Basically, local entities can choose to exempt cooperatives from certain taxes and some possible operations regarding the constitution of the cooperative from the taxes on capital transfers and documented legal acts, the economic activities tax, and the immovable property tax.

However, in my opinion, these are minor benefits, as the taxes on capital transfers and documented legal acts are just occasional taxes and the possible exemption only regards the constitution of the cooperative and not any other sort of operation. Moreover, they are minor taxes compared to others.

Regarding the economic activities tax, this possible exemption used to be important, but after the exemption was extended to all entities having a volume of operations under €1,000,000, it can no longer be said to be an exemption for cooperatives. Moreover, in relation to the immovable property tax, it is a negligible benefit, as it only concerns the exemption of payments relating to rural land and certain agricultural cooperatives, and only below a very low amount.

Over the last decade, the European Commission has decided that various fiscal benefits constitute state aid, so we have to analyze whether these fiscal policies relating to cooperatives at a local level may constitute state aid.

Regarding the immovable property tax—the only tax that is not occasional and that most enterprises pay—more than 95% of this tax revenue comes from what is called "urban property," with "rural" property making up just a tiny part of this tax. Concerning cooperatives, the benefit conferred to them applies only to agricultural cooperatives and only for rural properties of very little amounts. That is to say, we are only referring to a very tiny percentage of what this tax could mean. For the most part, particularly for the part that means most of its revenue, the immovable property tax does not have any sort of special benefit for cooperatives, so it could be considered a tiny part of a minor tax and fall under the consideration of "de minimis." We have to remember that aid amounts of up to €200,000 per undertaking over a three-year period are exempted from the state aid procedure. There cannot be a single case surpassing this sum, as the benefit falls way under the limit. The tax rebate granted needs to be calculated first so that there are clear numbers indicating what it really represents.

Thus, public policies regarding local taxes are not covered in the order of January 23, 2014, under the reference T-156/10 for Spanish agricultural cooperatives. This order does not enter into these issues, rather it merely denies the Spanish Confederation of Cooperatives and the Association of Agricultural Cooperatives legitimacy and status as interested parties in the matter. In my opinion, they would most probably fall under the category of "de minimis," so there is no risk in maintaining them.

Foral or Historical Territories' Tax Policies Regarding Cooperatives

Moving to the second level, we must first emphasize that each of the foral territories (Gipuzkoa, Bizkaia, and Araba) forming the Basque Country and Navarre is fully competent to legislate most of its taxes. Particularly important is the fact that legislative and applicative powers regarding both personal income tax and corporate income tax belong to each of the foral territories. In this way, foral territories have a clear say in these matters. Thus, direct taxation and many indirect taxation powers belong to these territories according to the Spanish Constitution and the Economic Agreement.[11]

The taxation of the cooperatives is based on the Basque tax system covered in the Economic Agreement, and the regional norms developed from this agreement regarding cooperatives belong to each of the foral territories or provinces. Public policies regarding these taxes are probably the most important ones. We have to highlight the fact that, even though other entities may have a say in certain taxes (such as we have seen with local entities) the most important tax for cooperatives, without any doubt, is company income tax—and this tax is the domain of the foral territories (Gipuzkoa, Bizkaia, and Araba). The obvious consequence is that within this level there are three coordinated systems. There are some small differences that might become important in some cases, but there is a certain coordination regarding the taxation of cooperatives in the different territories. This is probably because of the "Tax Coordination Organ," whose objective is to achieve a certain consensus over the basics of all taxes attributed to the three foral territories.

---

11. Additional Disposition no. 1, 1978, Spanish Constitution.

The main differences between taxation of cooperatives within the Basque Country and those in Spain are based in this tax. In this sense, cooperatives located in the Basque Country have a privileged situation compared with those in Spain, where the system is unnecessarily complicated, as a distinction is required in all operations between what is considered a cooperative operation and what is considered an extra-cooperative one. Needless to say, it is not always clear whether a particular operation can be characterized as one or the other. Such a distinction is the basis of a dual system in which the taxation of extra-cooperative results is different from the taxation of cooperative results. This situation generates very harsh indirect costs to cooperatives as the system becomes very burdensome, and thus it creates uncertainty.

Each of the Historical Territories has its income tax, and cooperatives have a so-called "special regime" regarding this tax. No distinction needs to be made between one sort of profit and the other, so all profits go to the same taxable base, as in any other sort of enterprise. However, as we have previously seen, there are certain substantive requirements regarding cooperatives that call for specificities relating to this tax—to begin with, the amounts that are compulsorily saved in the so-called "compulsory funds."

Each historical territory of the Basque Country has its own cooperative tax system, in which the regulation of the corporate tax applicable to the cooperatives is considered. In 2008, the corporate tax system of the Basque Country was reformed, establishing that small cooperatives should pay taxes at a rate of 18%, while large cooperatives should pay taxes at a rate of 20%, a reduction of one point with respect to the previous ones. Meanwhile, the tax rate applied to companies, generally speaking, has gone down from 32.5% to 28%, and for small and medium-sized companies, this rate has gone from 30% to 24%. This means that cooperatives do have privileged rates, but they are less privileged now than they were before, as we find a tendency toward convergence in the tax rates of cooperatives and commercial enterprises. This measure can be said to promote cooperatives, and should be considered in light of competition law.

The same has been happening in Italy over the last decade. Thus, article 12 of the 907/1977 Act of 16 December and articles 10 and 11 of the Presidential Decree have lost their attractiveness, as a series of laws has been passed in order to generally extend these benefits, and thus comply with EU law.

Apart from these differences in the tax rates, the cooperatives enjoy rebates regarding the taxable amount. Of the basic taxable amount, the yearly amounts saved in the Compulsory Reserve Funds are reduced by 50%, and the amounts dedicated to the Obligatory Cooperative Education and Promotion Fund can be totally reduced, provided that this fund is constituted with under 30% of the net surpluses. Again, this measure needs to be regarded under the light of competition law.

Other measures that were intended for cooperatives in the past have been broadly applied to other types of operations, such as in the case of depreciation allowances.

Cooperatives can be divided into two classes: protected cooperatives and specially protected ones. As regards the second category, such cooperatives enjoy a 50% tax rebate that, again, reflects a tax policy designed to benefit this sort of cooperative.

Again, we can learn some lessons about these measures from case law, as some of our measures are equivalent to others in Italy and Spain, and there already exist some pronouncements on the matter by the European Court of Justice (ECJ). Of particular importance is the ruling on Paint Graphos of September 8, 2011.[12]

Measures Concerning the Classification of Cooperatives

To begin with, an element that I personally think should be revised within our system is the division of cooperatives into three types: cooperatives without protection, the so-called "protected cooperatives," and those termed "specially protected." Cooperatives without protection are those validly inscribed in their register that have not complied with all the rules for cooperatives: for instance, they can lose their protection if they do not audit when they have an obligation to do so, when they have workers over 50% as compared to members, when their operations involving non-members surpass 50%, and so on.

The second category, specially protected cooperatives, includes agricultural, educational, consumer, labor, and in Bizkaia, home-building cooperatives. In the Basque Country, unlike in Spain, fishermen's cooperatives are not included in this category, whereas educational or housing cooperatives are not included in this category in Spain. Otherwise, the included groups are the same in the Basque Country and in Spain.

---

12. In two joined cases, C78/08 and C80/08.

The "protected" but not "specially protected" cooperatives include all others that do not form part of the previously described groups in the Basque Country. The only difference in taxation is the 50% rebate that the specially protected cooperatives have. In my opinion, this difference between one category and the other should not be maintained any longer, as it does not correspond to a real need to protect one type more than the others, and it is probably an issue that will raise objections under EU law. The fact that some cooperatives enjoy a 50% rebate while others do not, without specified justification, could possibly be considered state aid. The selectivity criterion is clearly fulfilled in this case, thus I would recommend its elimination. It is clearly a benefit and not a technical adjustment, and it would probably not last long if studied under EU competition law.

Deduction of Profits Compulsorily Allocated to Indivisible Funds

A second measure in our system that can be examined in light of EU competition law mandates that the amount that must be allotted to the Compulsory Reserve Funds is deductible in full or part. The amounts annually transferred into the Compulsory Reserve Fund are deductible at 50%, while the yearly amount devoted to the Educational Fund is totally deductible.

In my opinion, there is no justification for the differences between one and the other; both of them could be totally deductible, as they are both compulsory funds created for the general interest and are non-distributable, even in the event that the cooperative collapses. Owner–workers will never receive any of the profits compulsorily donated to these funds. We have to bear in mind that these funds amount to at least 30% of annual profits. In a way, these funds act as a parafiscal tax. This is why I cannot see any impediment to make them totally deductible.

At the EU level, this measure does not seem to pose a problem. Similar funds exist for Italian cooperatives, and they are also deductible. Again, recent cases give us an idea of what the Commission thinks about this issue. In the case of Coopitalia, one of the measures at stake is precisely the exemption for transfers to reserves. Regarding this case, the Commission has already expressed the following:

> [...] the deduction from taxable income of prevalently mutual cooperatives of the profits allocated to indivisible or divisible reserves corresponding to revenues generated from non-members of the cooperative. For large cooperatives and non-mutual cooperatives, the totality of

the deduction is considered to be aid, because where the members are not really involved in the cooperative the company seems more similar to a profit-making company. These deductions are, however, considered compatible aid for obligatory indivisible reserves and in the case of SMEs for all indivisible reserves.

We have to bear in mind that in the Basque case, we are speaking of obligatory and indivisible reserves that are non-distributable, even in the case when the cooperative collapses. Thus, they should be regarded as compatible with EU law even if the deduction of the annual profits devoted to the compulsory funds were total. Thus, there is a margin here to make the deduction of 100% in the case of transfers both to the Educational Fund and to the Compulsory Reserves Fund.

Lower Tax Rates

Regarding a third measure for cooperatives, the tax rate of 18% for small and medium-sized ones, as opposed to a 24% general rate for small and medium-sized companies and the 20% rate for all other cooperatives as opposed to a 28% general rate, there is a difference of six points in the rate for small and medium-sized companies and a difference of eight points in the rate for cooperatives and other types of companies, generally speaking.

However, the following should be highlighted: First, there is a tendency toward convergence of tax rates with this tax, as tax rates for other enterprises have gone down from 32.5% to 28%, and the tax rate for cooperatives has only been reduced by one point. Thus, generally speaking, there has been a reform reducing the rate for cooperatives by 4.5 points.

Regarding small and medium-sized companies, the general rate has decreased from 30% to 24%, while in cooperatives it has only been reduced by one point, from 19% to 18%. This means that the difference in most cases is four points, compared to the general rate for small and medium enterprises, which describes a vast majority of firms.

Second, the regime for cooperatives is just one of the special regimes, and there are many other special tax rates for other kind of entities, depending on their legal form. Although, under EU law, this difference might be seen as indicative of a selective aid, the same would happen with all other cases. This leads us to the instance of a compulsory harmonization of tax rates in EU cases—a compulsory harmonization of rates of a direct tax! This is not what the European

Union was created for, but the improper use of EU competition law and particularly of article 107.1 can lead us to this absurd conclusion.

However, differences in tax rates because of a different legal structure can be seen as state aids under EU competition law. A recent case proving this point in social economy and affecting a Basque association is the Commission's decision of March 7, 2014 concerning soccer clubs in the category of sports association clubs. There are four soccer clubs affected by this decision: the Real Madrid Soccer Club; the Barcelona Soccer Club; Osasuna, from the Navarre Soccer Club; and the Athletic, from the Bilbao Soccer Club. The Commission applies a difference in tax rate of 5 points from other clubs, as all the others are considered companies and are taxed at a 30% rate, while these clubs are considered sports associations and are taxed at a 25% rate, constituting state aid. What is more, the Commission highlights the fact that it is not only a state aid, but an unlawful one, as there can be no possible justification for it. Thus, in the end, different tax rates for different types of enterprises can be seen as constituting state aid.

Public Policies Relating to Cooperatives at the Basque Country Level

As Bakaikoa[13] states, almost all public policies in the Basque Country are supply-oriented, and much financial aid and tax aid is granted. According to his studies, public policies of the social economy developed by the public administration of the Basque Country have, to a great extent, been channeled toward the development, promotion, and consolidation of the Mondragon cooperatives: "It could be said that the current institutional and legislative framework of the Social Economy is a result of the demands made especially by Mondragon, thanks to its influence and social repercussion."

A large number of entities provide institutional recognition to cooperatives, help them through the creation process, and promote the cooperative movement. Among them are those devoted to social economy; furthermore, we can name the following ones specifically devoted to cooperatives:

- Directorate for Cooperatives and Council of Basque Cooperatives, a public entity with a consultative and advisory role within

---

13. Baleren Bakaikoa et al., "Public Policies for the Stimulation of Social Economy in the Basque Country," *The Emergence of Social Economy in Public Policy: An International Analysis* (Peter Lang: Brussels, 2013).

the Basque Public Administration and research centers in each university in order to promote the culture of cooperativism.

- KONFEKOOP, the Basque cooperatives confederation, an organization comprising the Basque cooperatives federations, set up in 1996 in order to promote the cooperative movement. It now represents 868 cooperatives, employing over 56,000 workers.
- The Directorate of Social Economy, included within the framework of the Organic Functional Structure of the Department of Employment and Social Affairs, manages the Register of Cooperatives and labor companies, training programs, and above all, it annually approves different aid programs for this sector.
- Oinarri, S. G. R., a mutual guarantee society in which the Council of Cooperatives of the Basque Country invests, which specializes in providing social economy entities and Basque small and medium-sized enterprises with financial and technical guarantors. It currently operates for *all types* of small and medium-sized enterprises.
- Elkar-Lan, a second-degree cooperative promoting the creation of employment in the cooperatives and offering free advice regarding not only the start-up process, but also mentoring for a period of one year following its establishment as a cooperative.
- ERKIDE, a federation of cooperatives that promotes certain types of cooperatives such as educational, labor, and credit coops.
- Bitartu: Administrative Dispute Resolution of Conflicts in Cooperatives (arbitration, reconciliation, mediation, and intermediation), an ADR, created to resolve conflicts among cooperatives, worker–partners, and cooperatives and their worker–partners. It belongs to the organizational structure of the Basque Council of Cooperatives.
- PROMOKOOP Foundation, devoted to the Promotion of Cooperatives. This foundation was established by Mondragon and the Confederation of Cooperatives of the Basque Country, and the Council of Cooperatives of the Basque Country has also joined it on equal footing. This foundation manages a fund aimed at defining and implementing cooperative projects of a strategic nature.

However, the Basque government's subsidy policy is what will most likely pose problems in relation to EU law, as Basque cooperatives not only benefit from general programs, but also from particular ones geared to them. Nevertheless, it is not the purpose of this paper to review the specific amounts or programs, as these are published annually and there is already a magnificent paper devoted to the subject by Bakaikoa, et al.[14]

Spanish Public Policies Affecting Basque Cooperatives

Several policies apply to all enterprises, others apply to small and medium enterprises as well as cooperatives, and still others are particularly intended for cooperatives. However, we will not delve into these here, because neither the substantive cooperative law nor tax law pertain to this level.

Measures at an EU Level

At an EU level, there has been a certain contradiction among the different documents promoting cooperatives and competition law. Among the earliest, we find the communication from the Commission on the promotion of cooperative societies in Europe,[15] and Regulation no. 1435/2003 on the Statute for the European Cooperative Society. However, until recently, these documents had never been applied in competition law. Theory is one thing; practice, another. The European Court's judgment of September 8, 2011 refers to these texts and highlights the need for cooperatives to stick to the principles of primacy of the individual, non-distribution of net assets and reserves, democracy, mutuality, and sharing of the profits in accordance with the activities carried out by the cooperative, thus changing course.

Interpretation of Article 107.1 TFEU Today

Over the last decade, different tax systems for cooperatives have been questioned in European cases as possible breaches of article 107.1 of the Treaty of Functioning of the European Union,[16] thus concerning certain tax measures and the system as it is a possible state aid. This has created uncertainty, not only for cooperatives, but also for all other entities within social economy.

---

14. B. Bakaikoa, et al.

15. COM (2004), p. 18.

16. Art. 107 regulates state aids as measures which are taken by some public body and which, by means of state resources, directly or indirectly, give a beneficiary undertaking an economic or financial advantage that it would not have had under normal circumstances, and that relieves the beneficiary undertaking of a burden to which its finances would otherwise normally be subject.

Some of the tax measures applying to cooperatives can be regarded as technical adjustments, others as pure tax benefits—the latter seeking the promotion of the cooperative model. Thus, every European member state has different substantive and tax regulations for cooperatives, which is seen as a problem for competition law, as it is not always clear when those differences are, strictly speaking, just technical adjustments and when those differences imply a benefit. For instance, national laws require different percentages of the activities of cooperatives to be shared among members in order to get a special tax treatment,[17] while others allow cooperatives the option to foresee in their statutes the possibility of acting with third parties, as long as these activities do not acquire more importance than the ones with members, such as in the cases of Holland and Norway. For instance, some national cooperative laws allow them to have members who are only interested in the return on capital, while others require that all their members are users or workers. In any case, remuneration of members for the capital subscribed is always limited. Regarding remuneration of members for transactions carried with them, a cooperative can only distribute returns *pro rata* to the number of these transactions. Thus, it is totally understandable that their contribution to the general budget, in the form of taxes, can be lower than that of other sorts of undertakings that, unlike cooperatives, do not internalize social costs and are subject to different tax policies depending on their constraints and context.

We can consider the uncertainty caused by the questioning of any system to be a potential risk for other countries, too. This uncertainty, particularly at times of crisis, can only cause problems. In some Member States in the European Union (such as Spain, France, and Italy), certain measures concerning cooperativism have been regarded as potentially suspicious when examined in light of state aid. The same thing has happened with countries of the European Free Trade Association, such as Norway. At this moment, certain tax measures concerning cooperatives are being carefully studied by the ECJ in order to ascertain their compatibility with competence regulations.

Keep in mind that the Commission undertakes economic analysis to determine whether state aid exists or whether state aid is compatible with the Treaty of Functioning of the European Union.[18] However, the balancing test is only applicable where compatibility

---

17. As in the cases of Italy, Spain, and Denmark.
18. From here on: TFEU.

guidelines provide for it or where state aid does not fall within the scope of existing compatibility guidelines.

Given that state aid control remains an essential tool to avoid unfair distortion of competition in the internal market, it is also true that until now, EU state aid policy has moved from a basic prohibition to a wide set of rules and case law, with a consequent increase in efficiency and difficulty. However, all that glitters is not gold, and article 107 can be said to have had undesired results for the achievement of the general interest in certain cases, as is the case with cooperatives.

Article 107(1) TFEU[19] establishes a general prohibition of state aid. According to this article, a measure needs to fulfill four cumulative criteria in order to qualify as state aid:

1. There must be an advantage.
2. State resources must be used.
3. The advantage must be selective.
4. The measure must effectively or potentially distort competition and affect (or threaten to affect) trade between Member States.

The First Condition: The Existence of an Advantage

The measure must confer an advantage to the recipient in order to constitute state aid. What can we consider to be an advantage? Even though not explicitly defined by article 107.1 of the TFEU, this is a very general concept that includes grants or interest rate rebates, loan guarantees, accelerated depreciation allowances, capital injections, tax exemptions, the purchase of land at less than the market price, the selling of land at higher than market price, privileged access to infrastructure without paying a fee, the obtaining of risk capital from the state on favorable terms, and so on. Thus, any possible benefit that an undertaking, a number of undertakings, or a sector have in comparison to others can be considered to be an advantage. In short, a measure entails an advantage when it reduces, even hypothetically speaking, a tax burden.

There are two important issues to be explored here: first, the concept of undertaking(s), and second, the framework of comparison, since, depending on that frame of reference, an advantage will or will

---

19. "Except as otherwise provided in the Treaties, any aid granted by a Member State or through State resources in any form whatsoever which distorts or threatens to distort competition by favoring certain undertakings or the production of certain goods shall, insofar as it affects trade between Member States, be incompatible with the internal market."

not be considered to be one (as we will see when we deal with the concept of selectiveness).

The TFEU does not define what it considers to be "an undertaking," so we need to refer to case law in order to define it. This point is crucial for the purpose of this paper, as some social economy entities cannot, strictly speaking, be considered undertakings. Thus, non-profit entities can be considered undertakings for this purpose because although they do not seek economic profit, that does not exclude them from state aid control, as far as they carry out an economic activity. In this sense, when an entity carries out both economic and non-economic activities, it is only considered an undertaking with regard to the former.

The ECJ resolved this matter in Klöckner,[20] which states that: "An undertaking is constituted by a single organization of personal, tangible and intangible elements, attached to an autonomous legal entity and pursuing a given long-term economic aim." Thus, what needs to be emphasized is that the legal nature of the beneficiary, or whether it is a public or private entity, is irrelevant. However, we have to make clear that even though the concept of cooperatives is fully included in the definition of undertakings, cooperatives have distinctive features that make them different, and some of the legal measures adopted in this sense are fully understandable and coherent with the system.

Article 54 of the TFEU recognizes the fact that there are different forms of undertakings. However, as regards the possible different rights of such undertakings, there is not always a clear approach.

The Second Condition: The Rise of State Resources

This requirement implies that there must be a consumption of public financial resources, including all levels of public authorities, regarding the different powers exercised by the executive, legislative, and judicial authorities. The legal nature of the institution granting aid can vary and can include not only public entities but also agencies, public companies under state control, and private entities directly or indirectly controlled by the state.[21] Thus, any sub-state entity, such as a region or local entity, can be a donor of state aid in the same way as federal or central authorities, as resolved in the so-called "Azores case."[22] What is important is the fact that there is no need for a real

---

20. See ECJ, *Klöckner v High Authority*, Joint Cases 17 and 20/61.

21. ECJ, *Helenic Republic v Commission*, Case C-57/86; ECJ, *Déménagements-Manutention Transport SA*, Case C-256/97.

22. CFI, *Territorio Histórico de Álava and others v Commission*, Joint Cases T-227 to

transfer of resources, as a subsidy; compliance with this condition is based on the possibility of an advantage if, hypothetically speaking, fewer resources could be raised because of a possible benefit.

The Third Condition: The Selectivity of the Advantage

There are two kinds of selectivity: material and territorial.

Material Selectivity

The advantage becomes state aid only if it is selective, meaning that it favors certain undertakings and not all of them. Therefore, general measures that apply to all sectors of the economy of a member state are not considered aid, as long as they do not have the ultimate effect of favoring certain undertakings, even if they follow objective criteria and are granted to an indefinite number of beneficiaries.[23] On the other hand, measures limited to an economic sector are materially selective. Moreover, measures that apply to different or all sectors of the economy can also be qualified as selective where they favor certain activities.

We need to know what the framework of comparison is in order to ascertain that there is an advantage. Two important issues arise here: first, the tax in question or the system as a whole, and second, the territory to be compared with. As regards the framework of comparison, the Surveillance Authority in a case of tax benefits for cooperatives in Norway considers that the comparison framework in regard to tax should be the corporate income tax.

In the Spanish case, we had two decisions. In the first, both personal income tax and corporate income tax had to be evaluated in order to ascertain the real tax. In the second one, only corporate income tax was the frame of reference.[24]

Regarding case law in Italy, regrettably, we also have two different considerations. In the communication of June 18, 2008, the Commission considered the following: "Since the measures considered constitute a derogation for Italian company Law it should be understood that the frame of reference is the Italian Company Tax."[25]

If the framework chosen is corporate income tax, it is the general regime of corporate income tax for capital-based companies and not any other sort of companies. As we can see, this conclusion leads us

---

229, 265, 266, and 270/01 *par.* 178.

23. GC, *CETM v Commission*, Case T-55/99, *par.* 40.

24. Pp.166–67.

25. EI/2008 of 18 June, p. 55.

toward an indirect harmonization of the different legal types of companies that need to be considered. It is obviously not a real objective of the EU treaties according to their wording, and it is clearly against the principle of neutrality.[26]

In relation to the first of the Italian cases where the Commission and the AG[27] said it was correct to consider the bonus as a cost to the cooperative, as it was possible to accept that the deduction responded to the logic of combining company tax with personal income tax, Alguacil[28] states the following: "We could not agree more with this argument. Moreover, it implies that a tax levy lower than the general rate, as happens in Spain, on non-distributed bonuses (which are earnings from operations with members above the market value) cannot be described as an incentive."

However, the ruling of the ECJ of September 8, 2011 concerning the Italian tax measures in relation to cooperatives adopts a different view because when dealing with the issue of selectivity it says that for the so-called "derogation test," the benchmark taken into account is the corporation tax. Moreover, it considers that there is an exception in the treatment of cooperatives.

Territorial Selectivity

Regarding the frame of reference as the member state of the company, there are also important issues to be dealt with here because of what is known as "territorial selectivity," which is of particular relevance to the Basque case. Generally speaking, the framework of comparison is that of the member state itself, unless certain criteria established in the Azores judgment are fulfilled. This is to say, the fact that there might be a 10% Company tax rate in Ireland does not matter if you have a 32.5% rate as compared to a 35% general rate in your member state. Thus, this last rate might be considered state aid if, in the framework of comparison that the ECJ uses, there is a higher rate, just initially happened with the 35% rate in Spain and the 32.5% rate in the Basque Territories.

Needless to say, nowadays, in a place where there is freedom of movement of persons, capital, and workers, a 10% company tax rate may attract companies to move there, while a difference of 2.5 points

---

26. Contrary to what is stated in the Opinion of the Economic and Social Committee on "Different types of enterprise," October 1, 2009, CESE 1454/2009.

27. Opinion of Advocate Jääskinen of July 8, 2010.

28. María Pilar Alguacil, "Tax Treatment of Cooperatives in Europe under the State Aid Rules," in *Genossenschaften im Fokus* (Vienna: 2011).

within a member state does not, as we are still speaking of a difference of more than 20 points between the rate of the European Union (not taking into account the existence of tax havens physically near the state) and a 2.5 rate.

This framework of comparison becomes particularly important in our example, as the exception confirms the rule in the Azores case.[29] Briefly, in the Azores' judgment, the fundamental question was whether the tax reductions at issue could be regarded as a measure of general application in the Azores, or whether it was, rather, a selective measure that was at issue, conferring an advantage solely on operators established in the Azores, as compared with those operating in Portugal. The ECJ considered that, in the Azores case,[30] three conditions had to be fulfilled in order to consider the measure of state aid in light of article 87.1 (now 107.1 TFEU): institutional, procedural, and economic autonomy.

Thus, first, the region must be autonomous in an institutional, procedural, and economic sense in order for it to be possible to consider the measure not of a selective nature.[31] Indeed, in the Azores judgment, the Court took the view that in order for a decision to be regarded as having been adopted in the exercise of sufficiently autonomous powers, it must have been made by a regional or local authority that has, from a constitutional point of view, a political and administrative status separate from that of the central government. Second, it must have been adopted without the central government's direct intervention regarding its content. Third and finally, the financial consequences of a reduction of the national tax rate for undertakings in the region must not be offset by aid or subsidies from other regions or the central government. The Court reiterated those principles, with certain clarifications, in the UGT-Rioja case. With regard to the third condition, it stated in particular that it was a question of "economic and financial autonomy."[32]

The judgment report pointed out that, although in the case of the Portuguese region the first two requirements might be fulfilled,

---

29. This question is studied in Susana Serrano-Gaztelurrutia, *El Concierto Económico vasco ante el juez comunitario* (Oñati: IVAP, 2012).

30. Case 088/03, *Portugal v.Commission* 2006, ERC I -7115 Azores.

31. 191.

32. B. Bahia Almansa, "El regimen fiscal especial de las cooperativas y su compatibilidad con la normativa sobre ayudas de Estado," *CIRIEC, España Revista Jurídica de Economia Social y Cooperativa*, 22 (December 2011), 67–72.

real economic autonomy does not exist in the case of the adopted fiscal measurement, since it is the Portuguese state that finances the decrease of income provoked by the reduction of the tax rate. Therefore, it is not the region that takes charge of this loss of income, which is evidence of economic dependency. Under these circumstances, the community Court decided not to sign the Portuguese theses. However, these three requirements are fulfilled in the Basque case, so the framework for comparison becomes that of the Basque Country, not that of the member state[33] or the Historical Territories.

Other important cases of regional taxation regarding sufficient institutional, procedural, and economic autonomy where we can learn about the ECJ criteria in relation to the Basque Country include Case C-428/06, UGT v. Basque Region, (2008) ERC-I 6747, Case T-211/04, Gibraltar v. Commission, (2008) ERC- I 3745; and C 106-09 P Commission v. Gibraltar, (2011) ERC-I nyr.

The Fourth Condition: The Distortion (or Threat of Distortion) of Competition and Trade Between Member States

This condition is, in reality, a requirement that ends up being taken for granted. Theoretically speaking, the definition of state aid requires that it distort competition. However, a very extensive interpretation of the letter of the law leads this condition to a merely potential one: the condition is fulfilled by the mere threat of distortion, and again, the need to affect trade becomes extended to a potential grade. Thus, even in cases where there has not been a distortion of competition affecting Member States, and even in cases where there is not even trade of this kind between Member States, its potentiality can be taken for granted. Thus, once the selective nature of the aid is declared, the Commission can assume that competition is likely to be distorted and trade is likely to be affected, without showing any kind of evidence.

This kind of automatic assumption of a distortive effect on competition forecloses the possibility of counterbalancing the wide application of selectivity. A narrower approach could consider that a measure does not constitute state aid if it does not effectively change the position of competing undertakings in comparison with the beneficiaries.

---

33. For further information, see Susana Serrano, "La incidencia de las ayudas de Estado en las cooperativas vascas," *Revista Vasca de Economía Social*, 7 (2011) 32–46.

Are Compatible Instances of State Aid Possible?

To determine whether an exception has been made, various instances of case law state that the existence of the exception needs to be determined by the effects of the measure and not by its motives or objectives.

According to the *Paint Graphos* judgment, a global consideration of the burdens and advantages of each regime is necessary to determine whether an advantage exists, and this means an open door for cooperatives, based on their principles. The principle of mutuality had been used by the Commission in the Italian case prior to this judgment. However, the fact that they only understood it in terms of purely mutual cooperatives was of no help.

Nevertheless, the judgment of the ECJ of September 8, 2011, concerning the Italian cooperatives (joint cases C-78/08 and C-80/08, also known as the *Paint Graphos* case)—against the opinion given by the Advocate General[34] in the matter—states that, regarding the comparability test, the cooperatives include features distinguishing them from other types of businesses and that would justify a different tax treatment. This was highlighted by Regulation no. 1435/2003 on the Statute of the European Cooperative Society and the communication of the Commission on the promotion of cooperatives in Europe.

These principles are seen in the second paragraph concerning the principles of Mondragon cooperativism: primacy of the individual, non-distribution of net assets and reserves, democracy, and mutuality. Thus, the Court, stating that "The profit margin of this particular kind of company is considerably lower than that of capital companies, which are better able to adapt to market requirements," considered that, cooperatives cannot, in principle, be regarded as being in a comparable factual and legal situation to that of commercial companies.

This is a very important case in regard to cooperatives; after the questioning of the Spanish and Italian systems and the extensive interpretation of all requirements in order to ascertain that there had been an advantage, the Court of Justice introduced some common sense to the situation. In effect, a truly important difference was established between *true* cooperatives and others. We have to bear in mind that, as we have seen, in many countries there has been a relaxation of the principles in cooperatives. However, Basque cooperatives have remained true to their principles, so the arguments in *Paint Graphos* must be welcomed, as "true cooperatives are those that conform to

---

34. Advocate General Jääskinen, July 8, 2010.

particular operating principles which clearly distinguish them from other economic operators."[35]

The characteristics that distinguish true cooperatives from other ones are those in the Statutes for a European Cooperative:

1. "Control of cooperatives should be vested equally in members, as reflected in our 'one man, one vote' rule. Reserves and assets are therefore commonly held, non-distributable and must be dedicated to the common interests of members."[36] Basque cooperatives strictly follow this.

2. As regards the operation of cooperative societies, in light of the primacy of the individual, "their activities should be conducted for the mutual benefit of the members, who are at the same time users, customers or suppliers, so that each member benefits from the cooperative's activities in accordance with his participation in the cooperative and his transactions with it."[37] Basque cooperatives do follow this principle, as there are restrictions to operations with third parties, solidarity, and a basic principle is that humans come first.

3. Cooperative societies have no or limited access to equity markets and are therefore dependent for their development on their own capital or credit financing. That is because shares in cooperative societies are not listed on the stock exchange and, therefore, not widely available for purchase. Moreover, as is also made clear by antecedent no. 10 in the preamble to Regulation No. 1435/2003, there is limited interest on loan and share capital, which makes investment in a cooperative society less advantageous.[38] Consequently, the profit margin of this particular kind of company is considerably lower than that of capital companies, which are better able to adapt to market requirements. As for Basque cooperatives, there are strict rules about it, so they can be said to comply with it.

In this case, it is remarked that the cooperatives compliant with the cooperative model "cannot, in principle, be regarded as being in a comparable factual and legal situation to that of commercial companies."[39]

---

35. Paragraph 55.
36. Antecendent no. 67.
37. Antecedent no. 68.
38. Antecedent no. 69–70.
39. Paragraph 61.

The national judge must ascertain if these requirements are complied with, and if the cooperative does not meet the necessary criteria, ascertain whether the measure at stake complies with the principles of consistency and proportionality, with a systematic interpretation of all tax law. Only when the national judge understands that the given measure is constitutive of state aid must he or she ask for the intervention of the European Commission against the state in the name of which he administers justice.

This is a common-sense and radically different new approach to state aid. It is true that it is just a particular case. However, the Commission and other judges should note this new interpretation of EU law because, with all the case law we have had until now, we were about to come to the point of harmonizing direct taxation for the sake of competition law and ended up with the other kinds of distinctions.

Case Law Concerning State Aid for Cooperatives

Although our system of public policies in relation to cooperatives has not been rejected yet, we have to admit that there are measures that need to be seen either as technical adjustments or as benefits. In the second case, our system could be seen as having State aid, according to article 107.1 TFEU.

The specificity of cooperatives in the ECJ case law as regards State aid has been recognized in very distinct cases. However, there is no clear tendency in the matter. By examining cases concerning different countries, we can see certain statements that can be considered for our case.

The Spanish system, without any doubt, is not only most similar to the Basque system, but also directly or indirectly affects our case most, as some of the measures are very similar and some general regulations can also be applicable to our case, since they coincide with those established by the 20/1990, of July 27, on Cooperatives' Fiscal Regime in Spain, which have already been questioned by the Commission.

Thus, I find it necessary to review a case concerning Spanish cooperatives that ended up questioning the whole system, although, theoretically speaking, it should only have pertained to certain measures for agricultural cooperatives. The case in question has been recently resolved by an order on January 23, 2014, avoiding most of the problems that were at stake, though they had not been named as such.

However, we can review the compatibility of these benefits with EU law according to the most recent case law. The case law that raises questions about these tax benefits at a local level began in 2009 when the General Commissioner annulled the decision regarding Spanish agricultural cooperatives, due to the Commission's lack of motivation with respect to advantages under the tax on capital transfers and documented legal acts, economic activities tax, and immovable property tax.

In short, there had been a complaint against the distribution of fuel to third parties carried out by agricultural cooperatives. An initial judgment of the Court of First Instance (CFI) of 12 December 2006, established the absence of an advantage contrary to competence regulations. However, the CFI annulled article 1 of the Commission's Decision.[40] The explanation of the subsequent judgment and its possible consequences became a terrible turning point in the matter and merits further examination.

We have to remember that Spanish cooperatives are obliged to distinguish between income from members and from non-member third parties, so that the first are taxed at a lower rate while the second are taxed at the general tax rate. Therefore, it is possible to identify which measures are technical adjustments to disadvantages caused by the attachment of a cooperative to its inherent principles. However, agricultural cooperatives are considered "specially protected cooperatives" that benefit from a 50% rebate of the payable tax, which is the sum of the tax payable from activities carried out with members and from activities with third parties. Thus, this measure can be considered a tax benefit aimed at promoting the cooperative model, in conformity with the Spanish system, in which the Constitution in article 129.2 establishes that cooperatives should be promoted.

The case is particularly important for Basque cooperatives because we have a similar classification; even though the cooperatives that fall into the category of specially protected ones are not exactly the same, the benefit is identical: a 50% tax rebate.

The Commission's decision of 11 December 2002[41] had previously declared that the tax advantages enjoyed by cooperatives must be seen in light of technical adjustment standards and the obligations

---

40. The Court declared that article 1 of the Commission Decision of 11 December 2002 on the measures implemented by Spain in the agricultural sector following the increase in fuel prices be annulled insofar as it found that the measures to support agricultural cooperatives provided for by Royal Decree Law 10/2000 on emergency support for agriculture, fisheries, and transport, did not constitute an aid within the meaning of article 87 (1) EC.

41. Case C-22/2001.

that these impose on cooperatives. Namely, cooperatives' dividends (returns) are subject to double taxation, and members are allowed a lower deduction on their income tax than shareholders of a company.[42] Cooperatives are also subject to mandatory reserves, which cannot be distributed even when the cooperative ceases to exist. Finally, the Commission stated that the tax regime of agricultural cooperatives had to be analyzed as a whole, and therefore no advantage was considered. As we can see, the frame of reference chosen as regards material selectivity is that of the whole system, keeping in mind the personal income tax and corporate income tax.

In April 2003, two different competitors, associations of service stations, brought an action for annulment against the decision of 2002 before the CFI (today General Court or GC). On 12 December 2006, the GC issued a judgment in Case T-156/03, *Asociación de Estaciones de Servicio de Madrid y Federación Catalana de Estaciones de Servicio v. Commission,* annulling the Commission's first decision. The Commission defended its decision by giving arguments to support that the tax treatment of Spanish cooperatives did not constitute selective state aid.

The Commission argued that with respect to corporate income tax, the fiscal regime applicable to cooperatives does not confer an advantage to them. First, the Commission stated that mandatory reserves of cooperatives are not equivalent to legal reserves of companies. Cooperative reserves are not in any case distributable. In addition, cooperatives must contribute to them 20% of benefits from activities with members and 50% of benefits from activities with non-member third parties.

We have to remember that in the Basque case, we do have this sort of reserve with different, lower percentages.

The Commission stated that even in the case where an advantage for cooperatives was identified, it would be fully justified by the nature or general scheme of the tax system, which requires different treatment for different realities.[43] Here, the Commission recognized the principles of equal treatment, progressivity, and ability to pay, enshrined in the Spanish tax system, as grounds for justification of cooperative tax benefits.

---

42. The Confederation of Spanish agricultural cooperatives argued that, "The advantage that a cooperative might have enjoyed as a result of the company tax rebate is offset by the double taxation on personal income imposed on cooperative members and the increase in their tax burden in this way." (Ibid., par. 90).
43. Ibid., par. 103.

However, the GC annulled the decision due to the Commission's lack of motivation with respect to advantages under the tax on capital transfers and documented legal acts, economic activities tax, and immovable property tax. The judgment did not question the Commission's argumentation regarding tax measures of cooperatives on corporate income tax. As we can see, there is only a lack of motivation in what we could call minor taxes that would fall under the "de minimis" category.

However, the Commission issued a new decision on December 15, 2009, with the radically opposite view of each of the criteria of Article 107(1) TFEU. The Decision goes beyond the GC's demand of motivation only with respect to taxes on transfer of property and documented acts, economic activities, and immovable property.

What is important is the fact that the judgment did not even question the Commission's argumentation regarding tax measures of cooperatives on corporate income tax. What also needs to be highlighted is the fact that more than 90% of the taxes cooperatives pay belong to this last tax, and all the others can be considered to be minor, as most of them (all except economic activities, which most enterprises do not usually pay because of a very high exempt minimum and immovable property tax) are only occasional and very low taxes, representing a minor proportion of tax for any sort of entity.

Regarding corporate income tax of agricultural cooperatives, the Commission states that the advantage must be reviewed at a cooperative level and not at a member level. Therefore, it does not accept the argument by which the different tax treatment compensates double taxation of cooperative returns.[44] This position is illogical, because the Commission itself recognizes in the Tax Notice that double taxation of cooperative returns needs to be taken into account, showing that a general view is necessary. As we can see, the frame of reference has changed, and now it only refers to corporate income tax.

Next, the Commission analyzed whether the comparability test was fulfilled. It concluded that only true mutual cooperatives (those that act only with their members) are not in a legal and factual situation comparable to capital-based companies, because these cooperatives do not obtain any benefit.[45] The effect created by the measures of a change in the fiscal treatment of cooperatives was enough to identify an advantage. In particular, the Commission concluded that agricultural cooperatives and companies are in a comparable situation with

44. Commission Decision on Spanish agricultural cooperatives 2009, par. 148–49.
45. Ibid., par. 163.

respect to compulsory reserves, and therefore to corporate income tax. The comparability test was also positive for the other three taxes, and thus the measures were declared selective, as they only applied to cooperatives.[46] This reference to purely mutual cooperatives would exclude Basque cooperatives, since even though they have substantive constraints because of the principle of mutuality, this does not mean that they cannot deal with third parties at all, only that there are limits, usually a 50% maximum of operations with third parties. Thus, they would not satisfy this condition and, if this argument were to be followed, some of our measures would be declared incompatible state aids.

The Commission acknowledged that the measures could be justified by proving that they compensated the higher burden caused by economic double taxation of cooperative income, first, through corporate income tax, and then through the income tax on members. Information provided by Spain was considered insufficient because it did not prove that this compensation existed. In addition, the objective of the measure (to allow farms to maintain their competitiveness in difficult economic conditions created by the increase in fuel prices) did not result directly from the founding principles or policy of its tax system.

Finally, none of the compatibility criteria of Article 107 TFEU was thought to be applicable. In particular, in light of the exemption of Article 107(3)(c) TFEU, the Commission discussed whether the said advantages of agricultural cooperatives were proportionate to the objective of promoting them and compensating their inherent limitations. Here, the only inherent element of cooperatives used was the principle of mutuality. The direct consequence of this partial appreciation was that only measures affecting tax treatment of cooperative results could be proportionate to their special characteristics. As the measures analyzed concerned extracooperative results, the Commission could not conclude that aid was given to eliminate inefficiencies in the market or to address other social or equitable objectives.

The Spanish Confederations of Cooperatives and of Social Economy brought an action for annulment on April 6, 2010 against this decision, which declared that the measures concerned constitute state aid incompatible with the internal market and ordered recovery.

The story ended on January 23, 2014, when an order was issued according to which the problems to be solved were only the legitimation by CEPES, the Spanish Confederation of Cooperatives and

---

46. Ibid., par. 176.

the Spanish Association of Cooperatives, and the restoration of aid. The new order does not enter into the problem of deciding whether the measures at stake are or are not possible state aids, or whether cooperatives are in the same factual and legal situation, so actually it does not shed any further light. However, strictly speaking, it is a good decision, as these measures had not been denounced in the first place and only the measures stated in Law No 34/1998, concerning the selling of diesel to third parties without the necessity of forming another kind of entity, had been denounced.

As regards legitimacy, the order says that neither CEPES nor the Association of Agricultural Cooperatives can be considered interested parties, an opinion that I do not share. In my opinion, the GC could have annulled the second decision as it deviated from the previous judgment's mandate to motivate the justification of the measures with respect to other taxes different from corporate income tax. Even if the GC had agreed on most of the points of the first decision, the Commission changed its whole argument and changed its view on issues that were settled, disregarding the differences pertaining to cooperatives.

Regarding the recovery of aid, it understands that it falls under the "de minimis" category, so, in the end, after ten years of questioning the system and creating uncertainty, and after having decided one thing and then the opposite, there is no problem for agricultural cooperatives regarding the matters outlined. We must remember that the measures considered had already been changed by the Law on Sustainable Economy.

However, as a general conclusion concerning the Spanish system that could be at issue when applying Article 107(1) TFEU to tax measures of cooperatives, the main concern from a competition point of view is whether the measure limits itself to compensating a disadvantage caused by an obligation of the cooperative to contribute to the general interest or not. If such a measure does not overcompensate the costs of performing that obligation, it should not be qualified as selective state aid.

For example, on the one hand, the Spanish tax benefits on the calculation of taxable income coming from cooperative results are compensating measures, because they only affect income coming from members, and exclude any economic activity capable of distorting the internal market.

On the other hand, the rebate that specially protected cooperatives get from their payable tax could be considered overcompensating because they get relief from income from both members and third parties. However, as not every tax measure specific to cooperatives can relate to a concrete cost or obligation, it is the task of the member state concerned to show its tax scheme of cooperatives as a whole system, separate from the general system of corporate income tax, that overall compensates cooperatives for their limitations to act in the market.

However, keep in mind that in the Basque case no distinction is made between cooperative and extra-cooperative results, so the lower tax rate applies to both. In my opinion, having seen the decision of March 7, 2014 on soccer-club associations, we are risking the consideration of this different rate as state aid. But if we bear in mind the *Paint Graphos* judgment, an exception could be made, considering that this benefit is proportionate with the burdens cooperatives have. Regarding Italy, the general characteristics inherent to cooperatives manifested in Regulation 1435/2003 on the Statute for a European Cooperative Society (SEC Regulation) and in the Commission's communication on the promotion of cooperative societies in Europe (communication on cooperatives), were pointed out by the ECJ in its judgment known as *Paint Graphos* of 8 September 2011. Among their operating principles: the primacy of the individual, the "one man, one vote" rule, the distribution of assets and reserves to another cooperative in the case of winding up, and the objective of mutual benefit of members. Among their disadvantages: no or limited access to equity markets, the limited interest on loan and share capital, along with the subsequent lower advantage of investing in them.[47]

In light of their specific characteristics, the Court held that cooperatives such as the ones involved in the proceedings "cannot, in principle, be regarded as being in a comparable factual and legal situation to that of commercial companies," provided that "they act in the economic interest of their members and their relations with members are not purely commercial but personal and individual."[48] Considering that the cooperatives within the proceedings acted to some extent with third parties, this statement could mean that the ECJ recognizes that predominantly mutualistic cooperatives are, together with purely mutualistic cooperatives, in a comparable situation to that of profit-making companies. However, the Court claimed that, "The nature or general scheme of the tax system in question can provide no val-

---

47. Ibid., par. 56–59.
48. Ibid., par. 61.

id justification for a national measure if it provides that profits from trade with third parties who are not members of the cooperative are exempt from tax or that sums paid to such parties by way of remuneration may be deducted."[49] This could be regarded as good news for Basque cooperatives, as they comply with the principles stated in the Italian judgment, and thus, they should not be compared with commercial companies.

However, I understand that under no circumstances would the 50% rebate for specially privileged cooperatives, as there is no valid legal reason for this very important difference from protected cooperatives that cannot have it. Thus, this tax policy should be revised, either by applying it to all kinds of cooperatives, if it can be regarded as a technical adjustment, or, in the worst case scenario, eliminating it and compensating all categories with the full deduction of profits allocated to Compulsory Reserve Funds, or other possible widespread measures, such as a smaller tax rate.

Conclusions

We live in a multi-level system where there are five levels of government, from a vertical point of view, and many more, from a horizontal point of view. Thus, various public policies need to be coordinated with the whole system, both vertically and horizontally. A revision of the cooperatives' taxes in the Basque Country should be carried out with this in mind, in order to coordinate with EU law and avoid being questioned in EU cases.

The selectivity framework established through the so-called "Azores case," followed by the 11 September 2008 or so-called "Basque case," includes the whole Basque Country. The institutional, procedural, and economic autonomies studied belong at this particular level. There is an urgent need to promote an internal harmonization among the three territories in order to comply with EU competition law. Although some important efforts are being made in this direction, there are still certain areas that need to be revised, such as that pertaining to the special regimes of corporate taxation.

Public policies concerning cooperatives are an example of it. There is a possible contradiction among policies at a Basque Country level and at a state level with EU law, as they are both constitutional mandates and statutory mandates to promote cooperatives and interdictions from state aid. As a result, we need to comply with the

---

49. Ibid., par. 72.

mandate of promotion of cooperatives, as it is a requirement under EU competition law. Thus, public policies need to be designed in compliance with both mandates. Further, there should be complete coordination among these public policies with EU law; otherwise, the public policies for cooperatives may be regarded as measures contrary to article 107.1 of TFEU.

Competition law, and particularly, state aids in relation to cooperatives, should be clarified in order to establish a secure legal framework that provides certainty. The internal market should be compatible with the general interest, and not the other way around.

Bearing in mind the various tax policies for the promotion of cooperatives in the Basque Country and the case law precedents we have to date, consider the following:

- Local taxes should fall under the "de minimis" category, as they can be considered to be minor.
- Regarding corporate income tax, the deduction of amounts allocated to the compulsory and nonreturnable funds should be considered to be technical adjustments, according to Advocate General Jääskinen's opinion on the joint Italian cases known as *Paint Graphos* (C-78/08 and C-80/08), an opinion that I fully share.
- Also regarding corporate income tax, the lower tax rates cooperatives have in relation to capitalist enterprises can be seen either as state aid—according to the latest case decision on soccer clubs in Spain of 7 March 2008, wherein a difference in the legal structure does not amount to a different tax rate—or as a compatible aid, if regarded in relation to the whole system of cooperatives, as seen in the *Paint Graphos* judgment.
- Again, regarding corporate income tax, the 50% tax rebate is hardly understandable as it now stands. The classification of cooperatives should be reviewed because such an important benefit can only be justified if it is widespread for all cooperatives. If not, it has no legal basis to justify it and can clearly be regarded as selective.

Bibliography.

Alguacil, María Pilar. "Tax Treatment of Cooperatives in Europe under the State Aid Rules," In *Genossenschaften in Fokus,* 1091–1105. Vienna: 2011.

Arana, Sofía. *Régimen Fiscal de Cooperativas*. Bilbao: Editorial Universidad del País Vasco/Euskal Herriko Unibertsitatea, 2012.

———. "El regimen fiscal de las cooperativas españolas en la Unión Europea: líneas de reforma del cooperativismo español," *Revista Vasca de Economía Social*, 7 (2010): 77–98.

Bahía Almansa, B. "Una aproximación a la fiscalidad de la transformación en el seno de las sociedades cooperativas," *Revista Vasca de Economía Social*, 6 (2010): 93–119.

———. "El regimen fiscal especial de las cooperativas y su compatibilidad con la normativa sobre ayudas de Estado," *CIRIEC, España Revista Jurídica de Economia Social y Cooperativa*, 22 (December 2011).

Bakaikoa, Baleren, Angel Errasti, Enekoitz Etxezarreta, and Ion Morandeira. "Public policies for the stimulation of Social Economy in the Basque Country," *The Emergence of Social Economy in Public Policy: An International Analysis*. Brussels: Peter Lang, 2013, 191–217.

Chaves, Rafael. "Public Policies and Social Economy in Spain and Europe," *CIRIEC, Revista de Economía Pública, Social y Cooperativa*, 62 (October 2008): 35–60.

Cusa, Emmanuele. (2011). "State Aid Law and Cooperatives in Europe," *Genossenschaften in Fokus*, Vienna: 2011: 1.105–1.021.

Garcia, Jesús María. *Contratación pública y Economía Social en Euskadi: 2010–2012*. PhD dissertation defended January 31, 2014 (unpublished as of 2015).

Rodrigo, M. A. "Reflexiones sobre la reforma de la fiscalidad de las cooperativas y sobre su compatibilidad con el Derecho comunitario," *Revista Vasca de Economía Social*, 6 (2010): 7–28.

Serrano, Susana. "La incidencia de las ayudas de estado en las cooperativas vascas," *Revista Vasca de Economía Social*, 7 (2010): 111–53.

Serrano-Gazteluurrutia, Susana. "Jurisdictional Defense of the Economic Agreement," in J. Agirreazkuenaga and E. Alonso (eds.), *Basque Fiscal Systems. History, Current Status and Future Perspectives*, 249–87. Reno: Center for Basque Studies, University of Nevada, 2014.

———. *El Concierto Económico vasco ante el juez comunitario*. Oñati: IVAP, 2012. pp. 539–654.

Suberbiola Garbizu, Irune. "Regimen tributario de las sociedades laborales. Propuestas de reforma," *Revista Vasca de Economía Social*, 10 (2013): 7–52.

13

EU Competition Law in Relation to Online Gambling Tax Policies in Spain and the Basque Country

Irune Suberbiola Garbizu*

Since its accepted practice by Royal Decree Law 16/1977, of February 25, amending its criminal, administrative, and fiscal aspects, gambling has a legal basis that does not reflect its social legitimacy. Indeed, gambling is a free and voluntary, uncertain and unproductive activity in which income is transferred between citizens, violating the virtues of work, patience, and saving supported by Catholic morality and driven in the long dictatorial period before it was legalized.

As we will see in this paper, taxation of the gambling industry has become an instrument through which the state and the autonomous communities regulate gambling with a clear, moralistic notion that—under the umbrella of the general usefulness of avoiding risky situations such as compulsive gambling, money laundering, or childhood protection—considers certain gambling as a clearly reprehensible activity in need of regulation.

The state "rate" on games of chance was introduced into the Spanish tax system by Royal Decree-Law 16/1977, which regulates all aspects of the games by broadening the tax base of the tax rate on raffles and gambling, which are regulated, in turn, by Decree 3059/1966, of 1 December.

With the advent of democracy, even before the promulgation of the Constitution, the possibility of organizing or lawfully holding games of chance, betting, or gambling opened up, expanding the tax-

* Member of Project financed by the Basque Government entitled "Tributación de las actividades económicas en el País Vasco: la incidencia del Derecho Comunitario," IT604-13.

able event of the tax rate on raffles, betting, and random games developed in casinos, bingo halls, and for amusement and slot machines. This moral perception is reflected in an increase in taxes on gaming, which have led to many disputes over its legal nature or even its constitutionality,[2] from the point of view of both the principles of tax justice and the role of autonomous communities in its management and policy development.

It should be recalled that the increase in the amount of the "rate" has been diversified by the participation of the Autonomous Communities in the shaping of the tax. Indeed, the "rate" on games of chance, which is the charge on the gaming machines, similar to taxes on raffles and gambling, may be assigned by the State to the Autonomous Communities. Article 11.i of the Organic Law 8/1980 of 22 September, which regulates the Financing of the Autonomous Communities (OLFAC), provides the possibility of this transfer. Specifically, after the amendment hold by the Organic Law 3/1996 of 27 December on the OLFAC, according to article 19 2e, in relation to these taxes, the autonomous communities may develop regulations on "determining exemptions, tax base, tax rates, fixed fees, bonuses and vesting powers and regulating the application of taxes"—that is, virtually all the main aspects of the tribute except the taxable event and the taxable subject.

Regarding the tax on games of chance, in the same sense expressed by the OLFAC, paragraph 7 of Article 3 of Decree-Law 16/1977, amended by article 32 of Law 14/1996, of 30 December, on the Transfer of State Taxes to the Autonomous Communities, states that the autonomous communities oversee the approval of bases, tax rates and fixed fees, accrual, exemptions, and tax rebates—again, nearly everything except the taxable event and the taxable subject. Thus, the rules on tax base, tax rates, and fixed charges and accruals, under Article 3 of Royal Decree-Law 16/1977, shall be applicable only in the absence of standards issued by the autonomous community or if it has not assumed legislative powers regarding this tax.

In fact, after the assumption of substantive and tax competences on gambling by the autonomous communities, this Article is almost empty of content, since most of them, with the exception of Ceuta and Melilla, are competent for the granting of authorizations in the area of games and have developed rules taxing this activity within the limits laid down in the aforementioned legislation: their territorial

---

2. Among them, the rulings of the Constitutional Court of July 16, 1987 and November 10, 1994, or that of the Supreme Court on December 28, 1998.

scope and the prohibition of regulating the tax fact and the taxable person. In other words, Royal Decree-Law 16/1977 shall be applied only when the game is developed in the autonomous cities of Ceuta and Melilla, or in the terms we will explain going forward.

When it comes to the Basque Country, after the substantive attribution made by Royal Decree 257/1982, of 15 October,[3] this tax attribution is made through the renewal of the Economic Agreement in 2002, approved by law 12/2002, of 23 May. Since then, and up until the renewal of the Economic Agreement in April 2014, article 36 of the Economic Agreement established that the taxes that apply to gambling have the character of approved regulatory autonomous taxes, if a license should be held in the Basque Country. However, the aforesaid article indicated that they were applied by the same standards as those established in each instance by the state regarding the taxable event and taxable subject.

As for the power to collect such taxes, article 37 of the Economic Agreement attributed this to the government of the territory where either the release or the realization of the taxable event should have been or was carried out among the three territories in the Basque Country. Holding to this qualification, the territorial governments of each Basque province approved their respective statutory rules for the tax on gambling: 5/2005, on 14 February in Araba; 3/2005, on 10 March in Bizkaia; and 1/2005, on 1 February in Gipuzkoa. These provincial standards are a response to the need for regulation of this matter by the foral institutions that previously had only addressed specific aspects of the same.

Within the Basque Country, the regulation of taxes on gambling has its origin in the substantive legislation elaborated by the Basque Autonomous Community, depending on the jurisdiction of exclusive character attributed by article 10.35 of the Statute of Autonomy.[4] In the development of that exclusive competence, the Autonomous Community of the Basque Country has issued various provisions governing gambling, including Law 4/1991, of 8 November, regulating gambling within their territory. Therefore, it was necessary to establish the range of powers that the institutions of the three Historical Territories were selecting, first, through the provisions of the Economic Agreement and, second, through the harmonized standards

---

3. According to which state services on casinos and gambling were passed on to the Autonomous Community of the Basque Country, fulfilling the substance of Article 10.35 of the Statute of Gernika.
4. With the exception of charitable sports betting.

within the Tax Coordination Body for the allocation of powers to levy and regulate them, in coordination with the powers of the Community of the Basque Country, which has had the authority to establish a regional surcharge on gambling since it was created by Act 6/1992 of 16 October.

It was also necessary to take into consideration the case law concerning taxation on gambling, especially according to the ruling of the Constitutional Court on 10 November 1994, and that of the Supreme Court on 28 December 1998, which state the nature of the tax "rate" on games of chance, gambling, or gaming. In addition, it was compulsory to respect the limits and history of the tax on gambling, appearing in the regulations regarding the Economic Agreement and the rules of the common system. Thus, as previously indicated, the same regulatory regime should apply to the regulation of taxes on gambling in the Basque Country, as in the state when it comes to the taxable fact and taxable person.

Gambling, however, is subject to constant evolution in the technologies used and the tastes and preferences of consumers. For this reason, in response to a social reality that demands the legalization of online gaming channels,[5] the Spanish state officially put into effect Law 13/2011, of 27 May, regulating games developed at the state level as well as those offered online. Title VII of this law sets a tax rate on the activities and services provided to operators by the National Gambling Commission regulatory body, which provides the necessary state authorizations and which has assigned all the powers necessary to ensure integrity, security, reliability, and transparency of gambling operations, as well as compliance with legislation and the conditions described for its exploitation. At the same time, Title VII determines the tax regime applicable to gaming activities developed by online channels, without prejudice to the maintenance of the above-mentioned provisions of Decree 3059/1966 and Royal Decree-Law 16/1977, which will remain in force regarding the assigned assessment in its area of competence.

Thus, instead of amending Royal Decree-Law 16/1977 with a special reference to online channels, a new statewide game tax[6] was created for online games as well as random drawings for advertising or promotional purposes.[7] It also regulates the participation of the

---

5. In terms of legality, gambling not specifically permitted by it is prohibited, and therefore condemned.

6. Which we will call the tax on gambling activities.

7. Although they are not strictly gambling, since no payment is required for a chance

autonomous communities in the new gambling tax via the assignment of the revenue obtained through payments made by the residents of each community. Meanwhile, the state reserves the income proceeds on behalf of non-resident players in Spain, for state sports mutual betting and state horse race mutual betting.

As we have said, the new tax is compatible with the existing rates on the games; it does not affect them, so their charges are still transferred to the autonomous communities in their entirety, in the way OLFCA specifies.

Note that the Spanish regulator, due to the technical characteristics of online gambling, has opted to create a new tax instead of broadening the existing tax regulated by Royal Decree Law 16/1977—something that, in our opinion, should be possible.[8]

To sum up, this new tax will be applied when the game is developed for online play or, rarely, in face-to-face games developed at the state level. As was necessary, this new tax was added to the Economic Agreement, in this case through modifications contained in Law 7/2014, of 21 April. According to the new redaction of article 36 of the Economic Agreement, the game activities tax is governed by the same substantive and formal rules as those established at any given time by the state.

Regarding the foregoing, with respect to the activities exercised by operators, organizers, or by those who develop the taxed activity and have tax residence in the Basque country, the competent institutions of the Historical Territories may raise tax rates up to a maximum of 20% of the rates established in each instance by the State.[9] This increase will apply, exclusively, to the proportionate share of the taxable base corresponding to the participation in gambling by fiscal residents in Basque territory. In addition, the competent institutions of the Historical Territories may adopt models of filing and payment that shall contain at least the same information as those of the common territory and set the payment deadlines for each settlement period, which does not differ substantially from those set by the administration of the state. In any case, taxpayers will be taxed, wherever they have their fiscal domicile, by the territorial governments, the State administration, or both administrations in proportion to the volume of operations performed in each territory during the exercise.

---

to play.

8. For a different perspective, see Juan José Zornoza, "El régimen tributario del juego remoto," *Revista Jurídica de deporte y entretenimiento*, 27 (2009): 29–43

9. This possibility is established in Law 13/2011 for all Autonomous Communities.

On the other hand, according to the new article 37 of the Economic Agreement, the rest of the taxes that fall on gambling—that is, the tax on games of chance and the tax rate on raffles and gambling—have the character of established regulatory autonomous taxes when the authorization must be given in the Basque country. At the same time, the Basque institutions should apply the same standards as established in each instance by the state regarding the taxable fact and subject.

When it comes to the tax on games of chance—when taxable in the Basque Country—it shall be levied by the provincial government, which is empowered by virtue of the territory. In the same way, in case the authorization of gambling must be given in the Basque Country, the tax on raffles and gambling shall be levied by the provincial government, competent by virtue of the territory.

Given these considerations, let us continue analyzing the main aspects of both taxes in the above mentioned statutory rules about the tax on gaming: 5/2005, of 14 February in Araba; 3/2005, of 10 March, in Bizkaia; and 1/2005, of 1 February in Gipuzkoa.

Tax Regulation on Gambling in the Three Provinces

As mentioned above, the Economic Agreement was renewed in April 2014. For that reason, until the transposition of the tax created by Law 13/2011 is completed, the only tax regulation on gambling is that developed on the basis of article 3 of Royal Decree Law 16/1977 and Decree 3059/1966. Nevertheless, as we will explain, the provincial regulators have introduced an amendment to their respective rules in order to take into account games provided through online channels.

Even though there are three statutory rules regarding the tax on gambling, one for each province, as their content is nearly the same, we will analyze them together. The three rules are divided into seventeen articles, a repealing provision, and two final provisions:

- Article 1 declares the indirect nature of the figure and determines that its aim is to tax gaming activities in the terms provided for in these provincial standards.
- Article 2 establishes the scope of application of the regulation and the jurisdiction for levying, stating that the taxes shall apply to gaming activities whose authorization must be given in the Basque Country, and establishing authorization should be requested through the historical territory where the operation of the game takes place.

- Article 3 regulates the taxable fact, something that has to be identical to that contained in Royal Decree-Law 16/1977 and that, indeed, is intrinsically linked to the substantive regulation in the field of games issued by the Basque Autonomous Community. According to this article, the authorization, organization, or performance of the following activities are meant to be taxable transactions of the tribute [tax] on gaming activities: casino games; bingo, including the modality of betting bingo; machine games; raffles, random combinations; or any other game included in the catalog of games of the autonomous community of the Basque Country. Note that, contrary to what happens with the State legislation, where a new tax was created by Law 13/2011 specifically for the games developed through online channels, the Basque tax is applied regardless of how the game is played, be it manually or through technical, telematics, electronic, or interactive media. From a practical point of view, it is easy to understand that the games offered by both online and offline operators form part of the same activity of gambling, regardless of their online or land-based settings. Moreover, even from a technical point of view, both online and land-based operators appear to be comparable in their technological platforms, formats, and parameters. This might be why the Basque regulator has considered it appropriate to amend the taxable event of the duty, broadening its scope to include those games developed by online channels.

- Article 4 declares the exemptions applicable in the case of the tax subject to regulation. Most of these are subjective exemptions and only affect raffles, betting, and random combinations.
- Article 5 determines the taxable persons of the tax.
- Article 6 refers to those who have a solidary liability, since it places responsibility on employers of premises, facilities, or premises where the game takes place.
- Article 7 contains the rules for the determination of the tax base, distinguishing a rule of general character in paragraph one and particular rules in paragraph two, according to the type of game and including the necessary qualifications for the correct determination of the database.
- Articles 8 to 14 regulate the tax rates applicable according to the type of game, establishing a general type in the case of

games that do not fall into existing categories, setting a fixed fee in the case of games operated by automatic machines, and assigning fixed tax rates for some types of games and progressive tax types for other modes of play. As with Article 4, there is no difference in the tax rate applicable depending on the way the game is developed: whether the game is online or offline, the tax rate will be always the same. Note that this does not occur at the State level, since, for example, in the case of casino games, Royal Decree Law 16/1977 settles a tax rate that can reach 55% of the gross receipts earned from the game,[10] while the online casinos are taxed at only 25%.

- Article 15 regulates accrual, laying out a general rule for the determination of the time of the accrual and a particular rule for the chargeable event for games played on automatic or slot machines.
- Article 16 contains rules about the formal obligations concerning the payment of the tribute, making a statutory remission for their development, without prejudice to the establishment of certain formal substantive obligations included in the same.
- Article 17 refers to the general statutory regulations relating to tax offenses and penalties, with the general rules therefore being applicable in this area.

The Basque operators who are licensed by the Basque government to develop gambling within the territory of the Basque Country will be held to this taxation system based on their fiscal domicile in Araba, Bizkaia, or Gipuzkoa.

At the same time, once development of the current Article 36 of the Economic Agreement is complete, and depending on where their fiscal domicile is located, taxpayers will be taxed by the territorial governments, the State administration, or both administrations, in proportion to the volume of operations performed in each territory during the exercise if they offer their services under the terms of Law 13/2001—that is, when they offer it at the State level, and are subject to State authorization. In any case, even if we wait for that development, it remains to be seen what the impact will be from a European perspective. The fact is that there are operators with licenses granted by the Basque regional authority who are subject to a 33% rate in the case of casinos, or a 10% rate for gambling. Meanwhile, the State-licensed operators, under Law 13/2011, could be subject to rates that

---

10. Article 3.4.1, Royal Decree Law 16/1977.

would rise to 25%. These differences could be considered as State aid and therefore be rejected by EC Law.

Tax Regulations on Gambling and EC Law

Gambling seems to be immune to European Community harmonization. The initiative taken by the Commission on the basis of the study *Gambling in the Single Market. A Study of the Current Legal and Market Situation*[11] was abandoned in 1992 under pressure from some Member States. Gambling has also been out of range of further harmonization efforts, among them the E-Commerce Directive and the Services Directive.

In any case, far from the intention of the Member States to maintain control of gambling, by reasons of social policy, money laundering, and so on, the lack of harmonized regulation has only led to the Court's decision about whether or not national regulations regarding gambling are compatible with EU freedoms, particularly the freedom to provide services and freedom of establishment. As has occurred in other areas, the evolution of the jurisprudence of the Court has been slow and gradual, suffering, at times, particularly significant fluctuations. The initial court case[12] on the limitations to the provision of gambling services recognizes that advertising import bans, monopoly schemes, licensing restrictions, and so on are real limitations to the freedom to provide services, even as it establishes that the limitations are justified for reasons of social policy and fraud prevention.

This traditional jurisprudence begins to break in the *Gambelli*[13] case, in which the Court analyzes the Italian monopoly on sports betting attributed to the Italian National Olympic Committee. Thus, the Court questioned the restrictions traditionally imposed on gambling services in the name of social policy, noting that to the extent that national authorities incite and encourage participation in gambling in order to receive more tax revenues, the desire to reduce gambling opportunities cannot be considered a public or social reason.

In subsequent rulings, the Court repeats the arguments made in the *Gambelli* case. Notably, in the *Placanica*[14] case, the Court notes

---

11. *Gambling in the Single Market. A Study of the Current Legal and Market Situation* (Luxembourg: Office for Official Publications of the European Communities, 1991).
12. See *Schindler* case, sentence of 24 March 1994 (C-275/92); *Läärä* case, sentence of 21 September, 1992 (C-124/97); and *Zenatti* case, sentence of 21 October 2001 (C-67/98).
13. *Gambelli* sentence of 6 November 2003 (C-243/01).
14. *Placanica* sentence of 6 March 2007 (C-338/04, 359/04 y 360/04).

that although the limitations on the freedom to provide gambling services may not be consistent with the objective of reducing gambling opportunities in a context of expansion of gambling by the authorities, these limitations may be appropriate to prevent the holding of gaming activities for criminal or fraudulent purposes. Thus, in the *Santa Casa*[15] and *Sporting Exchange Ltd*[16] cases, the Court reinforces the importance of preventing fraudulent activities enabled by the special circumstances of Internet gambling, that is, the lack of direct contact between the consumer and operator.

In any case, this statement, to consider that fraud is consubstantial to online gaming, cannot be absolute because in its judgment on the case *Ladbrokes Betting and Gaming Ltd*,[17] a case of online gaming, the Court stresses the need to justify the real dangers of fraud, which indicates a clear tendency toward the removal of internal gambling services' regulatory hurdles.

In terms of the Spanish and Basque case, beyond nonsubordination of state level lotteries proclaimed in article 48.2 of Law 13/2011,[18] the fact is that both the current configuration of the tax on face-to-face gaming and the referral to electronic gaming raise difficult problems from the point of view of European freedoms. This is so to the extent that the possible violation of community freedoms in this field depends on discriminatory treatment of resident and non-resident operators—an unequal treatment that in the indicated cases does not exist since they project similar requirements regardless of the place of residence of the tax subject. However, the fact that a measure is non-discriminatory does not mean that it is consistent with European law, particularly in terms of the application of the State aid regime. From this point of view, it is advisable to consider whether unequal tax treatment of offline and online gaming in Spanish regulations can be construed as the type of State aid prohibited by article 107 of the Treaty of the Functioning of the European Union.

We can therefore take into account what has happened in a similar case regarding the Danish rules for online gaming, in which the Commission initiated an examination procedure culminating in the Commission Decision of 20 September 2011,[19] currently being ana-

---

15. *Santa Casa*, sentence of 8 September 2009 (C-42/07).
16. *Sporting Exchange Ltd.*, sentence of 3 June 2010 (C-203/08).
17. *Ladbrokes Betting and Gaming Ltd.*, sentence of 3 June 2010 (C-258/08).
18. Which eventually could cause problems from the perspective of community freedoms.
19. C 35/2010 (ex N 302/2010).

lyzed by the Court of Justice of the European Union, which reviewed the case on 30 April 2014; a verdict is expected mid-autumn.

On July 6, 2010, the Danish authorities announced, pursuant to article 108 (3) of the Treaty on the Functioning of the European Union (TFEU), the Legislative Proposal L 203 on Gaming Duties (the "Gaming Duties Act"), adopted on June 25, 2010. At the same time, the Commission received two separate complaints with regard to the proposed Gaming Duties Act. The first complaint was submitted by the Danish Amusement Machine Industry Association (DAB) on July 23, 2010. The second complaint was submitted by a land-based casino operator, the Royal Casino, on August 6, 2010.

According to articles 2–17 of the Gaming Duties Act, the games subject to a duty are, among others, land-based casinos and online casinos, and they have different tax rates depending on whether the games are provided in online casinos or in land-based casinos. Holders of a license to provide games in land-based casinos are subject to a basic charge of 45% of their Gross Gaming Revenues (GGR—stakes minus winnings), less the value of the tokens in the tronc, and an additional charge of 30% for GGR (less the value of the tokens in the tronc), which exceeds DKK 4 million (calculated on a monthly basis), while holders of a license to provide games in an online casino are subject to a charge of 20% of their GGR. In this context the European Commission opened the formal investigation procedure laid down in article 108(2) of the TFEU with respect to the measure at issue on the grounds that the measure could entail state aid within the meaning of article 107(1) TFEU.

In particular, the Commission considered that the measure could be regarded as selective within the meaning of the jurisprudence. Recall that, when assessing the selectivity of the tax measure, one should analyze whether a given measure favors certain undertakings in comparison with other undertakings that are comparable in a legal and factual situation, and in light of the objective pursued by the scheme in question. Given the nature of the games offered online and on land-based premises, the social experience provided by gaming activity in both platforms, and the socioeconomic profiles of the consumers, the Commission doubted whether the differences between online and land-based gaming were important enough to consider them as not being comparable in law and in fact, for the purposes of their tax treatment under the Gaming Duties Act.

In order to determine whether the measure should be defined as state aid contrary to the TFEU, several aspects have to be considered:

the presence of state resources; the existence of an advantage; the possibility of distorting competition or the effect of the measure on trade; whether it is a selective measure or not; the system of reference; the departure from the general tax system; the justification of the measure by the logic of the tax system; and finally, the compatibility of the measure on the basis of article 107(3)(c) TFEU.

As we know, article 107(1) TFEU provides that any aid granted by a member state or through state resources in any form whatsoever, which distorts or threatens to distort competition by favoring certain undertakings or the production of certain goods and affects trade among Member States, must be considered incompatible with the internal market. Number 1 of article 107 TFEU requires that the measure be granted by a member state or through state resources, and, in this sense, a loss of tax revenue is equivalent to consumption of state resources in the form of fiscal expenditure.

By allowing online gambling undertakings to pay taxes at a lower rate than face-to-face casinos, the Danish authorities forego revenue constituting state resources. Furthermore, the measure should confer a financial advantage to the recipient, something that covers not only positive benefits, but also interventions that, in various forms, mitigate the charges normally included in the budget of an undertaking. Under the Gambling Duties Act, online gambling undertakings are liable to pay a tax rate substantially lower than the rate applicable for land-based gambling operators. Therefore, online gambling undertakings benefit from an advantage consisting in the reduction of their tax burden. Consequently, the measure under review involves an advantage for undertakings providing online gambling services.

According to article 107(1) TFEU, the measure must affect intra-EU trade and distort or threaten to distort competition. In the present case, online gambling providers that establish themselves in Denmark will be exposed to competition and intra-community trade, and therefore the Gaming Duties Act necessarily affects intra-Community trade and distorts or threatens to distort competition.

In order to be regarded as state aid within the meaning of article 107(1) TFEU, the measure should be found selective inasmuch as it favors certain undertakings or the production of certain goods. However, the notion of selectivity is interpreted by the European Court of Justice in such a way that the measure is selective if it is "intended partially to exempt those undertakings from the financial charges arising from the normal application of the general system of compulsory contributions imposed by law."[20] In other words, the measure is selective if it constitutes a departure from the application of the general tax framework, a situation that leads to a comparison of it with other undertakings in a comparable legal and factual situation.

If the measure is considered to depart from the general tax system, the next step is to analyze whether such differentiation results from the nature or the general scheme of the tax system of which it forms a part. In other words, one should examine whether the measure in question, which appears *prima facie* to be selective, is justified in light of the logic of the tax system. In the Danish case, the system of reference is none other than the taxation system for Danish gambling activities. The Gaming Duties Act aims to regulate the payment of duties of all gambling activities provided or arranged in Denmark, be they online or through land-based activities. Therefore, it settles the reference tax system where the measure at issue should be assessed. In this regard, note that the games offered by land-based and online gaming operators are equivalent.[21]

Based on the foregoing, one can conclude that online and land-based casinos are legally and factually comparable. Accordingly, the measure at issue introduces a differential tax treatment in favor of online gambling operators, to the detriment of land-based casinos. Thus, since it constitutes a departure from the general tax regime, the measure under review should be regarded as selective within the meaning of article 107 TFEU. Once we have noticed that the measure is selective, we have to determine whether it can be justified by the nature and general scheme of the system, since its guiding principles or rationales can be relied upon to justify the selectivity of the measure. When it comes to the Danish case, the Commission[22] has considered that the selectivity of the announced Act is not justified in light of the logic of the tax system, and it is, therefore, considered state aid for the providers of online gambling services.

Paragraphs (2) and (3) of article 107 of the TFEU provide for rules under which certain aids shall be compatible with the internal market. Hence, in order to be compatible, an aid measure must pursue an objective of common interest in a necessary and proportionate way, balancing the positive impact of the measure in reaching an objective of common interest against its potentially negative side effects,

---

20. Case 173/73, *Italian Republic v. Commission of the European Communities* (1974).
21. Including roulette, baccarat, punto banco, blackjack, poker, and gaming on gaming machines.
22. Paragraph 101 of the Decision on the Measure N° C35/2010 (ex N302/2010).

such as distortion of trade and competition. According to the State Aid Action Plan,[23] this test is based on a three-stage examination, in which the first two steps address the positive effects of the state aid and the third addresses the negative effects and resulting balancing of the positive and negative effects. The balancing test is as follows:

1. Is the aid measure aimed at a well-defined objective of common interest? According to the Commission, if we take into account that the Danish measure will liberalize the market and allow Danish and foreign online gambling operators to provide their services to Danish residents, while ensuring that they will fulfill the necessary conditions to be licensed by the Danish authorities, it serves a well-defined objective of common interest.

2. Is the aid well-designed to deliver the objective of common interest? In other words, does the proposed aid address a market failure or other objective? In particular:

   • Is the aid measure an appropriate instrument, or are there other, better-placed instruments? In the Commission's opinion, a lower tax rate applicable to online gambling activities is an appropriate instrument to attain the liberalization objectives of the new Gaming Act. Therefore, an aid measure will ensure that online operators wishing to provide gambling services directed at Danish residents will apply for a license and comply with the applicable national regulations.

   • Is there an incentive effect? That is, does the aid change the behavior of potential beneficiaries? From the Commission's point of view, the Danish measure "is capable of modifying the behavior of foreign providers of online gambling services, since the lower tax rate applicable to online gambling activities is an appropriate instrument to attain the liberalization objectives of the new Gaming Act. The aid measure will ensure that online operators wishing to provide gambling services directed at Danish residents will apply for a license and comply with the applicable national regulations."[24]

   • Is the aid measure proportional? That is, could the same

---

23. "State Aid Action Plan—Less and Better-Targeted State Aid: A Roadmap for State Aid Reform, 2005–2009," COM(2005) 107 final.
24. Paragraph 129 of the Decision on the Measure N° C35/2010 (ex N302/2010).

change in behavior be obtained with less aid? In the words of the Commission, "The tax rate of 20 percent of GGR applicable to online operators is not lower than is necessary to ensure that the objectives of the Gaming Act are achieved."[25] Consequently, when it comes to the Commission, the Danish aid measure meets the proportionality requirement set out in the case law of the Court of Justice.

3. Are the distortions of competition and effect on trade limited, so that the overall balance is positive? To answer this question we have to take into account the impact of the aid measure distinguishing possible distortions at the level of the trade between Member States as well as distortions of competition within Denmark. With regard to trade between Member States, no negative impact is to be expected, since the Gaming Act provides Danish residents with the possibility of legally gambling on websites of licensed online gambling operators that are not restricted to Danish resident users but may be accessed by residents of all EU Member States, subject to the restrictions imposed by their national law. On the other hand, with regard to distortions of competition within Denmark, the Commission says, "The measure will potentially benefit a considerable number of different Danish and foreign online gambling operators which up to now were prohibited from providing their services to Danish residents,"[26] and this liberalization will further increase overall competition in the market. In any case, note that in its analysis, the Commission forgets the distortion with regards to the already existing land-based gambling operators, which have to suffer the competence made by the online operators, who are able to pay more for prizes and to undertake large advertising campaigns, since they are not obliged to pay higher rates.

As mentioned above, the measure is currently being reviewed by the Court of Justice. It remains to be seen whether or not the Court considers a measure consistent with a lower tax rate for online gambling operators to be contrary to the TFEU.

---

25. Paragraph 137 of the Decision on the Measure N° C35/2010 (ex N302/2010).
26. Paragraph 140 of the Decision on the Measure N° C35/2010 (ex N302/2010).

Conclusions

We have analyzed the current tax regulations on land-based and on-line gambling both in Spain and in the Basque Country, taking into account the distribution of powers in this special field both from a substantive and a tax point of view, on the basis of the Constitution, the Autonomic Statute, and the Economic Agreement.

Among the different taxes levied on gaming, the tax on games of chance, the tax rate on raffles and gambling, and the Game Activities Tax, we have mainly referred to the former, since it is regulated by the Historical Territories of Araba, Bizkaia, and Gipuzkoa. In this sense, until the transposition of a new Article 37 of the Economic Agreement is complete, there are no differences among the taxes applied to online and face-to-face games, and, therefore there is no risk of European intervention in the name of Article 107 of the TFUE. We have seen that at a state level, a different tax rate is applied for games under the umbrella of Law 13/2011 and for those developed in the scope of Royal Decree Law 16/1977—that is to say, online and land-based games.

The Spanish and Basque legislators should be aware that Community law prohibits such discrimination. Gaming activities, either online or face-to-face, cannot be subject to different charges; they are comparable competing activities and they should compete in equal conditions.

At this point, we have to take into account that even if no formal complaint is made in courts by land-based operators against these tax rates, the response by the European Court of Justice in the Danish case, even given the differences of the Spanish and Danish regulations, will confirm, or not, the legality of the measure in light of European law.

Final words

From the date on which the writing of these lines was completed, several rules and pronouncements have been published by European institutions, which modulate their contents. The Spanish Government has approved the basic rules of slot machine games through Order HAP/1370/2014 of 25 July, allowing the online practice of this type of game. At the same time, when it comes to the Basque Country, the Provinces have approved two Statutory Rules, Rule number 23/2014, of 9 July, in Araba, and Rule number 7/2014, of 11 June, in Bizkaia, in order to apply the latest reforms of the Economic Agreement and regulate the new tax contained in Gaming Act 13/2011, of 27 May. Gipuzkoa's Statutory Deputation, even without previously having approved any Statutory Rule that regulates it, has published the Statutory Order 445/2014, of 28 July, regulating the model that liquidates the tax.

On the other hand, in September 2014, the Court of Justice delivered its judgment in the case *Dansk Automat Brancheforening v European Commission*, rejecting the presented resource for procedural reasons. In addition, the European authorities have had occasion to declare on the Spanish case. Thus, the Commission, in a decision that would by itself need a detailed analysis, concluded in March 2015 (SA.34469 2014/NN ex 2012/CP), that the selectivity requirement set out in Article 107(1) TFEU was not fulfilled, and that the tax rates provided in Article 48, paragraph 7, first indent, 1° to 12°, of the Gaming Act 13/2011 do not constitute State aid granted to online gambling providers with respect to land-based gambling providers. This conclusion is without prejudice to the case-by-case study, should any Autonomous Community (or Basque Province) decide to increase tax rates established in the Gaming Act, as per Article 48(7) of the Gaming Act 13/2011. At the moment, no Autonomous Community has made use of this provision, and it is yet to be seen what the Court may decide about the issue.

Bibliography

Agoués Mendizábal, C. "El control judicial de las restricciones al principio de la libre prestación de los servicios de juego en línea. La STJUE de 8 de septiembre de 2010 (Carmen Media Group)." *Administración y justicia: Un análisis jurisprudencial: Liber amicorum Tomás-Ramón Fernández*. 1st ed. Thomsom Aranzadi, Cizur Menor, 2012.

Andrés Álvez, R. "Comentario sobre la sentencia del tribunal de justicia de la unión europea (gran sala) de 8 de septiembre de 2009 en el asunto C-42/07, que tiene por objeto una petición de decisión prejudicial planteada, con arreglo al artículo 234 CE, por el tribunal de pequena instância criminal do porto (Portugal), mediante resolución de 26 de enero de 2007, recibida en el tribunal de justicia el 2 de febrero de 2007, en el procedimiento entre la liga de fútbol portuguesa contra el Estado portugués y la Santa Casa de la Misericordia." *Revista Jurídica de Deporte y Entretenimiento: Deportes, Juegos De Azar, Entretenimiento y Música*, 28 (2010): 653–64.

Artetxe Palomar, E. "La evolución de la jurisprudencia europea en materia de juegos de azar." *Justicia Administrativa: Revista de Derecho Administrativo*, 39 (2008): 19–38.

———. "Los juegos de azar y el derecho de establecimiento y la libertad de prestación de servicios en el derecho europeo." *Revista Vasca de Administración Pública Herri-Arduralaritzako Euskal Aldizkaria*, 78 (2007): 37–82.

Barba Sánchez, R. and D. García Rivas. "Derecho comunitario y juego online." *El juego on line*. 1st ed. Cizur Menor: Editorial Aranzadi, 2001.

Ferrero, J., and M. Serrano. "Un paso más en la delimitación de la relación entre las libertades fundamentales de la unión europea y el negocio del juego y apuestas ligadas a eventos deportivos: Comentario a la sentencia del Tribunal de Justicia de las Comunidades Europeas de 6 de noviembre de 2003, asunto c-243/01 (caso Gambelli)." *Revista Jurídica de Deporte y Entretenimiento: Deportes, Juegos de Azar, Entretenimiento y Música*, 12 (2004): 511–19.

García Caba, M. M. "Los modelos europeos del juego on line." *El juego on line*. 1st ed. Cizur Menor: Editorial Aranzadi, 2011.

González Vaqué, L. "El TJUE declara compatible con el derecho de la UE una normativa nacional que prohíbe la publicidad de juegos de azar organizados en otros estados miembros (sentencia "Sjöberg y Gerdin")." *Unión Europea Aranzadi*, 10 (2010): 15–25.

Hörnle, J., and B. Zammit. *Cross-border online gambling law and policy*. Cheltenham (UK): Edward Elgar Publishers, 2010, 273–82.

Jiménez Ramo, E., and J. Vicente Matilla. "Tributación de las apuestas y de los juegos desarrollados a través de internet desde la perspectiva de la fiscalidad internacional." *Cuadernos de Formación IEF*, 10 (2010): 55–97.

Leal Marcos, A., J. López Laborda, and F. Rodrigo Rodríguez. "Faites vos jeux! efectos transfronterizos de los tributos regionales sobre el juego." *XVIII encuentro de economía pública*, Málaga. Economía Pública, 18 (2011):1–22.

Manteca Valdelande, V. "El régimen del juego en el ámbito de la Unión Europea." In *El nuevo régimen jurídico de los juegos de azar: Comentario a la ley estatal 13/2011, de regulación del juego*, Coord. por Olga Ortiz Arraiz, 725–85. Las Rozas: Editorial La Ley, 2012.

———. "Regulación del juego en la unión europea (I)." *Unión Europea Aranzadi*, 1 (2011): 7–17.

Miguel Kühn, W. "La conformidad con el derecho europeo de la integración de las disposiciones nacionales relativas a la explotación económica de juegos de azar: Un análisis de la jurisprudencia supranacional europea." *Revista Española de Derecho Europeo*, 24 (2007): 485–517.

Padrós Reig, C. "El tahur de luxemburgo. La jurisprudencia reciente del tribunal de justicia sobre juegos y apuestas." *Revista Española de Derecho Europeo*, 26 (2008): 151–190.

Ruiz Almendral, V., and J. J. Zornoza Pérez. "La necesaria eliminación de la tributación especial sobre el juego en España." *Régimen del juego en España*. Coord. por Alberto Palomar Olmeda, 217–56. Cizur Menor: Editorial Aranzadi, 2006.

Ruiz-Navarro Pinar, J. L. "La libre prestación de servicios de juegos de azar: La normativa europea y reflexiones sobre la futura legislación española del juego online." *Asamblea: Revista Parlamentaria de la Asamblea de Madrid*, 19 (2008): 213–70.

Zornoza Pérez, J. J., and A. Báez Moreno. "La fiscalidad del juego remoto y la nueva ley de regulación del juego. Un análisis constitucional y comunitario del impuesto sobre actividades de juego." *El juego on line*. Coord. por Alberto Palomar Olmeda, 585–616. Cizur Menor: Editorial Aranzadi, 2011.

———. "El régimen tributario del juego remoto." *Revista Jurídica de deporte y entretenimiento*, 27 (2009): 29–43.

14

Resilience in Tax Matters: The Case of Basque Foral Tax and Legal Conflict Context

*Susana Serrano-Gaztelurrutia**

Given the resilience of Basque self-government public finance and facing the current crisis, in considering the issue of political funding of public institutions at various levels in the Basque Country and elsewhere in Europe, we must not forget that coexistence of "human communities" (states, regions, provinces, counties, departments, cantons, autonomous regions, and so on) presupposes living together. And that cohabitation does not have to be peaceful, because it is still subject to standards recognized by all parties; the interpretation of these rules does not need to be (and it is not) the same, nor peaceful.

We briefly explain the geopolitical situation in the Basque Country and its fiscal relationship with the state, and the problems of this *status quo*. The problem is not new, and throughout history the Basque territories have been avoiding it, until now. It is in these settings to "get ahead" or survive where the question engages with the resilience referred to at this 13th Annual International Conference held on March 26 and 27, 2014 at the Center for Basque Studies at the University of Nevada, Reno.

* This work forms part of the Research and Training Unit 11/05, the project "Taxation of economic activities in the Basque Country: The Impact of Community Law", IT604-13, and the Draft Tax coordination from the perspective of the *foral* system of the Basque Country, DER2012-39342-C03-02.

Conceptual Issues on the "Basque Tax Resilience" and Framework

In Spanish, *resilience* means the ability to flexibly assume human extreme situations and overcome them,[1] and on the Internet, we find other definitions of the term as meaning the ability of individuals to overcome periods of emotional pain and adversity; an individual or group able to do so is said to have adequate resilience to overcome setbacks or even be strengthened by them.[2]

In a social-political context, for Agirreazkuenaga the concept of resilience has evolved from Holling. The resilience of a system must be analyzed according to some attributes, factors, or indicators that influence and govern the system dynamics. In social-ecological systems, there are three attributes that determine future trajectories: resilience, adaptability, and transformability. Resilience is the ability of a system to absorb disturbance and reorganize while experiencing a change in order to retain the proper function of the system to maintain an identity, structure, and feedback. Adaptability is the ability of the actors in the system to influence resilience and strength to play its management. Transformability is the ability to create an entirely new system when ecological, economic, or social structures of the system are unsustainable.[3]

In our area of study, we can understand the resilience as the capacity of the Basque Historical Territories to overcome periods of political and economic changes and adverse situations, including pressure to assimilate these territories within a homogeneous unit as the Spanish state. Focusing on this approach, we will refer only to the tax-financial-fiscal framework, or what we call "Basque or *foral* tax resilience."

We focus our study on the financial and tax environment; for all other matters relating to resilience and the history of the Basque territories, we refer to reference works.[4] In the legal-political field

---

1. *"Resiliencia,"* Real Spanish Academy of Language (RAE, Real Academia Española), http://lema.rae.es/drae/srv/search?key=resiliencia.[AU: Please include access date, as you have included it for the next note.]
2. "Resiliencia," Wikipedia, http://es.wikipedia.org/wiki/Resiliencia_%28psicolog%C3%ADa%29, last modified on 16 May 2014.
3. Joseba Agirreazkuenaga, "Resilient People, Resilient Planet" (The Report of the United Nations Secretary-General's High-Level Panel on Global sustainability) A Future Worth Choosing (www.galeuscahistoria.com/congreso2/1.pdf), p. 1.
4. Joseba Agirreazkuenaga Zigorraga, *Vasconia, Euskal Herria, Euskadiizena eta izana denboran barrena*, Ed. Jakin, no. 183–184, (2011), pp. 93–116; "Exploring Resilience Patterns Amongst National Minorities: From the Historical Representative As-

CAÑO, without using the term *resilience*, is also referred to the way in which the Basque territories have "been and remain" throughout history.[5]

Throughout history and up until recent times, the Basque territories have known how to accommodate circumstances (with more or less success) in order to survive while other territories were losing autonomy, rights, and to identity. Currently, within the Spanish state are some territories that have lost autonomy, rights, and identity and others that have not, for better or worse. This problematic heterogeneity arises because the alleged unity of the state did not materialize. Because where there is no uniformity, it is necessary to coordinate, agree, and be willing to accept that equality is not all the same but unique for each territory, including in terms of regional funding, which must not only demonstrate ability to manage and spend funds responsibly.

Let us start with a brief description of the situation. The Basque Country is an Autonomous Community (AC) within the Spanish state (one of 17). The current Constitution (1978) reserves tax matters for the State, while recognizing that the Autonomous Communities may impose and levy taxes in accordance with the Constitution and the law (art. 133). Therefore, the original regulatory authority belongs to the state, which yields to the Autonomous Communities, in what is known as a "common funding scheme."

The same Constitution also recognizes that some territories have historical rights, respected and taken refuge, in its update within the framework of the Constitution and the Statute of Autonomy (First Additional Provision), which has come to assume recognition of tax regulatory parallel power to the state in these territories: Araba (Álava), Bizkaia (Biscay), Gipuzkoa (Gipuzkoa), and Navarra. Navarra is itself an Autonomous Community, and Álava,

---

semblies (1812–1877) to the Basque Parliament (1980)," *RIEV, Revista internacional de los estudios vascos/Eusko ikaskuntzen nazioarteko aldizkaria/ Revue internationale des ètudes basques/International journal on Basque studies*, no. Extra 6 (2010) (Ejemplar dedicado a: Cuadernos 6: The making of Parliaments: 19th and 20th century, Europe and America): 73–90; "El Estado Vascongado triple y uno: de la "Constitución foral" (1808) al Estatuto de autonomía de Alava, Bizkaia y Gipuzkoa (1919)," *Hermes: Pentsamendu eta Historia Aldizkaria/Revista de Pensamiento e Historia*, no. 17 (2005) (Ejemplar dedicado a: Euskal autonomiaren bidarriak eta giltzarriak/Hilos y claves de la autonomía vasca), pp. 2–10.

5. Javier Caño Moreno, *Teoría institucional del Estatuto Vasco. Concepción institucional e interpretación normativo-institucional del Estatuto de Autonomía del País Vasco* (Bilbao: Universidad de Deusto, 1997), pp. 30–98.

Bizkaia, and Gipuzkoa together make up the Basque Country's Autonomous Community.

Coordinating in Financing System in the Spanish Kingdom

The issue is part of the regional financing both common systems as autonomous system. And though lately the functioning of the system has been questioned in the state, regional funding has enough roots so we can consider it an intrinsic competence of the Autonomous Communities.

On taxation, although the EC itself states that the primary power to tax is solely for the state by law (art. 133.1 CE'78), what is remarkable about this point is the issue of "primary power" and exclusivity. Because in the opposite sense, it is an "original" power to tax, which is not unique to the State, and which is embodied in recognizing in the Autonomous Communities and local corporations the ability to establish and levy taxes, in accordance with the Constitution and laws (art. 133.2 CE'78).

Therefore, regional tax competition has its foundation in the art. 133 SC, where, after establishing the primary power of the state itself to create taxes, provides regional competition in their own territory.

Article 133: Tax Powers

The primary power to raise taxes is vested exclusively in the State, by law. Autonomous Communities and local Corporations may impose and levy taxes in accordance with the Constitution and laws.

In addition, the Spanish Constitution of 1978 (SC'78), in order to protect the historical rights of these territories, established a statutory basis for tax competition and tax matters. And among those rights is particularly relevant the subject matter of our analysis.

First Additional Provision: Historical Rights of Foral Territories

The Constitution protects and respects the historic rights of the foral territories. The general updating of the foral system will be implemented, where appropriate, within the framework of the Constitution and the Statute of Autonomy. Therefore, since the Constitution was expected that it could get decentralization in tax matters, although apart from the listings autonomous powers provided for that purpose (article 148 SC).

This tax decentralization *per se* implies the co-existence of different competence levels in the same subject (tax, in this case). Within the financing system of common rules, this relationship is vertical (state–autonomous community) and horizontal (autonomous community–autonomous community). And a certain order regulating this relationship, which is what is known as "coordination" (or vertical cooperation between state and autonomous communities), known as a constitutional principle (art. 156.1 SC) is necessary.

Article 156 SC

1. The Autonomous Communities shall enjoy financial autonomy for the development and execution of its powers, under the principles of coordination with the State Treasury and solidarity among all Spaniards.
2. Autonomous Communities may act as delegates or collaborators of the State for the collection, management and settlement of the State's tax resources, in accordance with the laws and Statutes.

As Bayonne of Perogordo and Soler Roch (1989) note, this principle of coordination by the State Treasury implies "dependency and mutual subordination and, in turn, nested, so to speak, a pyramid among the various treasuries (State/Autonomous Communities/ Corporations local), such that the action of the principle of financial autonomy and, in particular, the different degrees to which is configured, structurally and functionally different public treasuries not be properly interpreted, but integrating it into the principle of coordination."[6]

The Spanish Constitutional Court (SCC) repeatedly argues that with coordination what is sought is the integration of the diversity of parts or subsystems in the assembly or system, avoiding contradictions and dysfunctions reduced, that, if survive, respectively prevent or hamper the reality of the system pursued (SCCJ 32/28 April 1983 and 42/1983 of May 20, 1983).

According to the SCC, that power must be understood as fixing means for exchange of information, technical standardization and establishment of the competent authorities, so that the integration of partial acts on the totality of the system is achieved. To do this, some media may be creating collaborative bodies only if they are governing or advisory; development of sectorial plans ,which are defined as supra interests, and objectives, priorities, and requests for information are set in form of relief between aadministrations (SCCJ 76/1983 of 5

---

6. Bayona de Perogordo and Soler Roch (1989), pp. 245–246.

August 1983, about the Organic Law of the Autonomy Process Harmonization, OLAPH).

As outlined, the general approach for coordinating statewide had to focus on the area of the Basque *foral* funding, that is, coordination or vertical cooperation between the Basque Autonomous Community (BAC) and the Historical Territories.

Fiscal Coordination with the Basque Country: The Economic Agreement

In regards to seeking ways to *coordinate*,[7] the Basque territories have shown to have internalized this way of understanding reality, both in the past and more recently. Thus, while each *foral* territory until then had remained "independent" with respect to the others, the Spanish Constitution of 1978 (SC'78) created a common block, and financial relations that had hitherto been independent (with different monarchs or Lords) came to be regulated jointly under the the the "Economic Agreement."

The importance of this unification cannot be overemphasized. It should be noted that this matter had historically been the responsibility of each of the Historical Territories. The creation of a common Basque political subject, the Basque Country's Autonomous Community (BCAC), is an important milestone in Basque historiography. This new subject certainly assumes those SC'78 skills set for the Autonomous Communities (art. 148 and 149 SC'78), but also some specific to the Historical Territories.

Therefore, when we talk about *coordination*, think of an organized multiplicity. In the case of the Basque Country, this term is appropriate, because there are four different co-estates; one for each historical territory and another general one for the entire Basque Country's Autonomous Community—and that is without including the local forms. And each of these levels corresponds to a level of competence with different legal basis.

Regardless of autonomy that the assumption of these materials may pose themselves, we must not forget that in the case of the Basque Country and Navarre they pose greater autonomy. That is, in terms of the higher powers assumed by the Basque Country's Autonomous Community, as the state does not cover these services, the quota to be delivered is reduced. The more powers are transferred, the lower quota that must be paid to the state (the State revenues will

---

7. Coordinate; (From lat. *co, por cum,* con, y *ordināre,* ordenar). 1. Tr. Have things methodically. Two. Tr. Make media endeavors, etc., For common action. RAE, visited on 04.07.2014, http://lema.rae.es/drae/?val=coordinar.

be lower). And that is something to be avoided at all costs, delaying competences devolution.

Peculiarities of Basque Foral Financing

The normative power of Historical Territories, also known as tax normative capacity, establishes a different and differentiated tax regime from that prevailing in the state.[8] Embodied in several basic principles, some internal system itself and others are configured to govern the relationship with the state:

- Principle of power or normative autonomy: Each territory has its own normative system. The cohesion among the various Historical Territories is achieved through tax harmonization rules. Each normative system regulates its own taxable transactions.
- Principle of fiscal separation and non-fiscal overlay: It is not possible that the same taxable event is subject to various charges related to many other tax jurisdictions; separation operates by applying certain connection points, which define when a chargeable event is submitted to the competent Basque authority.
- Principle of separation of boxes *versus* single box principle from the rest of the state: The difference (positive or negative) between the actual collected revenue and the collection taken as mean (for the Agreement, proportional to their income level) may be referred to as "income benefit."
- Principle of matching: Given the usual gap between revenues collected and assumed powers, the need for vertical equalization is inherent to the system. The amount of the quota (as a mechanism for vertical correction) decreases with increasing financial importance of the powers assumed by the Basque Country. In the Basque Economic Agreement, it is assumed that the Interterritorial Compensation Fund (ICF, a quintessential mechanism for horizontal equalization in the Spanish system) is a general burden of the state. This corresponds to the central Treasury operationalizing the redistributive function.
- Principle capacity *versus* benefit principle: This is enshrined in the contribution to the financing of the general burdens (or not taken), which is basically an indicator based on income. The

8. Moreno Portela (1997), pp. 166–182. Regarding the possible application to other Autonomous Communities, see Zubiri Oria (2000), pp. 127–146.

same approach is used in the allocation of the share of non-subsidized income to be attributed to the Basque Country ("offsets"). The financing of competences that are transferred is also determinated based on an indicator of income. The (positive or negative) difference between the actual cost corresponding to the territorializing in the Basque Country of the competence at the time of the transfer, and the cost that results from applying the income indicator above average cost can be called "benefit spending."

Capacity and responsibility set the tone for the Agreement regime and make it a *rara avis* even in the context of existing federalism systems in Europe today.

From the perspective of tax administration, the procedure for levying and tax management, in all its phases, lies with the Historical Councils, primarily, and is not assigned to them.[9] As such, its own power can be exercised, if appropriate, in collaboration with other tax administrations.[10]

General Principles of the Basque Agreement

The general principles of the tax system of Historical Territories are enshrined in article 2 of the Economic Agreement:

- Respect of solidarity in the terms provided in the Constitution and the Statute of Autonomy.
- Attention to the general tax structure of the state.
- Coordination, fiscal harmonization, and cooperation with the state, according to the rules of the Economic Agreement.
- Coordination, fiscal harmonization and mutual cooperation between the institutions of the Historical Territories according to the rules, to that effect issued by the Basque Parliament.
- Submission to international conventions or treaties signed and ratified by the Spanish state or to which it adheres. In particular, it is stated that the territories must comply with the provisions of international conventions signed by Spain to avoid

9. This autonomy also have common regime Autonomous Communities, but because the state has yielded. See Ramos Prieto (2007), pp. 365–386; Grandal Pita (2008), pp. 201–230.

10. Obviously, as is universally recognized, control over fiscal and tax system itself has been a key element in the economic development of the Basque Country due to leeway involved in economic policy. See Aizega Zubillaga (2003), pp. 163–173; also Beldarrain Garín, Escribano Riego, and Ugalde Zaratiegui (1996).

double taxation and tax harmonization rules of the European Union and must take appropriate returns to practice following the implementation of these Conventions and rules.[11]

In turn, the financial relations between the state and the Basque Country are governed by the general principles set out in article 48 of the Ecomic Agreement. These principles are:

- Fiscal and financial autonomy of the institutions of the Basque Country, for the development and execution of its powers.
- Respect of solidarity, in the terms provided in the Constitution and the Statute of Autonomy.
- Coordination and collaboration with the state's fiscal stability
- Basque contribution to state burdens not assumed by the Basque Autonomous Community, in the manner determined in the Economic Agreement.
- Financial guardianship of the local authorities, which corresponds to the institutions of the Basque Country and whose level of autonomy in no case be lower than those under the common regime.

In terms of collaborative principles, article 4 of the Economic Agreement provides that the competent institutions of the Historical Territories shall inform the state administration, with due notice of its entry into force, the draft tax legislation regulations. Similarly, the State administration practice identical communication to those institutions. Regarding the participating institutions of the Basque Country in international agreements affecting the implementation of the Economic Agreement, the state shall develop mechanisms to allow this, and the state and the Historical Territories, in the exercise of its responsibilities to them—management, inspection, and collection of taxes—shall provide each other, in a timely and appropriate manner, any information and records deemed necessary for the best tax charge. In particular, both administrations, through their data processing centers, will provide all necessary information.

In summary, the general criteria for harmonization between state and *foral* tax systems could be classified into two groups. On the one hand, as a general principle, these systems would respect the solidarity in the terms provided by the Spanish Constitution and the Basque

---

11. On these principles, understood as limits, see Barbara Martinez (2003), pp. 115–121.

Country's Autonomy Statute: attention to the tax structure of the state; coordination, harmonization, and cooperation both with the state as contained in Economic Agreement and and with the Historical Territories, as dictated by the Basque Parliament; and submission to international treaties and conventions signed by Spain. In terms of early tax harmonization, the following stand out: the adequacy (not uniformity) of historical rules to Spanish General Tax Law; the classification of economic activities in the common territory; the stipulation that historical rules cannot involve impairment of business competition or distort allocation of resources and the free movement of capital and labor, and the requirement that the overall effective tax burden is equivalent to the state.

Unilateral Risk

The Agreement system establishes a model of decentralization of both income and expenditure. It means self-sufficiency—that is, the Historical Territories and Basque Autonomous Community manage themselves without state assistance or funding. Therefore, the financial capacity assumed responsibility for the management of revenues and expenditures, without state intervention, which does not participate in the revenue obtained in the Basque Country. And as separate from the funds raised by the Historical Councils, it also assumes coverage of public expenditure of the Autonomous Community, so there is no option to use the state to meet the public expenditure. This "self-sufficiency" means that the profit or loss arising from a good or bad tax management pertains exclusively by the *Foral* Treasures (and by extension the Basque Autonomous Community).

In addition, the contribution to the general expenses of the state (quota) are based on expenditures contained in the state budget, in relation to the powers not assumed rather than in relation to the revenue collected by the Historical Territories. The principle therefore implies that both the State Treasury and the Basque Autonomous Treasury unilaterally assume the risk arising from the management of its tax jurisdiction, and the quality of management in collection will benefit or harm each of the two public treasuries. And lower collection by the Autonomous Treasury of the Basque Country results in a decreased ability to manage its interest, because the percentage of the general expenses of the state that the Basque Autonomous Community is assigned an attribution rate objective, which has been constant since 1981 (6.24%). However, the principle of unilateral risk applies only with respect to the state, since within the Basque Autonomous Community the risk is shared between all institutions (autonomous, *foral*, and local), because the distribution of resources is made between them after paying the quota.

The Quota

The quota is the amount the Basque Country delivers to the State Treasury in payment for the powers not assumed and the services provided by the state (skills not transferred, the army, the crown, foreign representation, etc.). This quota reduces Basque Country's financial capacity as conferred by the current model Agreement, which is determined by the sum of income plus additional agreement (from horizontal leveling or any other state fund distribution) under the quota (as a positive liquid balance). That is, the valuation methodology of charges not assumed by the Basque Country is to assign to each budget appropriation of government spending.

Therefore, as a concept, the quota is the economic contribution of the Basque Country to the state, consisting of the global quota, composed corresponding to each of the Historical Territories as a contribution to all the charges do not assume the Basque Autonomous Community (art. 49, Econic Agreement).

Tax Coordination in the Basque Country: Basque Autonomous Community—Historical Territories

Within the Basque institutional framework, each of these institutional settings has its powers defined by the Economic Agreement. Thus, based on the three policy areas (State, Basque Autonomous Community, and Historical Territories), three levels of "power" are established: General Treasury of the Basque Country, whose revenues are divided into ordinary and extraordinary income; Institutions of the Historical Territories, covering tax management in all its phases (charge, management, liquidation, taxation, review and collection, and specific rules for each tax agreement); and the state.

In agreement taxes, the Basque Country (the Historical Territories) assumes full autonomy and freedom in the management and charge thereof, which are within its jurisdiction, its area of responsibility, and its share of risk. In accordance with the provisions of article 42.2 BCAS, financial autonomy resides in the Historical Territories more than in the Autonomous Communiteis; this mainly affects expenditure autonomy. This is not a constitutional conflict incompatible with article 156.1 SC; on the contrary, as the Basque financial autonomy rests on the 1st Additional Provision SC.[12]

And to avoid inconsistency, as noted even in the Judgment of the Court of Justice of the European Union (JCEU) of 11 September 2008 (Joined cases C-428/06 to C-434/06), this division of powers requires close cooperation between the various entities. As already mentioned, this is the governing principle of coordination between the General Treasury of the BAC and the financial activity of the Historical Territories, contributing to the maintenance of all general burdens of the Basque Country. The system assumes that as each of the Historical Territories raises its taxes, the quota is provided to the state and much of that revenue is transferred for the support of commons institutions and assumed autonomous powers. In addition, this transfers to the municipalities the necessary function of the powers conferred spending amounts. And, obviously, the respective *foral* institutions must deal with their own powers and expenses.

Decisions about how each Historical Territory bears the common expenses—that is, determining the allocation of resources or calculation of the contributions of each Historical Territory—are made by the Basque Council of Finance, which also corresponds to the enforcement tax collection under Historical Territories Law (HTL). This assessment is performed according to the volume of skills or services that each agency holds in accordance with the law, and shall pursue a policy of global current expenditure per capita, equity, and solidarity.

The most problematic competencies around which the *foral* financing is limited are the local administration, the Basque language, civil functions, highways and roads, education, and self-policing. These powers also include *Osakidetza* (Basque Health Service),[13] which is certainly one of the most expensive budget items, and claimed Social Security, which despite being considered deficient by the state, is still pending transfer.[14]

General Treasury of the Basque Country

The General Treasury of the Basque Country (autonomous) has its basis in individual state laws and autonomous law: the Statute

---

12. This matter was resolved by the Constitutional Court in STC 123/1984, of December 18, and STC 76/1988, of 26 April.
13. Article 18.1 Statute of Autonomy of the Basque Country (SABC).
14. Article 18.2 SABC.

of Autonomy of the Basque Country (SABC),[15] the Organic Law on Financing of the Autonomous Communities (OLFAC),[16] and what is known as the Historical Territories Law (HTL).[17] As such, the regulatory principles of the General Treasury are set out in Legislative Decree 1/1997.[18]

Although, as noted above, the Economic Agreement provides that the power to regulate taxes and management corresponds to the Historical Territories, this does not necessarily imply that the tax system of the Basque Country (as such Autonomous Community) is completely limited. Thus, in principle, the BAC would be able to set its own taxes (article 42.b of the SABC), which are established by the Basque Parliament, pursuant to the provisions of article 157 of EU the and the OLFAC.

Technically, the internal system of the BAC does not avoid, totally and absolutely, the exercise of tax jurisdiction by the Basque Common Institutions. A different matter is how the use (or not) of this competition is done, and how it performed. However, the principle of coordination was established to articulate these competent institutions. As noted above, the Spanish Constitutional Court itself understands that cooperation aims to "integrate the diversity of parts or subsystems in the assembly or system, avoiding contradictions and dysfunctions reducing that to survive, prevent or hamper, respectively, the reality of the system" (JSCC 70/1997, of 10 April). In fiscal matters, this implies the need to ensure that the exercise of the financial autonomy of each territory does not distort or duplicate between the financial systems of other entities with taxing power, and thus this is connected to the actual distribution of sources taxation between the various units of government.

Given the institutional and jurisdictional settings of and in the Basque Country, it is clear that the principle of coordination has particular relevance. Recall that in the autonomous institutions themselves must be added for each Historical Territory and the local authorities. This institutional framework may result in overlapping functions (which, in tax matters, can result in double-taxation, for example).

---

15. Organic Law 3/1979 of 18 December.
16. Organic Law 8/1980 of 22 September.
17. Law 27/1983 of the Basque Parliament on relations between public institutions of the Autonomous Community and *foral* organs of their Historical Territories.
18. Legislative Decree 1/1997, of 11 November, approving the revised text of the Law on Principles Governing the General Treasury of the Basque Country.

Obviously, tax legislation of the three Historical Territories is abundant, and to promote the harmonization, coordination, and collaboration between the Basque tax institutions, the Appellate Tax Coordination (ATC) was created.[19]

Foral Tax Treasure

The Additional Provision 1 of the Spanish Constitution protects and respects the historical rights of Historical Territories, while the overall renovation of historic rights is ordained under the Constitution and the Statute of Autonomy.

The powers of the Historical Treasury are governed by the Economic Agreement and the Historical Territories Law. In turn, the local treasuries are regulated by the Economic Agreement and the Foral Rules of Local Taxation.

When talking about "*Foral* treasury," we refer primarily to the competence of the General Assemblies of Araba, Bizkaia, and Gipuzkoa to create tax rules (legislative power), and more specifically to the management of these agencies perform the relevant *Foral* Deputations of each Territory.[20]

Limits Concerted System

The power of the taxing power of the Historical Territories (through the legislative work of the General Assemblies, and the executive of the Foral Deputations), is embodied in the authority to maintain, establish and regulate within its territory, taxation (art. 1.1 EcAgr). This implies the co-existence of three distinct regional tax systems in each Historical Territory (Álava, Bizkaia, and Gipuzkoa), to which must be added the regional tax system in the Basque Country Autonomous Community itself and those for local entities. Only intern level, or *ad intra*. Noting the general principles of the tax system of the Historical Territories, and pointed out the coordination, fiscal harmonization and collaboration ad extra (with the state). And even, one might add

---

19. The Appellate Tax Coordination (ATC) can be accessed online and even compared to the Foral Tax Code that integrates all the rules of Euskadi. http ://www. ogasun.ejgv.euskadi.net/r51-5472/es/contenidos/enlace/codigo_fiscal_foral/es_ 10655/es_indice.html.

20. For example, while the Basque Country governs the Cooperative Societies, each Historical Territory has its own rules of taxation of these companies. See Sofia Arana, *Taxation of Cooperatives* (Bilbao: UPV / EHU, 2012). Sofia SPIDERMAN, Sofia, "The fiscal regime of Spanish cooperatives in the European Union: Spanish lines reform cooperatives.", Basque Journal of Social Economics, No. 7, 2010, pp. 77-98.

a third relation, ad above, regarding the relationship with the European Union.

Limits ad extra: State

Basically, the regulation on tax matters as Historical Rights protected by the SC 1st AP, references to state law are recurrent. And while the tax law is a very broad power competition (especially when compared with what they may have as a common regime with other Autonomous Communities), no longer a competition subject, ultimately, to the State, that limits thereof.

The financial-tax between the Basque Country and the Spanish state relations are regulated by the Economic Agreement. The Economic Agreement is the rule (state law) agreed between the Historical Territories, the Basque Country´s Autonomous Community and the Spanish State[21]. It basically sets the agree taxes, which assumes that the taxes collected shall be governed by foral legislation respecting a number of general principles:

- Respect of solidarity.
- Attention to the general tax structure of the State.
- Coordination, fiscal harmonization and cooperation with the State.
- Coordination, fiscal harmonization and mutual cooperation between the institutions of the Provinces.
- Adjustment to the Tax Code in terminology and concepts.
- Maintain an overall effective tax burden equivalent to that in the rest of the State.
- Shall respect and ensure freedom of movement and establishment of persons and the free movement of goods, capital and services throughout the Spanish territory.
- They will use the same classification of artistic common ground in ranching, mining, industrial, commercial, service, and professional.

---

21. The Law 12/2002 of the Economic Agreement is not any law. Its content is agreed between the parties on the call Joint Commission on the Economic Agreement: Historical Territories (one representative from each Territory: Alava, Bizkaia and Gipuzkoa: 3), as many of the Basque Country (3), which form known as the "Basque representation", consisting of 6 members, and many others (6) by the state. The resolutions adopted saved an exquisite balance between the interests of all parties (technically 5 different interests), so it passes the legislative approval process can only be done by accepting or not accepting the whole law, unable to get to do amendments (since in this case the principle of covenant would step).

Within these parameters, therefore, based on the recognized in the Constitution tax capacity (SC 1st AP), taxes (Economic Agreement) was concluded for each of the legislatives chambers of the Historical Territories (General Assemblies) may make rules corresponding tax.

This tax legislation of the Historical Territories capacity makes that in the State co-exist five different state tax systems, with different rules and different tax rates.

The problem has led to the foral tax resilience is precisely that policy-tax non-uniformity within the Spanish state. Many do not want to accept that being different does not necessarily mean a discrimination or a violation of equality.

So in addition to the principles already outlined the system, it should be recalled, for example, that all that can be related to customs and relations with the exclusive competence of the State. However, the leasehold system is fairly complete; enough as to function autonomously if the case came.

Limits ad supra: European Union

The limits that Spain's membership of the European Union supposed to foral taxation have been widely tested. Remember, nothing more, than an agreement system itself has repeatedly appealed to European authorities for alleged breach of European Law. Some examples are known as "Basque tax holidays" and appeals from Foral Rules of Income Tax (FRIT) of each of the Historical Territory.

In the case of "tax holidays" it was certain fiscal and tax measures adopted by the relevant General Assemblies incurred in the regime of illegal State aid referred to in arts. 107 and 108 of the Treaty on the Functioning of the European Union (TFEU).[22] As noted by the European Commission itself, such measures could have been legalized if it had followed the required procedure (i.e., before taking the measures in question, seek authorization from the Commission itself, art. 108.3 TFEU). When this requirement has been avoided, measures were automatically illegal, so proceeded to urge recovery and assume appropriate sanctions for breach of European Law. The JECJ 13, 2014 closed this issue by establishing a fine of 30 million euros.

As for appeals against Foral Rules of income tax of each Historical Territory, some bordering Autonomous Community, basically because the reported tax rate was slightly lower than that in the State

---

22. Previous art. 87 and ss. TEU.

common territory applied (32.5% foral *vs.* 35% State) claiming assumptions prejudices besides alleged breach of the State aid regime for territorial selectivity. After appropriate journey (interpretation of European law by the Spanish High Court included), the Superior Court of Justice in Basque Country's (SCJBC) opted to seek a preliminary ruling. What was whether Art. 87.1 TEU (now 107.1 TFEU) should be interpreted as meaning that the measures adopted by the General Assembly of Biscay in the General Corporation Tax should be considered selective with lace on the notion of State aid and should therefore be communicated to the Commission. The "triple test of autonomy" was established as a parameter of mandatory state standards known infra JCEU of September 11, 2008.

- Institutional autonomy: institutions adopting the challenged rules are independent of the State.
- Procedural autonomy: that the adoption of the contested rules not bound by State intervention.
- Economic autonomy: the lowest possible income from those contested measures is not compensated by the State.

As a national court of the question with the sentencing guidelines, the Superior Court of Justice in Basque Country's determined that this test was satisfied and therefore not incurred in territorial selectivity. With this, the question was settled by the "legality" of infra-state tax systems with different types (lower) than the rest of the State territory. And Economic Agreement *as infra* system reaches full legal status under the EU law.

Closed these issues, however, the statutory funding model is no exception to the limits established by European legislation for the Member States. Assume the same limits and obligations; even without being part (and therefore subject responsible, because only the Member States are represented) to the European institutions, respects and pay the penalties for breach of European law (the defendant is the Spanish State, the EU does not fall in the internal organization of Member States, or how powers and responsibilities are divided, the EU responds to the State, and internally operate the internal rules).

Therefore, settled the issue of territorial selectivity in tax matters as State aid, there are still (or may become, if need be give) without solving many fronts; remember that the regime of State aid can be violated in other areas such as free movement of people, capital, goods or services, and also the exercise of the power to tax (whether national, regional or leasehold) is conditioned by the framework set by harmonization directives in the field of indirect taxation (VAT and Special Taxes, basically) and direct taxation (dividends, interest and royalties paid between parent-subsidiary mergers, savings) or by homogenizing standards as regulations common Customs Tariff and related charges.

Limits ad intra: BAC

The internal relationship between institutions and between Historical Territories and autonomous institutions, governed by rules, to that effect issued by the Basque Parliament, then Historical Territories Law.[23] As already noted above, the HTL engages the existence of a new political and administrative organization (the BAC, a common government and a Parliament that set up the HHTT[24]) with ancestral Historical Territories. These new institutions articulate with respect to proprietary legal regimes and historical powers of the General Assemblies and the Foral Deputations of Bizkaia, Gipuzkoa and Alava[25].

The HTL proved a controversial rule that was appealed to the Spanish Constitutional Court, although the "path" that finally made it in the same was not as much as originally claimed.[26] Basically the complaint focused on that 54 Senators understood that law generated a abolitorio transfer Competencies HHTT for the Autonomous Community against the SC 1st AP, and considering that the Basque Parliament was not competent to make the distribution since only the Statute of Autonomy was entitled to update the Foral regime and Historical Rights. The part of the judgment dismissed the appeal, as remembers Caño Moreno (2007), stating competition Basque legislature not only for the update performed at HTL, but to perform it in correctly both as regards holders or subject (subjective novation) and to the powers (objective novation).[27]

---

23. Law 27/1983 of the Basque Parliament on relations between public institutions of the Autonomous Community and foral organs of the Historical Territories
24. Art. 1 SABC.
25. Art. 3 SABC and art. 1 LHT.
26. SCC judgment of 26 April 1988 on the LHT
27. Moreno Cano (2007), p. 202 And, as this author points out, the LHT had close political and institutional backbone of the country and, therefore, opt for one of only two possible models: empowerment of Common Institutions to consolidate the BAC as a new political subject or enhance competence by Autonomous Institutions exempt redoubts higher than initially anticipated and constitutional and statutory due. In other words, deepen the national way of art. 2nd SC or follow the provincial road of SC 1sr AP. The political representatives of both bodies (regional and foral) started

By regulating the division of powers between the Common Institutions of the BAC and the Foral Institutions of their HHTT in ownership and exercise, in accordance with the provisions of the Constitution and the SABC[28], the objective of the HTL was to harmonize and balance the demands of the two levels of competition (the autonomic and foral).[29] Since this law autonomic beginning (1983), and having already more than five decades, today is spoken to reform and update. As observed Basañez Larrazabal (2008), in the HTL intangible competencies core *foralidad* or forality plus any tasks of the Basque Autonomous Community Parliament decided to transfer to HHTT with a closing clause (art. 6.1 LTH) develop establishing a residual clause in favor of the common institutions, which was expressly endorsed by the aforementioned Spanish Constitutional Court Judgment. Updating the HTL could happen, so for a change in the powers of the Historical Territories that could increase or decrease.

Given the unique institutional architecture in the State of the BAC, the "legislative" power in the Basque Country is divided between regional and Historical institutions. In all other Autonomous Community the only organs that can make rules with force of law are the legislative assemblies, and other institutions (county councils, city councils ...) can only issue regulations (without implying any problem since, obviously, and county councils and city councils have powers conferred on subjects in which is established the principle of legal reserve). In the Basque Country, however, the art. 25.1 SABC said

---

from different conceptions of the final model of institutional structuring. Ibid., Pp. 196-197. To Larrazabal Basañez (2008), p. 28, an open and flexible mechanism that allows to increase the powers of the Historical Territories was established, probably because at that time there were other priorities and was not entirely clear to which model internal structuring was going to tender.

28. Section 1 LHT. Recall that its origin is the recognition of the historical rights of Provincial Territories expressed in art. 3 SABC, which States that Bizkaia, Gipuzkoa and Araba may "maintain or, where appropriate, restore and update your organization and custodial institutions of self-government" but reserving to the Basque Parliament and the Basque Government, the political and institutional supremacy administration of Basque Country or Euskadi (art. 2).

29. The LHT incorporated in Title I allocations of HHTT according to foral tradition explicitly recognized in the Statute. It also establishes the legal mechanisms needed to adapt skills to new situations that may arise in the future, setting the legal mechanisms through which it may transfer or delegate new materials to improve the delivery of public services to citizens. Thus the absence of inflexible or rigid approaches that may be inappropriate for social, economic and political development of the country itself is guaranteed. However, the "partnership" between foral and autonomic institutions has not always been peaceful, as stated doctrine. For an overview of the problem, see, Among others, Corcuera Atienza (1985).

that "the Basque Parliament exercises legislative power (...) without prejudice to the powers of the institutions referred to in art. 37" (foral organs of the Historical Territories).[30] This is because the legal institutions hold tax capacity, being competent to regulate the essential elements of taxes, and the establishment of rebates and exemptions on them, and this can only be done by law (Art. 133 SC).[31]

The bodies performing this financial and tax work are the Basque Council of Finance (as a body of encounter, dialogue and agreement between the BAC Treasury and foral treasuries), and the Appellate Tax Coordination of Basque Country (created to articulate the tax relationship between the four Basque treasuries), with equal representation of the various institutions represented.[32] And as the regulatory body *ad intra* jurisdictional conflicts in the Basque Country the Arbitration Commission (not to be confused with the Arbitration Board, which is an ad extra body in relationship between the BAC and the State), with equal representation chaired by instituting President of SCJBC, which is responsible for mediating between the autonomous and foral institutions, as discussed in the following section. To complete this general overview, it should be noted that bodies exist to articulate the relations (*ad extra*) of the BAC with the State in this matter are the Joint Commission Quota, the Coordination Committee and the Arbitration Board.

With the foregoing, it is clear that the principle of coordination is an essential tool that should be examined exhaustively in the statutory tax regime of the Basque Country, for the consolidation and demarcation of the responsibilities of each entity based on concrete manifestations of economic capacity and perfectly differentiated, avoiding duplication.

Resilience: Conflict Statutory Tax

The plurality of competent institutions in this taxation materia is a

---

30. Institutional Foral Rule of Biscay in January 5, 1983; Institutional Gipuzkoa Foral Rule of 26 February 1983 on Institutional Organization province of Gipuzkoa, replaced by the Foral Rule on Institutional Organization and Administration Government the Historical Territory of Gipuzkoa, adopted by the General Meeting on July 1, 2005; Institutional and Foral Rule of Álava, March 7, 1983.

31. See, Alonso Arce (1998), pp. 3-4.

32. For a discussion of these organs, see Aranburu Urtasun (2005), p. 67-71, Reta (2002), p. 183-189; Vivanco (2002), p. 192 et seq. More recently, on the occasion of the 25th anniversary of the LHT, see Bilbao Eguren (2008), p. 4-12; Arrese Olano (2008), p. 14-20; Agirre Lopez (2008), p. 22-24; Larrazabal and Basáñez (2008), p. 26-34.

complexity not only in his explanation, but was accepted despite having almost 40 years working in the current constitutional framework. Even with constitutional protection, the foral tax system has been constantly resorted to the courts, trying to establish tax harmonization rules (set out in the statute of Autonomy of the Basque Country and in the Economic Agreement). Do not forget that the core is attacked is the normative capacity of the Historical Territories, using the Foral rules dictated by the respective General Assemblies in this matter. Since the late 90s of the twentieth century the State Bar filed more than 75 resources, many of them relying on breach of the principle of fiscal harmonization.

It came to a multilateral agreement in the Joint Committee on the Economic Agreement, where respect of tax harmonization was committed.[33] While the conflict since the State was solved with this "tax peace", then were the neighboring Autonomous Communities who were devoted to resort tax foral rules. And as there was no room to say that the Spanish law is violated (because the foral financing system is constitutionally valid within the Spanish State), the argument against this duality regional financing (common and foral) was that violates European Union law. It was argued that the rules difference between areas within the same State is a violation of State aid scheme "territorial selectivity." And the European Union had to rule on that issue and others related to the Basque foral taxation. Issues that have highlighted the strength of the Historical tax resilience.

New Space for Historical Tax Resilience: Harmonization

The issue was highlighted by the judgment of the Court of Justice of the European Union of 11 September 2008 is the harmonization. In the Spanish State coexist 5 tax systems: the State system (which applies in the 15 Autonomous Communities of common system), and the foral system from Álava, Bizkaia, Gipuzkoa and Navarre. In this coexistence is the *quid* of the matter in this work.

We have already noted that we focus only on the Territories that make up the Basque Country (Alava, Bizkaia and Gipuzkoa). But, no doubt, harmonization is an issue that is also relevant in the context of the European Union, composed of 27 Member State and (at least) as many tax systems. Without going on, remember that harmonization comes from the EU makes it through various means: regulation of the Treaties, the ECJ jurisprudence, *Shoft Law*, Codes of Conduct and

---

33. Agreements Joint Commission Conn January 28, 2001, known as "Tax Peace."

policy on aid state. We won't go into these issues.

In the Spanish State there is harmonization, particularly in relations between the State and the Basque Country, harmonization is a general principle to be respected by the tax systems of the Historical Territories, in their relationship with the State tax system (development art. 41.2 SBCAC and arts. 2 and 3 EcAgr). With a special mention to the work of the Committee on Evaluation and Policy Coordination (EcAgr).

So, we reduced our scope of analysis, the internal of the Autonomous Community of the Basque Country. In this *ad intra* harmonization, it must achieve and maintain a delicate balance between the exclusive jurisdiction of the Historical Territories to maintain, establish and regulate the system or tax regime[34] and competition from the Basque Country to make rules for coordination, tax harmonization and cooperation (art. 42.a SBCAC, art. 2 EcAgr., and art. 14.3 HTL).[35]

Technically, harmonize is to bring harmony, or consonance or make two or more parts of a whole, or two or more things that must be in the same order are rejected. For several administrations with competences in the same subject, one might think that the higher institutions are imposed on the lower. But that's not harmonized, since it can not send what it do not have skills, because that creates constant tensions. Harmonization of negotiating and agreeing, but sometimes, partisanship makes it very difficult and also promotes institutional loyalty essential to reach a reasonable settlement in these times.

The essence of tax harmonization, as a limiting principle of the regulatory capacity of Historical Territories in the XXI Century, which is simply to enable the complex financial and tax Basque model (federalist features, unique in Comparative Law, rooted in History the Basque people and engine of actual Basque Country or Euskadi), works correctly in any of the legal plans in which is inserted: European Union, Spanish State, Basque Autonomous Community.

Facing the *ad extra* harmonisation with and in the European Union, in 2010 there was an agreement for Basque representatives participate actively integrating the delegation of Spanish State in the Working Groups of the ECOFIN in which issues related to the competencies are addressed tax of Historical Territories. They are instru-

---

34. About this foral jurisdiction of the Constitutional Court itself has laid an established doctrine, according to which the foral tax system "is part of the intangible nucleus of the *forality*" SCCJ 76/1988 (Full Court) of 26 April, Legal Basis 6).
35. This competition has been developed by Act 3/1989 of 30 May the Basque Parliament, harmonization, coordination and fiscal cooperation.

ments intended to tax harmonization approach of the tax laws of the Member State in corporate taxation. Since April 2011 Basque representation is present too.

Bibliography

Agirreazkuenaga, Joseba. (2012), Exploring Resilience Patterns in National Minorities: From the Historical Representative Assemblies (1812-1877) to the Basque Parliament (1980), page 11, in www.galeuscahistoria.com/congreso2/ 1.pdf.

————. "Resilient People, Resilient Planet" (The Report of the United Nations Secretary-General's High-Level Panel on Global sustainability) A Future Worth Choosing (www.galeuscahistoria.com/congreso2/1.pdf), 1.

————. *Vasconia, Euskal Herria, Euskadiizena eta izana denboran barrena*, Ed. Jakin,, N°. 183-184, 2011

————. "Exploring resilience patterns amongst national minorities: from the historical representative assemblies (1812-1877) to the Basque Parliament (1980)", *Revista internacional de los estudios vascos = Eusko ikaskuntzen nazioarteko aldizkaria = Revue internationale des études basques = International journal on Basque studies, RIEV*, N°. Extra 6, 2010

————. "El Estado Vascongado triple y uno": de la "Constitución foral" (1808) al Estatuto de autonomía de Alava, Bizkaia y Gipuzkoa (1919), *Hermes: pentsamendu eta historia aldizkaria = revista de pensamiento e historia*, °. 17, 2005

Aizega Zubillaga (2003), "La utilización extrafiscal del tributo por las instituciones vascas", en Alonso Arce, I. (coord.), *Reflexiones en torno a la renovación del Concierto Económico vasco*, Ad Concordiam, Bilbao, 2003, pp. 163-173

Agirre López, Xabier. "Una elección acertada", en *Hermes, pentsamendu eta historia aldizkaria = revista de pensamiento e historia*, n° 28, 2008 págs. 22-24

Alonso Arce, Iñaki. "Naturaleza de las Normas Forales de los Territorios Históricos del País Vasco y su posición en el ordenamiento jurídico", *Forum Fiscal de Bizkaia*, n° septiembre.

Arana Landín, Sofia, *Taxation of Cooperatives*, ed. UPV / EHU, Bilbao, 2012 Arana Landín, Sofia, "The fiscal regime of Spanish cooperatives in the European Union: Spanish lines reform cooperatives.", *Basque Journal of Social Economics*, No. 7, 2010, pp. 77-98.

Aranburu Urtasun, Mikel. *Provincias exentas. Convenio-Concierto. Identidad colectiva de la Vasconia peninsular (1969-2005)*, Fundación para el Estudio del Derecho Histórico y Autonómico de Vasconia, Donostia-San Sebastián, 2005.

Bayona de Perogordo y Soler Roch, María Teresa. *Derecho financiero*, Vol. 1 (2ª ed.), Compás, Alicante, 1989.

Beldarrain Garín, M., Escribano Riego, M., and P. Ugalde Zaratiegui, P. *La autonomía fiscal en Euskal Herria*, Manu Robles Aranguiz Institutua, Bilbao, 1996.

Bilbao Eguren, José Luis. "La LTH desde el actual marco jurídico-político", en *Hermes, pentsamendu eta historia aldizkaria = revista de pensamiento e historia*, nº 28, 2008 págs. 4-12.

Caño Moreno, Javier. Teoría institucional del Estatuto Vasco. Concepción institucional e interpretación normativo-institucional del Estatuto de Autonomía del País Vasco, Universidad de Deusto, Bilbao, 1997.

————. *Derecho Autonómico Vasco*, Universidad de Deusto, Bilbao, 2007.

Corcuera Atienza, Javier. "Notas sobre el debate de los Derechos Históricos de los Territorios Forales", *REPNE*, nº 46-47, julio-octubre, 1985.

Holling, C.S. "Resilience and stability of ecological systems." in: *Annual Review of Ecology and Systematics*. Vol 4 :1-23, 1973.

Larrazábal Basáñez, Santiago. "Reflexiones sobre la Ley de Territorios Históricos en su XXV aniversario", en *Hermes, pentsamendu eta historia aldizkaria = revista de pensamiento e historia*, nº 28, 2008.

Martínez Bárbara, Gemma. Armonización fiscal y poder tributario foral en la Comunidad Autónoma del País Vasco, Premio Leizaola 2013, ex equo. IVAP, Oñati, 2014.

————. "Del nuevo Concierto Económico y de sus normas generales", *Forum Fiscal de Bizkaia*, nº marzo, 2003 (Ref. 035.110).

Moreno Portela (1997), págs. 166-182. Respecto a la posible aplicación al resto de CCAA, *vid.*, Zubiri Oria (2000), págs. 127-146

Olano Arrese, Markel. "Lurralde historikoen Legearen 25, urteurrena", en *Hermes, pentsamendu eta historia aldizkaria = revista de pensamiento e historia*, nº 28, 2008, págs.14-20

Pita Grandal, A. M. "La organización de la gestión tributaria en los estatutos de autonomía", en Pita Grandal, A. M. and Aneiros Pereira, J. (Coords.), *La financiación autonómica en los estatutos de autonomía*, Marcial Pons, Madrid, 2008.

Ramos Prieto, Jesús. "La distribución de las competencias de gestión, recaudación, inspección y revisión en materia tributaria y la reforma de los Estatutos de Autonomía", *Revista de estudios regio-*

nales, nº 78, 2007 (Ejemplar dedicado a: Modelos de financiación autonómica y financiación de los servicios básicos: Educación, Sanidad y Servicios Sociales).

Reta, E. "Las relaciones de los Territorios Históricos en el ámbito tributario", en Aizeaga Zubillaga, J. M. (coord.), *Concierto y Convenio Económico Jornadas de estudio,* Cuadernos de Derecho Azpilcueta, 18. Sociedad de Estudios Vascos, Donostia, 2002.

Serrano-Gazteluurutia, Susana. El Concierto Económico ante el Juez europeo. La judicialización de las Normas Forales tributarias en el ámbito jurídico europeo. Situación vigente (ayudas de Estado) y perspectivas de futuro. Premio José Mª Leizaola 2011, IVAP, Oñati, 2012,

————. Defense of the Economic Agreement in National and European context", edited by Joseba Agirreazkuenaga and Eduardo Alonso Olea, *The Basque fiscal system: history, current status, and future perspectives,* Coll. Basque Politics Series, nº 7, Center For Basque Studies, University of Nevada, Reno University of Nevada (USA), 2013.

Vivanco, J.L. "La litigiosidad del Concierto Económico: la relación de los Territorios Forales con la Administración estatal", en Aizeaga Zubillaga, J.M (coord.), *Concierto y Convenio Económico Jornadas de estudio,* Cuadernos de Derecho Azpilcueta, 18. Sociedad de Estudios Vascos, Donostia, 2002.

15

Bringing the Basque Economic Agreement to School: First Steps in Democratic Citizenship Education and Open Government Using New Technologies

Joseba Iñaki Arregi

This chapter will describe a workshop developed in 2014 in the Teacher Training School at the University of the Basque Country in Vitoria. This practical training initiative was part of the Didactics of Social Sciences course I am currently teaching. One of the main goals of the course is to develop a sense of democratic citizenship among future Basque teachers, through the use of history and related social sciences.

Democratic citizenship involves critical thinking[1] and participation in public affairs.[2] Democratic decision-making and participation should be based on consistent arguments, defended in a peaceful manner and with a profound attitude in favor of dialogue and debate.[3] According to Levstik, "Democratic citizenship develops best when students learn how to protect and celebrate diversity without losing the sense of connection and unity that makes sharing public spaces possible."[4] Here is where the Social Sciences make an important con-

---

1. Eva Brodin, *Critical Thinking in Scholarship. Meaning, Conditions and Developments* (Lund: Lund University, 2007).
2. Tina Nabatchi, *A Manager's Guide to Evaluating Citizen Participation*, ed. IBM Center for the Business of Government, Fostering Transparency and Democracy Series (Syracuse: IBM Center for The Business of Government, 2012).
3. Joan Pages and Antoni Santisteban, "Una mirada del pasado al futuro en la Didáctica de las Ciencias Sociales," in *Una mirada al pasado y un proyecto de futuro. Investigación y Didáctica en la Didáctica de las Ciencias Sociales*, ed. Joan Pages and Antoni Santisteban (Barcelona: Servei de Publicacions Universitat Autónoma de Barcelona, 2014) 24.
4. Lind S. Levstik, "What can history and social sciencies contribute to civic educa-

tribution, since there is a common belief that our current democratic systems "will not be sustained unless students are aware of their cultural and physical environments; know the past; read, write and think deeply and act in ways that promote the common good."[5] But in doing so, it should be remembered that just "teaching about events relevant to the present, but not making those connections explicit, for instance, is unlikely to support the transfer from past to present circumstance.[6]

The field of didactics of Social Sciences has as its constant practical and academic goal to promote a variety of topics as well as changes in the ways they are taught. These changes are needed in order to bring the content closer to the real needs and aspirations of current students and future teachers of primary school in the Basque Country. Taking into account the above-mentioned ideas, and since knowledge of the history and the institutional framework of Euskadi is part of the Basque curriculum for primary education, we have focused on the case of the Basque Economic Agreement (from now on BEA). Keeping in mind that "some combinations of instructional purposes and practices or stances appear more likely to support transfer and produce civic outcomes than others,"[7] the BEA provides a great tool to connect history with the needs and interests of our contemporary Basque society. Actually, such a tool could help students to "better understand the ways peoples have arranged to live together, the consequences of such arrangements and their applicability to civic responsibility."[8]

All the aforementioned ideas were combined in an educational initiative that started with a short historical presentation linking the Fueros with the Economic Agreement, and followed with a web tour through the *Ad Concordiam* and ITUNA (Documentation Center of the Basque Fiscal Agreement and Foral Treasuries) websites. These two websites are part of a public initiative to make the BEA better known to Basque society.

Basque Resilience in the Making

tion?" in *Una mirada al pasado y un proyecto de futuro. Investigación y Didáctica en la Didáctica de las Ciencias Sociales*, ed. Joan Pages and Antoni Santisteban (Barcelona: Servei de Publicacions Universitat Autónoma de Barcelona, 2014), 43.

5. National Council for Social Studies, *The College, Career and Civic Life (C3) Framework for Social Studies State Standards: Guidance for Enhancing the Rigor of K-12 Civics, Economics, Geography and History* (Silver Springs, MD: National Council for Social Studies, 2013), 82.

6. Levstik, "What can history and social sciencies contribute to civic education?" 45.

7. Ibid., 45.

8. Ibid., 47.

The BEA constitutes the political-economic backbone of Basque autonomy since it embodies the exercise of powers and services corresponding to the Basque Country under the Statute of Autonomy approved in 1979.

The tax relationship between Spain and the Basque Country is governed by the BEA, which grants revenue-collecting powers to the Basque Country under a Treasury system. Actually, Chapter III of the Statute of Basque Autonomy bestows its own Autonomous Treasury on the Basque Country. Due to this fact, the Basque Country has the power to regulate, manage, and collect taxes. All this entails the existence of a specific Basque tax system, with its own peculiar way of regulating taxes that includes: a general tax system, encompassing, among others, the Income Tax, the Company Tax and the Value Added Tax.

According to the Statute of Autonomy and the BEA, the Basque Country pays a quota to the Spanish Treasury to cover general expenditures in areas of common interest between the Kingdom of Spain and the Basque Country. These areas include foreign affairs, defense and the armed forces, customs, and general transport networks.

The Basque Country pays the quota to the Spanish government in accordance with the state's general burden, and not according to its available resources. Therefore, the Basque Country contributes according to its capacity and relative revenue, as the quota is calculated by applying the Basque contribution capability ratio to general Spanish expenditure.

A Politically Highly Relevant Instrument and Object of Controversy

The president of the Basque Parliament, Bakartxo Tejeria, in the introduction of a seminar organized by this prominent institution, offers some clues to better understand the political relevance of the BEA.

- It is a Bilateral Agreement
- It is based on non-dependency
- It is fundamental for the economy, but also for politics
- It predates the Spanish Constitution
- It gives Basques a comparative advantage in a globalized world

In addition to all this, the BEA embodies 125 years of resilience in the making,[9] since "the strengthening of the federal tax systems in the nineteenth century reflects a resilient structure, not only in terms of the will to self-govern, but also because of their management capacity and the benefits gained by those paying into the systems."[10] This is still true today.

Agirreazkuenaga and Oleas' proposal linking the BEA and political resilience constitutes the main inspiration for our attempt to bring such a fundamental issue to a class made up of future teachers in the Teacher Training School of Vitoria, at the University of the Basque Country.

Taking these factors into account helps us to understand why the BEA is a singular system that attracts so much interest and generates such a big controversy. This has been the case in both the European Union and the kingdom of Spain. As Rubi Cassinello states, the BEA has undergone severe questioning "within the European Community, criticized by the rest of the Autonomous Communities in Spain (which see it more as an unjustified privilege than as an instrument of responsibility and self-government) and by state representatives by means of an ongoing appeal for judicial review, continually calling into question each and every one of the measures exercised by the foral institutions pursuant to the powers granted by the Agreement."[11]

This controversy is especially relevant in the Kingdom of Spain, where part of the Catalan challenge was generated after Madrid denied the possibility of implementing such a system in Catalunya[12]

Outside the Spanish Kingdom, Scotland also has taken the BEA into account when thinking of advanced self-goverment. Actually, the document published by the Scottish Government to promote and explain their bid for independence makes a reference to this Basque tool of self-government. Under the heading "Is further devolution an alternative?" the following is stated:

> With the agreement of Westminster, devolution could be

---

9. Joseba Agirreazkuenaga and Eduardo Olea, *The Basque Fiscal System: History, Current Status and Future Perspectives* (Reno: Center for Basque Studies, 2014).

10. Agirreazkuenaga, *The Basque Fiscal System*, 33.

11. Jose Rubi Cassinello, "Ten Years of the Ad Concordiam Association," in *The Basque Fiscal System. History, Current Status and Future Perspectives*, ed. Joseba Agirreazkuenaga and Eduardo Olea. (Reno: Center for Basque Studies, University of Nevada, 2014), 184.

12. La Voz de Barcelona, "Rajoy le dice a Mas que el concierto económico no cabe en la Constitución," *La Voz de Barcelona*, 2012.

extended within the UK to cover all domestic and economic matters and to provide full fiscal responsibility for
Scotland. This would mean that Scotland would collect
our own taxes and make a payment to Westminster for
common services such as defense. Such a system operates
in the Basque country and Navarra in Spain. However,
all the indications are that the Westminster Government
believes that further devolution of taxes should be strictly
limited. It is also unlikely that any significant elements
of the welfare system will be devolved. Without further
devolution in these key areas, Scotland will not have the
powers needed to grow our economy or to deliver a fair
society that meets the aspirations of the Scottish people.[13]

Didactics of Social Sciences 1: When History Meets Citizenship

Didactics of Social Sciences 1 as an academic subject aims at offering
a view of social change, taking into account its historical and geographical implications; building democratic citizenship; appreciating
the goods of material and non-material heritage; using ICTs and different languages; and promoting interculturality.

In summary, our students participate in and analyze issues linking history and their personal experiences. They learn by locating,
discussing, analyzing, and evaluating a variety of existing social studies teaching resources. In this proccess they are exposed to a variety of instruction strategies (case studies, cooperative learning, and
activities using primary sources). The goal is to encourage critical
thinking processes, from a multicultural perspective, through concept development and integration with other subjects, and by incor-
porating technology into the learning of social studies.

But mere lecturing about history and current institutions is not
enough, since "making the leap from disciplinary ways of knowing
to civic engagement . . . requires explicit attention to connecting disciplinary study to current civic issues, and examining these issues in
terms of available agency and constraints in the agency so that students can identify appropriate interventions and associations that
might be employed in initiating and responding to change."[14] The

---

13. Scottish Government, "Scotland's Future. Your Guide to an Independent Scotland." (Edinburgh: Scottish Government, 2013), 335.
14. Levstik, "What Can History and Social Sciences Contribute to Civic Education?"
48.

BEA offers a case where history, institutions, Basque agency and its constraints can be studied and appropriate associations and future interventions can be imagined and designed in response to social change. These factors are key for civic engagement.

Controversial Topics as a Teaching Tool

Controversial topics such as the BEA offer the opportunity to link history with hot, current social and political debates. The relevance of this link is at the very heart of the current debates in the field of didactics of social science. Indeed, connecting social sciences with current issues and students' lives proves to be a key challenge when approaching the teaching of social sciences.[15]

According to Oxfam,[16] discussing highly emotional and controversial issues encourages students to develop the following thinking skills:

- *Information-processing skills.* Students learn how to gather, sort, classify, sequence, compare and contrast information, and to make links between pieces of information.
- *Reasoning skills.* Students learn how to justify opinions and actions, to draw inferences and make deductions, to use appropriate language to explain their views, and to use evidence to back up their decisions.
- *Enquiry skills.* Students learn how to ask relevant questions, to plan what to do and how to research, to predict outcomes and anticipate responses, to test theories and problems, to test conclusions, and to refine their ideas and opinions.
- *Creative thinking skills.* Students learn how to generate and extend ideas, to suggest possible hypotheses, to use their imaginations, and to look for alternative outcomes.
- *Evaluation skills.* Students learn how to evaluate what they read, hear, and do, to learn to judge the value of their own and others' work or ideas, to not take all information at face value, and to have confidence in their own judgments.

The BEA offers a new way to put all these skills into practice. It

---

15. Juan Delval, "Ciudadanía y escuela. El aprendizaje de la participación," in *Educar para la participación ciudadana en la enseñanza de las ciencias sociales* (Sevilla: Asociación Universitaria de Profesorado de Didáctica, 2012).

16. Oxfam, *Teaching Controversial Issues* (Oxford: Oxfam Development Education, 2006), 5.

also tackles a key issue in our current political, economic, and social reality. It is the center of a hot debate, and it can be an effective method of enabling students to take an active part in their own learning through the preparation and presentation of their own work, and confronting that of their peers. This supports pedagogic theory which proposes that students learn effectively when they learn cooperatively, through interaction with others, and when they develop critical thinking.[17] Davidson[18] suggests five characteristics of a cooperative learning technique that must be taken into account: a learning activity suitable for group work; a small-group–based project (2–5 people); tasks that encourage cooperative behaviors; student interdependence; and individual student accountability and responsibility for task completion.

Taking all this reasoning into account, our goal was to offer a practical training activity covering key areas of the history, current affairs, and debates around the BEA. In doing so, it was our aim to offer access to relevant resources and bibliography that could be used by our students when dealing with issues related to the BEA. In this manner, our students were able to develop fundamental skills related to Basque democratic citizenship education and civil responsibility, since the BEA is based on unilateral risk, good management, liberty with responsibility, and bilateral agreement.

Getting to know the BEA

Students were divided into groups of 2 to 5 people in order to be able to perform the different tasks involved in the practical seminary. The first session started with a set of questions about various aspects of the BEA, in order to assess previous knowledge around some of the relevant issues. After that, a Google search was launched in order to find what Basques know about the BEA. The goal was to identify surveys made by institutions or other relevant sources working on this topic. The students received two main surveys on the BEA, one made by the Basque government in 2008 and another by the *Ad Concordiam* in 2012. The results were compared and the level of knowledge

---

17. Jacqueline Sue Thousand, Richard A. Villa, and Ann Nevin, *Creativity and Collaborative Learning: A Practical Guide to Empowering Students and Teachers* (Baltimore: Paul H. Brooks, 1994).

18. Neil Davidson, "Cooperative and Collaborative Learning: An Integrative Perspective," in *Creativity and Collaborative Learning: A Practical Guide to Empowering Students and Teachers*, ed. Jacqueline Sue Thousand, Richard A. Villa, and Ann Nevin (Baltimore, MD: Paul H. Brooks, 1994).

about the BEA assessed, focusing on the strong and weak points related to the public's knowledge of the Agreement. Issues about who collects taxes, who has more taxing power compared to whom, and who litigates against the BEA were addressed by the different groups. In the following task, groups were asked to compare the results with the situation experienced by the members of each group in their close social environment. Finally, each group was asked to report back and participate in a class debate on the question: What do Basques actually know and think about the BEA?

One major issue came out of this discussion: a gap existing between the perception of high relevance and actual knowledge of its history, mechanism, and related aspects. This lack of factual knowledge was identified as a great obstacle. Most students describe themselves as history haters, mistrustful of politicians, and disinterested in any institution of any sort, but all of them have heard about the BEA and consider it good. At this point, we reached the cognitive conflict level and were ready to go on.

This complex reality marked the starting point for our initiative. The goal was to teach them about Basque history and resilient political institutions, using ICTs, and making them active participants and protagonists in this knowledge search.

Mass Media Says...

During the second session, with the intention in mind to assess public knowledge and to understand why the BEA is such a controversial issue, students Googled information in order to answer the following search-triggering question and hot issue of debate: Is the BEA a right or a privilege? In order to assess our fundamental question, students were asked to compare and analyze mass media information taking into account who in the Spanish and Basque Media says right or privilege. After that, they were asked to gather information published by institutions, going to Irekia (the public information service of the Basque government) and to the Basque Diputaciones.

Most of the students used Spanish as a main search language and found that the combination of the search words Basque+Agreement+right+privilege showed a total of 167,000 entries. The prevailing view in the Spanish-speaking media was that the BEA was a privilege. Once the search was finished, the results were shared and a discussion was held based on the results. The goal was to make clear who said what, the difference between Basque and Spanish views, and the arguments and sources that were quoted.

What You Like Is What You Bring

During the third session, the main task was to visit *AD CONCOR-DIAM* and ITUNA. These two associations offer new resources exploring different ways to make the BEA accessible to both an expert public and an ordinary one. Our goal was to identify and assess possible resources susceptible to being included in future didactic proposals to bring the BEA closer to the education world, paying special attention to the opportunities offered by the use of ICTs and languages.

ITUNA and AD CONCORDIAM: Two Sisters in the BEA

These two institutions offer an interesting case where a Basque Public University and the Private Jesuit University of Deusto are working together with the Foral Diputation of Bizkaia on issues of general public interest. In addition, the above-mentioned institutions combine the expert knowledge aspect with a desire to reach the public, by using different strategies that can inspire those of us involved in the didactics of social sciences. These strategies used in open government initiatives are considered important for future teachers since they offer a variety of ways to bring a complex economic and political reality to non-experts and the Basque constituency in general.

Starting with a Little History of the Project

Before starting with our virtual tour, a short history of the project and the two institutions involved was offered. The *AD CONCORDIAM* Association for the Promotion and Dissemination of the Economic Agreement is a private, non-profit organization legally constituted in 2000, having the Foral Deputation of Bizkaia, the University of the Basque Country (UPV-EHU), and the University of Deusto as its main partners. Its chief goal is to tackle a formidable challenge arising from both ignorance of the BEA and great indifference regarding it, resulting in civic disengagement. This initial situation brings us to a scenario where past and current positions on a highly controversial issue can be followed and the root causes explored.

While previously, the mere mention of our unique foral system aroused passions of unconditional support, the institutions of Basque society were now viewed by the majority of citizens with a high degree of indifference. Added to this was a general ignorance with regard to the meaning, essence, and history of those institutions.[19] To tackle this phenomenal institutional and democratic challenge, in 2000 the Department of Treasury and Finance of the Foral Deputation of Bizkaia moved to address this state of affairs by including in the General Budget of the Historical Territory a new program called "The Economic Agreement." This program aimed at preparing the citizens and institutions of the historical territory of Bizkaia to effectively ensure a process of renewal of such a unique instrument of self-government.[20] Sentiment and appreciation were considered key to civic engagement.

We feel that it continues to be a matter of urgency to renew a collective sentiment of support for the Economic Agreement and an appreciation of its importance for the Basque Country. But this goal will only be achieved if we can get the citizens of Euskadi to understand that the Economic Agreement is good for everyone. For this purpose we need to use all of the means at our disposal to reach these citizens. This includes students of all ages,[21] communications media, scientific institutions, and universities.[22] The UPV-EHU (Universidad del País Vasco-Euskal Herriko Unibertsitatea, or University of the Basque Country) through its Department of Social Sciences, and the University of Deusto through the Institute of Basque Studies responded to the challenge by stating their will to participate. This alliance gave birth to the two sisters in the BEA: *AD CONCORDIAM* and the Economic Agreement Center and Foral Treasuries (UPV-EHU).

A Virtual Tour

After a brief introduction, and in order to make the general goal achievable, these three operational objectives were agreed to:

- *Search for knowledge:* Providing critically important data regarding the Economic Agreement.
- *Universalization in mind:* Getting citizens to see that the Agreement is a tool from which all Basques derive benefit.
- *Raising awareness:* Making citizens aware of the strategic importance of the Agreement for the Basque Country,[23] in order to promote action and civic engagement in support of the BEA.

---

19. Jose Rubi Cassinello, "Ten Years of the Ad Concordiam Association," 184.
20. Ibid., 186.
21. Emphasis added.
22. Rubi Cassinello, "Ten Years of the Ad Concordiam Association."
23. Ibid.,187

Introducing the Previous Groundwork

After making it clear that these were the operational objectives, students were introduced to various initiatives that *Ad Concordiam* set in place. Several of them are familiar to teachers since they are regular external didactic resources. In this realm, the exhibition "Historia eta Sentzazioak" was highlighted. My goal was "a renewed appreciation of the basic importance of the Economic Agreement through activities aimed at fostering, on the one hand, a general awareness of the origin, history, and meaning of our historical rights, and their evolution until the present time, and, on the other hand, knowledge of those rights within a contemporary social and political context."[24] The exhibition was completed with a series of didactic tools such as conferences, courses, seminars, distribution of didactic material, publishing-media advertising, as well as a CD and a board game focusing on the history of the BEA.

The web format was the main target of the activity due to its potential to attract students and future teachers and for its ability to make the BEA accessible for all citizens. Divided into several groups and testing the multilingual character of the information involved, students were invited to navigate and experience the web firsthand. Groups tested the Ad Concordiam web in Basque, Spanish, and English, with the goal of seeing if it could be useful as a tool to spread knowledge about the BEA, make the BEA universal, and raise BEA awareness. The knowledge dissemination part had more to do with the expert, academic side of the BEA and civic engagement. This skill was emphasized for undergraduate students. Indeed, the goal was to achieve transposition in citizenship education.[25] The groups were asked to navigate and experience the virtual Ad Concordiam site and the Center of the Economic Agreement and the Foral Treasuries site, and then report back to the group.

AD CONCORDIAM

The Ad Concordiam groups navigated through the four layers of the web site. The first layer is called "To Make a Long Story Short"; this level is dedicated to general information such as the origins of the BEA, its main characteristics, introducing the current Agreement and its purpose, and explaining what the quota is. It is a first contact

---

24. Ibid., p. 188.
25. Tristan McCowan, "Curricular transposition in citizenship education" *Theory and Research in Education* 6, no. 2 (2008).

section with basic surface level information and mainly written information.

The second layer of search was called "In Detail." This particular section is geared toward students in need of deeper knowledge of the BEA: its meaning and its contents. This area displays a variety of resources that allow our students to move beyond citizen education to economics, including mathematics (another important subject or skill according to the Basque curriculum). This level allows students to find information on general regulations, tax relations, financial relations, committees, and legal texts.

Finally, students went to the third level called "Documentation." This is the expert level for academics and professionals needing the latest state-of-the-art information for such a complex and controversial matter. Rubi Cassinello describes the richness and complexity of this in-depth level of information, which includes, among other details, the administrative foundations of the Economic Agreement; specifically, information regarding the Tax Authority Council consultation with the Coordinating Committee regarding the Economic Agreement; court resolutions; decisions of the European Commission; material related to jurisprudence; and various relevant expert and academic publications.

Ad Concordiam offers all these services mainly in a "pull-mode," so that those interested have to enter the web and find the information, but also include a "push-mode" via RSS or e-mail alerts.

The Center for the Economic Agreement and the Foral Treasuries

As in the previous case, several groups of students searched and navigated through this virtual center which has a profound academic and expert vocation. Since 2007, this Center has been involved in the gathering, storage, and spreading of knowledge regarding the BEA.[26] It is run from a scholarly viewpoint with emphasis on history. This characteristic proved problematic for many students, who were not very interested in bibliographic and biographical materials, so students were asked to focus on other levels and formats of information including the blog, Wikipedia, the monitoring of printed and digital press activity, and the electronic newsletter and the Facebook group as push-services.

---

26. Eduardo Olea,"Thirty Years of Economic Agreement," in *The Basque Fiscal System. History, Current Status and Future Perspectives*, ed. Joseba Agirreazkuenaga and Eduardo Olea. (Reno: Center for Basque Studies, University of Nevada, 2014), pages?.

What They Concluded

After completing the tasks of searching and navigating, each group was asked to choose a speaker to communicate their results and conclusions to the general class-group. Students that worked with the *Ad Concordiam* website found it attractive, colorful, and full of resources that could be used in primary school, secondary education, high school, or even at University levels. In terms of primary school education, the majority thought that specific material suited for this level and designed in a more accessible way needs to be developed. However, they considered the use of audiovisual material using infographics a very effective way to explain the Financial Agreement and the quota. They also found the dynamic timeline that described the history of the BEA attractive.

Participants saw ITUNA as providing a lot of history and information about the BEA that is complex and suited only for experts. On the contrary, Wikipedia, the newsletter, and the Facebook group were highly valued. These last two resources offer a friendly way to access complex data in an easy manner, in several layers of information, and with direct access to the sources for those desiring to enter the in-depth expert level. Many highlighted the contrast between *Ad Concordiam's* colorful design and the Center's more solid, cooler and austere look.

Overall, both sites were considered a good resource offering expert information and various resources to address such an important and controversial issue. The use of dynamic audiovisual resources and easy-to-access text articles were considered key for socialization and for transposition of citizenship education. Indeed, all the groups mentioned that the texts were hard to understand, especially those found in the legal section and news sections of *Ad Concordiam*. On the contrary, the Ituna newsletter was considered a positive asset as a tool to communicate and access expert information and relevant sources on the topic. Many also liked the Facebook format because they could share those news items they found interesting and interact with others.

Conclusions

The use of controversial and complex issues such as the BEA opens the path to exploring new ways to bring social sciences to the classroom by linking history and current affairs. This link between past and current institutions is very important since the BEA is a key instrument of Basque resilience and self-government. This is why it is a fundamental topic that should be taken into consideration when teaching Basque history, politics, and institutions. Its relevance is even greater in the case of the Teacher Training School. Introducing this issue into the curriculum means taking a step forward in the right direction for the future of our institutions, promoting a model of citizenship based on knowledge and rational commitment.

The workshop described presents an experience exploring a new setting in which the professor becomes a mere organizer of the activity. This format offers an active way of learning instead of the traditional preaching-lecturing format dominating many social sciences classes in the Basque Country. Identifying two very relevant resources that can help future teachers and society in general with historical and legislative arguments has been fundamental. Besides, these two digital resources offer a variety of formats that make it appealing for education professionals.

More experiences like this, and more investigation into resources to create awareness of the BEA, are needed. Our initiative takes a first step on the long road to encounter methods for building democratic citizenship in the Basque Country and the world.

Bibliography

Agirreazkuenaga, Joseba, and Eduardo Olea (eds.). *The Basque Fiscal System. History, Current Status, and Future Perspectives*. Reno: Center for Basque Studies, University of Nevada, 2014.

Brodin, Eva. *Critical Thinking in Scholarship. Meaning, Conditions and Developments*. Lund: Lund University, 2007.

Cassinello, Jose Rubi. "Ten Years of the Ad Concordiam Association." In *The Basque Fiscal System. History, Current Status and Future Perspectives*, edited by Joseba Agirreazkuenaga and Eduardo Olea, 183–97. Reno: Center for Basque Studies, University of Nevada, 2014.

Davidson, Neil. "Cooperative and Collaborative Learning: An Integrative Perspective." In *Creativity and Collaborative Learning: A Practical Guide to Empowering Students and Teachers*, edited by Jacqueline Sue Thousand, Richard Villa, and Ann Nevin, 410–17. Baltimore: Paul H. Brooks, 1994.

Delval, Juan. "Ciudadanía y escuela. El aprendizaje de la participación." In *Educar para la participación ciudadanía en la enseñanza de las Ciencias Sociales*. Sevilla: Asociación Universitaria de Profesorado de Didáctica de las Ciencias Sociales, 2012.

La Voz de Barcelona. "Rajoy le Dice a Mas que el Concierto Económico no Cabe en la Constitución," 2012.

Levstik, Lind S. "What Can History and Social Sciencies Contribute to Civic Education?" In *Una Mirada al Pasado y un Proyecto de Futuro. Investigación y Didáctica en la Didáctica de las Ciencias Sociales,* edited by Joan Pages and Antoni Santisteban, pages?. Barcelona: Servei de Publicacions Universitat Autónoma de Barcelona, 2014.

McCowan, Tristan. "Curricular Transposition in Citizenship Education." *Theory and Research in Education,* 6, no. 2 (2008): 153–72.

Nabatchi, Tina. *A Manager's Guide to Evaluating Citizen Participation.* Fostering Transparency and Democracy Series. Edited by IBM Center for the Business of Government, 2012.

National Council for Social Studies. *The College, Career, and Civic Life (C3) Framework for Social Studies State Standards: Guidance for Enhancing the Rigor of K–12 Civics, Economics, Geography and History.* Silver Springs, MD: National Council for Social Studies, 2013.

Olea, Eduardo. "Thirty Years of Economic Agreement." In *The Basque Fiscal System. History, Current Status and Future Perspectives,* edited by Joseba Agirreazkuenaga and Eduardo Olea, 197–205. Reno: Center for Basque Studies, University of Nevada, 2014.

Oxfam.*Teaching Controversial Issues.* Oxford: Oxfam Development Education, 2006.

Pages, Joan, and Antoni Santisteban. "Una Mirada del Pasado al Futuro en la Didáctica de las Ciencias Sociales." In *Una mirada al pasado y un proyecto de futuro. Investigación y didáctica en la didáctica de las ciencias sociales,* edited by Joan Pages and Antoni Santisteban, pages? Barcelona: Servei de Publicacions Universitat Autónoma de Barcelona, 2014.

Scottish Government. "*Scotland's Future. Your Guide to an Independent Scotland.* Edinburgh: Scottish Government, 2013.

Thousand, Jacqueline Sue, Richard A. Villa, and Ann Nevin. *Creativity and Collaborative Learning: A Practical Guide to Empowering Students and Teachers.* Baltimore: Paul H. Brooks, 1994.

About the Contributors

Joseba Agirreazkuenaga is full professor of contemporary history at the University of the Basque Country (UPV-EHU) and head of the University Research Group on *Biography & Parliament* and President of the International Commission for the History of Representatives and Parliamentary Institutions (ICHRPI). William A. Douglass Distinguished Visiting Scholar for the 2013-2014 academic year.

Eneka Albizu, professor of Business Administration and Strategic Human Resources Management at the Industrial Relations Faculty of the University of the Basque Country (UPV-EHU).

Eduardo J. Alonso Olea, is permanent researcher and professor of history in the Department of Contemporary History, University of the Basque Country (UPV-EHU).

Sofia Arana is Professor of Tax Law at the University of the Basque Country (UPV/EHU). International Projects Director University of the Basque Country (UPV/EHU). Member of the Economic and Administrative Court of Donostia-San Sebastian

Mikel Aranburu, official of the government of Navarre and since 2015 minister of Economics and Financial Policy of the Navarre government cabinet.

Andrés Araujo, full professor of Business Administration, Industrial Organization and Managerial Economics at the Business School at the University of the Basque Country (UPV-EHU). Vice-minister of the Economy and Finance Policy of the Basque Government (2009-2012).

Joseba Iñaki Arregi. Associate Professor at the Departament of the Didactics of the Social Sciences at the University of the Basque Country

Imanol Basterretxea, professor of Business Administration at the Business School at the University of the Basque Country (UPV-EHU).

Mikel Erkoreka, PhD candidate in the Department of Contemporary History of the University of the Basque Country (UPV-EHU).

Juan Jose Ibarretxe is Director of Agirre Lehendakaria Center for Social and Political Studies at the University of the Basque Country and Visiting Professor of Economics at Universidad Interamericana in Puerto Rico; former President of the Basque Country (1999–2009); former Vice-President of the Basque Government and Councilor of Finance and Public Administration (1995–1998)

Jon Landeta, professor of Business Administration and Strategic Human Resources Management at the Business School at the University of the Basque Country (UPV-EHU). Director of the Human Resource Management and Innovation research team of the UPV-EHU

Gemma Martínez is official of the Regional government or Deputation of Bizkaia, since 2000 Head of Tax Policy of the Department of Treasury and Finances. Representative of the Basque Institutions in the ECOFIN working groups (Economic and Financial Affairs Council of Europe). Treasurer of Ad Concordiam. Regular professor in post-graduate programs at the University of Deusto and the Chamber of Commerce of Bilbao. Visiting Fellow at the Center for Basque Studies in 2015 according to the agreement between the Deputation of Bizkaia and University of Nevada.

Javier Muguruza, Lawyer, National Expert for the Tax General Direction in The European Commission in Brussels (1993-1997) Director of the Department of Treasury and Finances of the Regional government or Deputation of Bizkaia (1999-2003), since 2009 one of the three member of the Arbitration Board of the Economic Agreement

Elliot Parker is Professor of Economics, Director of the University Core Curriculum, and Associate Dean, Undergraduate Programs and Administration at the University of Nevada, Reno.

José Gabriel Rubí is official of the Regional government or Deputation of Bizkaia, since 1995 General Secretary of the Department of Treasury and Finances. Representative of the Basque Institutions in

ECOFIN working groups. (Economic and Financial Affairs Council of Europe). President of Ad Concordiam, Association for the Promotion and Diffusion of the Economic Agreement.

Antoni Segura is a full professor of the University of Barcelona, Director of the Director of the Center for International Historical Studies (Cehi, Centre d'Estudis Històrics Internacionals) at the University of Barcelona from 2005 to 2016. Since January 2017 President of Barcelona Centre for International Affairs (Cidob)

Susana Serrano-Gaztelurrutia is Professor of Tax Law, at the University of the Basque Country.

Irune Suberbiola is an Associate Professor at the Public Law Department of the University of the Basque Country